Neurotherapy and Net

The fields of neurobiology and neuropsychology are growing rapidly, and neuroscientists now understand that the human brain has the capability to adapt and develop new living neurons by engaging new tasks and challenges throughout our lives, essentially allowing the brain to rewire itself. In *Neurotherapy and Neurofeedback*, accomplished clinicians and scholars Ted Chapin and Lori Russell-Chapin illustrate the importance of these advances and introduce counselors to the growing body of research demonstrating that the brain can be taught to self-regulate and become more efficient through neurofeedback (NF), a type of biofeedback for the brain. Students and clinicians will come away from this book with a strong sense of how brain dysregulation occurs and what kinds of interventions clinicians can use when counseling and medication prove insufficient for treating behavioral and psychological symptoms.

Theodore J. Chapin, PhD, teaches courses on divorce, family mediation, and group therapy. He serves as the president and clinical director of Resource Management Services, Inc., a private business consulting and counseling firm. Dr. Chapin is an expert in custody evaluations and has written widely about neurofeedback, mediation, and clinical supervision, most recently in *Clinical Supervision: Theory and Practice*, which he co-authored with Dr. Russell-Chapin.

Lori A. Russell-Chapin, PhD, is a professor and associate dean of the College of Education and Health Sciences at Bradley University in Peoria, Illinois. She is also the co-director of the Center for Collaborative Brain Research at Bradley University, where she facilitates collaborative research in the areas of cognitive research, brain imaging, and neural feedback. In 2013, she was the recipient of the national Linda Seligman Counselor Educator of the Year Award, and she currently maintains a private counseling practice and is the co-author of six books, including *Clinical Supervision: Theory and Practice*.

Neurotherapy and Neurofeedback

Brain-Based Treatment for Psychological and Behavioral Problems

Theodore J. Chapin and Lori A. Russell-Chapin

Routledge
Taylor & Francis Group

NEW YORK AND LONDON

First published 2014
by Routledge
711 Third Avenue, New York, NY 10017

and by Routledge
27 Church Road, Hove, East Sussex BN3 2FA

Library of Congress Cataloging-in-Publication Data
Chapin, Theodore J.
    Neurotherapy and neurofeedback : brain-based treatment for psychological and behavioral problems / Theodore J. Chapin and Lori A. Russell-Chapin.
        pages cm
    Includes bibliographical references and index.
    1. Biofeedback training. 2. Mental health. 3. Neuropsychology.
4. Neuropsychiatry. I. Chapin, Ted. II. Title.
    BF319.5.B5R87 2014
    615.8'514—dc23
    2013023602

ISBN: 978-0-415-66223-9 (hbk)
ISBN: 978-0-415-66224-6 (pbk)
ISBN: 978-0-203-07252-3 (ebk)

Typeset in Abode Caslon
by Apex CoVantage, LLC

Printed and bound in the United States of America by Sheridan Books, Inc. (a Sheridan Group Company).

This book is dedicated to everyone who finds the human brain fascinating. Neurofeedback has made such a difference in many people's lives. Thank you to our children, Elissa and Jaimeson, who trusted us enough to allow neurofeedback into their lives.

CONTENTS

FOREWORD

After reading, I am shamelessly impressed by the scholarly and creative work of Drs. Lori Russell-Chapin and Ted Chapin. This book offers both the basics of neurofeedback and, equally important, a superb summary of current discoveries on the brain and neuroscience research. While oriented to those interested in neurofeedback, it is also an ideal introduction to brain basics for anyone who wishes to bring science into counseling and psychotherapy.

Neurofeedback's history goes back to 1924, when the German psychiatrist Hans Berger attached electrodes to the scalp and detected small currents in the brain. His research became the foundation for what is occurring today. In the 1960s, Joe Kamiya brought neurofeedback into more popular attention through his pioneering study of alpha brainwaves. It has taken some time, but now more sophisticated equipment at a reasonable price for what it provides has made neurofeedback and neurotherapy available to professionals and to the lay public.

The Chapins' book is also pioneering, even seminal, in several ways. First, it defines and summarizes the nature of neurofeedback clearly and succinctly. Next, it is the first book that brings together neuroscience as the foundation of neurotherapy. The definition of neuroscience is wisely broad, as neuroscience is the most integrative of all science disciplines. In this book, you will discover a raft of implications for neuroscience and neurofeedback. Among these are how diet and exercise impact the brain and the importance of Bowlby's attachment theory as a central aspect of neuroscience, as well as many brain basics.

I could go on at great length reviewing and discussing each chapter. For those who want to learn essentials of neurofeedback, you may want to start by reading Chapters 5 and 6. Here you will learn about the several types of neurotherapy interventions, the relation of operant and classical conditioning to neurotherapy, and the latest computerized software including electroencephalograph (EEG) instrumentation.

Assessment and treatment follow in Chapters 8 and 9. It is impressive to read the clear summary of how neurofeedback can be used for training with therapeutic challenges such as ADHD, depression, anxiety, and chronic pain. There is evidence for its effectiveness with post-traumatic stress disorder (PTSD).

Neurofeedback *normalizes* dysregulated brains. However, neurotherapy must be conducted by an ethical and well-trained professional. Sadly, there are many "certification" programs that run through the many complexities of neurofeedback much too quickly. Quality technical equipment that is fully up to date is required. Ethical practice demands that neurotherapists be licensed in their helping profession, seek the BCIA certification, and receive supervision from a certified neurotherapist. The Chapins emphasize these points quite well.

Now, let me return to the superb discussion of the brain and neuroscience you will find in Chapters 3 and 4. These two chapters alone are worth the price of the book. Although I write and present on neuroscience around the world, I have never seen such a useful and clear description of the basics in such a small space. I like these two chapters so much that I intend to reread them several times. They are ideal introductions for both beginners and advanced professionals. Included are the basics for further study and further growth.

The National Institute of Mental Health is currently funding projects and research that will lead us to a fully developed brain-based counseling and therapy system within 10 years. This project will include specifics for recommended treatments as well as assessment and diagnosis, thus possibly changing the *Diagnostic and Statistical Manuals* of the American Psychiatric Association.

The Chapins provide the reader with a real sense of neurofeedback and neurotherapy in action. The concluding chapters "ice the cake" with a summary of key research and what we can anticipate from this field in the next several years.

Neurotherapy and Neurofeedback: Brain-Based Treatment for Psychological and Behavioral Problems will make a difference in both your understanding and practice, whether you work in medicine, psychology, counseling, social work, or any field where human communication and development is central.

Kudos to the authors. Read on!

Allen E. Ivey, EdD, ABPP
Distinguished University Professor (Emeritus),
University of Massachusetts, Amherst;
Courtesy Professor, University of South Florida

1

INTRODUCTION TO NEUROTHERAPY AND NEUROFEEDBACK

The human brain is estimated to have about a hundred billion nerve cells, two million miles of axons, and a million billion synapses, making it the most complex structure, natural or artificial, on earth.
—Tim Green, Stephen Heinemann, Jim Gusella

When the authors of this book combine their past counseling work experiences, we have an amazing and varied clinical counseling history. Ted has been a licensed clinical psychologist for several decades and has been in private practice for the past 25 years. Lori has been counseling as a licensed clinical professional counselor and teaching graduate counseling courses for the past 25 years. During this time period, discussions inevitably evolve to outcome-based questions such as, "Does counseling actually work? If so, how do helping professionals know that it works?"

These questions stimulate wonderful personal and classroom debates about counseling's efficacy. The conversations usually go something like this: There have always been counselors and a variety of other helping professionals throughout the history of mankind. From the village shaman to the wise sage to local pastors to licensed clinical professionals, people have been seeking out experts to help sort out the problems of daily living. In the beginning, the answer to "Does counseling work?" seemed a bit obvious.

Yes, counseling does work because "clients" come back and say they are feeling better in some way. When probing a bit more deeply, the answer is narrowed down further by specifically stating that the problem was gone or the presented behavioral symptoms have been reduced. Through research on counseling effectiveness, the largest predictor of counseling success is therapeutic alliance, over gender of therapist to theoretical orientation (Smith & Glass, 1977; Landman & Dawes, 1982; Lambert & Cattani, 1996).

Sometimes when cognitive therapy does not seem to be helpful, we then turn to medicine and psychopharmacology to assist us in reducing symptoms. Results of meta-analyses indicate that often the combination of counseling and medication is the best solution for many of our depressed adolescent clients (Bhatia & Bhatia, 2007). In the past, counseling and medication have been the two mainstay approaches for the treatment of behavioral and psychological symptoms.

Just as discussions revolve around counseling efficacy concerns, every year discussions arise about the brain. For years, we have been saying that in the future the advances in neuropsychology, neurobiology, and neurorehabilitation will change the way we all conduct counseling. That future has arrived with the advances in neuroscience and fMRI research. We were correct; this new information has changed our thinking about counseling. It must change how we conduct our counseling strategies and interventions. These advances in neuroscience allow clinicians to understand more fully the above beliefs about why clients change and how symptom reduction occurs.

Fortunately we have a third option for treatment of behavioral and psychological symptoms, neurotherapy and neurofeedback.

Therefore, the main purpose of this book is to provide a thorough understanding of many of the aspects surrounding the world of neurotherapy and neurofeedback. In Chapter 1, *Introduction to Neurotherapy and Neurofeedback*, we will discuss in general terms the definition of neurotherapy (NT) and neurofeedback (NFB), the goals of neurotherapy and neurofeedback, and the basic principles. In-depth analysis of those topics will be covered in separate chapters. Chapter 2, *The History of Neurotherapy*, offers the reader an historical perspective of neurotherapy and neurofeedback. Then we showcase several of the pioneers in this field who have dramatically influenced the progress of neurofeedback. In Chapter 3, *Sources of Brain Dysregulation*, a thorough explanation of many of the reasons our brains become dysregulated are presented, from genetic predisposition to chronic illnesses. Chapter 4, *The Neurophysiology of Self-Regulation*, provides essential information to better understand the biological underpinnings of neurotherapy and neurofeedback, explaining the functions of the autonomic nervous system and the polyvagal system. The remaining six chapters offer specific information about NT and NFB. For example, in Chapter 5, *Strategies for Self-Regulation*, distinct categories of NT are presented from biofeedback to neurofeedback. Chapter 6, *Basic Concepts and Principles in Neurofeedback*, describes the needed instruments, computers, electroencephalographs, and the learning principles of operant and classical conditional that allow NFB to work. Chapter 7, *Assessment, Treatment Planning, and Outcome Evaluation*, outlines the step-by-step procedures and processes necessary to conduct NFB. This chapter describes the expectations and types of assessments needed to gather information on each NFB client. Following a logical order, Chapter 8, *Neurofeedback Training, Protocols, and Case Studies*, delineates actual NFB protocols designed for specific symptoms from ADHD to Peak Performance. We offer several NFB case studies to illustrate the needed protocols and presenting symptoms. Chapter 9, *Neurofeedback Efficacy Research*, offers essential and useful information about efficacy ratings and NFB research. Chapter 10, *The Future of Neurotherapy and Other Professional Issues*, is our final chapter advocating for further NFB research, available resources, and ethical codes. We briefly visit the world of epigenetics and its impact on NFB.

NEUROTHERAPY AND NEUROFEEDBACK DEFINED

Neurotherapy is a form of neuromodulation. Neuromodulation simply means the alteration of some aspect of neuronal functioning. This could happen because of a variety of experiences, whether that occurs through physical exercise, learning a novel task, or neurofeedback. In future chapters, we will go more in depth about differing types of neurotherapy, but for now we will focus on neurofeedback (NFB), a type of neurotherapy involving a brain-computer interface (BCI) that maps certain aspects of a client's neurophysiology (e.g., brain wave amplitudes for various frequency bands) to some form of feedback, usually audio or video, that allows the brain to monitor and manipulate the underlying EEG activity. NFB, sometimes called EEG operant conditioning, is a type of self-regulation training (Swingle, 2010). Sometimes neurofeedback is labeled biofeedback for the brain, noninvasive brain surgery, or a neurological tune-up. When applied correctly, NFB has been found to lead to clinical improvements in several mental health disorders (Yucha & Montgomery, 2008). According to Yucha and Montgomery's thorough reviews, the authors rated the combined efficacy of biofeedback and neurofeedback a Level 4—"Efficacious" for anxiety reduction, attention disorders, chronic pain, epilepsy, and headaches. NFB "reinforces an optimal baseline of central nervous system self-regulation" (Legarda, McMahon, Othmer & Othmer, 2011, p. 1050). In addition, this self-regulation often decreases the need for multiple medications.

THE GOALS OF NFB

Many neurotherapists believe that because of living life and allowing life to happen, our brains become dysregulated. Chapter 3 will emphasize many of the occurrences that may cause dysregulation. For this discussion, though, here are a few examples for dysregulation: high fevers, accidentally falling on your head, personal trauma, or misuse of alcohol and drugs. These situations may cause three very different categories of brain states: overarousal, underarousal and/or unstable arousal. Overaroused persons may have symptoms ranging on a continuum from highly anxious to chronic pain. Underaroused persons may have symptoms from depression to ADHD, and the unstable aroused persons may be prone to anything from migraines to bipolar concerns.

The goal of NFB for any of these arousal states would be to reregulate and normalize brain functioning. Neurofeedback has the capacity to restore brain efficiency and begin to optimize personal and behavioral performance once again. This is accomplished with the principles of operant and classical conditioning. A neurotherapist will select a reinforcement brainwave target for a particular symptom such as ADHD. Perhaps there is not enough low beta in a child with ADHD, so the reinforcement target might be around 12–15 Hertz. Because the brain loves to be challenged, it will search for that targeted brainwave. When it hits that specified brainwave, it will be reinforced with a reward such as a full puzzle unfolding or a game moving forward. This is the action behind the principles of operant conditioning and learning in general.

There may be excess brainwaves causing symptoms as well. This same child with ADHD may have excess in theta and high beta. The neurotherapist might need to set two inhibits to help condition the brain to lower theta and high beta. These inhibits could have sounds attached to them, such as birds chirping, to remind the client there is too much theta. To remind them there may be too much high beta, a foghorn-like sound could be associated with high beta. When the client hears these sounds, it is a reminder, consciously and unconsciously, to lower those brainwaves. The brain wants those noises to go away and wants its goal to occur. Often, a client might work too hard or try too hard to make these sounds go away or make the puzzle unfold. The neurotherapist then has to teach the client to allow this natural process to occur. This may mean teaching the client some basic relaxation techniques or heart rate variability techniques. Eventually the brain wins out, and reinforcement and inhibit goals are achieved. Again these are basically the same principles of classical and operant conditioning and the principles of learning that change any behavior. These conditions all work together to assist the dysregulated brain to function in a more normal, regulated, and efficient manner.

NEUROPLASTICITY AND NEUROGENESIS

Through the advances of neuroscience, we better understand the brain, its functions, and its capabilities. In the last decade, brain research has debunked some old ideas, validated other existing beliefs, and offered new and encouraging interventions for helping people grow and learn. For years, educators and helping professionals believed that the brain matured around 12 years of age. Now with the help of functional magnetic resonance imaging (fMRI), researchers know that the adolescent brain is fully developed in the middle twenties (Giedd, 2004). However, neuroscientists now understand that the brain has the capability to adapt and develop new living neurons up until the very end of our lives, according to Dr. Norman Doidge, a psychiatrist at

Columbia University Center for Psychoanalytic Training and Research in New York. This process is called neuroplasticity. "Neuroplasticity can result not only in one region of the brain colonizing another—with remarkable effects on mental and physical functions—but also in the wholesale remodeling of neural networks" (Doidge, 2007, p. 16). A brain can rewire itself, as authors Schwartz and Begley demonstrate in their 2003 book called *The Mind and the Brain: Neuroplasticity and the Power of Mental Force*.

The brain is no longer considered a stagnant organ, but rather three to four pounds of plastic, fluid, and malleable tissue. Human beings can change their brains and develop new pathways through repetition and learning new skills. Challenging and taxing the brain with new tasks such as learning a foreign language can forge different pathways in the brain. The capacity to restructuring our brain allows our brain span to match our life span. The old adage, "you can't teach an old dog new tricks," no longer holds true.

One of the early neurorehabilitation pioneers, Dr. Paul Bach-y-Rita, recounts a poignant, personal story about his beginnings in the world of neuroplasticity (Bach-y-Rita, 1980). His father, Pedro Bach-y-Rita, a 65-year-old widower, had a disabling stoke. Pedro was paralyzed and unable to speak. Dr. Bach-y-Rita's brother, George, a medical student at that time, took his father in and was determined to help him recover. George first taught Pedro to crawl through painstaking and frustrating incremental movements. Then they begin to work on daily survival tasks such as washing dishes. They turned normal daily activities into life exercises. After months of struggles, Pedro slowly got better and better. Three years later, Pedro was able to return to his love of writing, poetry, and teaching. Pedro even remarried and became active in traveling and hiking. This story in itself has a wonderful and unique ending, but the best part of the story is yet to come. When Pedro was 72, he died of a heart attack while climbing in the high mountains of Colombia. Paul, curious about his father's astonishing recovery, requested an autopsy. He wanted to see slides of his father's brain. Paul's emotions ran from shock to amazement. Paul could actually see the part of his father's brain that had the lesion from the stroke. Ninety-seven percent of the nerves that went from his cerebral cortex to his spine were destroyed. The remainder of the slides, however, showed Pedro's brain had reorganized itself and built new nerve growth that restored his higher life functions. Pedro's brain slides dramatically demonstrated the devastation from the stroke and the creation of new growth. His determination, struggle, and hard work were clearly worthwhile. This dramatic story and countless other research results can also be read in Dr. Doidge's remarkable 2007 book, *The Brain That Changes Itself*.

Our brains are changeable and malleable organs for the positive and negative, and we know we can reorganize and maintain our brains for the better. Negative neuroplasticity can occur through trauma, repeated negative events, poor environmental conditions, and even constant negative thinking. Positive neuroplasticity can develop by challenging the brain with a new task such as learning a musical instrument, physical exercise, and even counseling.

The research and stories described above are only the beginning of this exciting new frontier into our changing brains and neurorehabilitation. Neurofeedback is just one more way we can help our brains. Swingle stated, "The mind is capable of astounding regeneration, growth and change" (2010, p. 31). Having the capacity to build new neuronal pathways, or neurogenesis, has far-reaching implications for all of us.

JAIMESON'S STORY

This story will seem all too familiar. Meet Jaimeson, a small, 7-year-old boy, who is bright and energetic. He is well liked in his class, very verbal but easily distracted. He is busy and constantly on the go. His teachers send home notes about his conduct, behaviors, and falling behind in homework. Jaimeson's parents are well educated and concerned about his learning in general. Many academic tests are administered, and all are in the normal ranges. His IQ is 130. Finally, his parents take him to a psychiatrist for additional testing. A Single Photon Emission Computer Tomography (SPECT) is done, along with several computerized continuous performance tests. After much discussion, the diagnosis was possible ADHD.

Jaimeson's parents decided not to place him on medication and began the long and arduous task of structuring his environment with behavioral modification plans. The psychiatrist supported their decision but warned that when their son hit puberty and his testosterone was in full motion, that his symptoms might progressively worsen. Providing structure and finding physical activities that Jaimeson enjoyed such as drumming, music, and Tae Kwon Do seemed to work, especially in coordination with the school system. His academic performance was average, but Jaimeson began not enjoying school.

During the eighth grade, Jaimeson became discouraged and struggled academically. His parents finally relented and placed him on a stimulant medication. After the first day of medication, his mom picked him up from school. He declared, "This is what it feels like to be focused!" His grades began to improve slowly, but contraindications from the stimulant were discouraging. Jaimeson lost weight, had difficulty sleeping, and had an even more difficult time getting up in the morning. Of course, this created emotional distress among other family members in the house.

Entering high school was even more difficult for Jaimeson. He lacked confidence in his learning skills, and that generalized to diminished social skills. An individualized education plan (IEP/504) was developed, allowing for special testing and homework tactics. Jaimeson detested having an IEP and being labeled as a "special needs student." Along the way, he had many tutors and camps to assist him in learning better skills. It seemed as if nothing truly made a substantial difference.

During Jaimeson's junior year in high school, his parents bribed him into doing 40 sessions of SMR neurofeedback (NFB)! They offered to purchase a new drum that he dearly wanted, after completing his 40 NFB sessions. The lure of a new drum enticed him, but he was scared that somebody would be "messing" with his brain. One day he mentioned that he basically liked his personality and didn't want to be changed through neurofeedback. This concern was discussed with his neurotherapist, and he wisely stated, "Your personality will not be changed. NFB only makes you a better you, a more efficient Jaimeson!" This alleviated some of Jaimeson's fears, so he reluctantly began his sessions. He was taught several beginning biofeedback interventions, Heart Math and skin temperature control. Then his NFB sessions began.

Around session number 20, his mom noticed that Jaimeson seemed to get out of bed more easily, and his general demeanor seemed more relaxed. By session 30, Jaimeson's entire life seemed to go more smoothly. He had the courage to begin a 20-hour-per-week job, maintained Bs and a few As in classes, and had a steady girlfriend. His mother commented that his life was like the Claritin commercial on television. In that commercial anyone with allergies lives a very foggy and cloudy lifestyle, but when Claritin is introduced into the system, that veil of fogginess is lifted away. That described Jaimeson's new life. He began to live life with clarity and ease.

The story does not end here. During his senior year of high school, Jaimeson earned the distinction of Dean's Honor Roll for the first time and graduated from high school. He began weaning off his stimulant medication, becoming medication-free during the summer. He surprised his parents by requesting to take a study skills class before entering college. He completed that series and began his freshman year in college at a small, private university. He is majoring in finance and the prelaw curricula. He successfully completed his first semester of college with all As and Bs and also competed in mock trials with other universities. The reader needs to know, however, that Jaimeson would not contribute his success to NFB. He believes it certainly helped, but it was he who made the difference.

As a practicing neurotherapist, I agree with Jaimeson's statement. It was that young man who made the difference, but it was NFB that gave him the needed neurological foundation and stability to put that ever-maturing brain into action. This is only one success story that will be discussed throughout this book, but it gives the reader an example of the power and hopefulness that NFB offers.

There is one additional component to this particular story that is important. Jaimeson is the son of the book authors! He gave us permission to share his story, and all three of us are thrilled with the results of NFB. We truly believe that NFB was the essential turning point for Jaimeson's successful life journey.

AN INITIAL NFB SCREENING FOR THE READERS

This final section of Chapter 1 is a short screening assessment titled "Neurological Dysregulation Risk Assessment" (Chapin, 2013). Read through the tool thoroughly and check off any of the categories that might apply to your life. Score the screening, and then read the bottom to see if NFB might be appropriate for you. Each one of these dysregulation categories will be explained further in Chapter 3.

NEUROLOGICAL DYSREGULATION RISK ASSESSMENT

Name (or Child's Name): _____ Age: _____ Date: _____

Current Problem, Symptom, or Complaint: _____

Please read each potential source of neurological dysregulation and indicate whether or not it may be a risk factor for you or your child.

	Yes	No
Genetic Influences: Grandparents, parents or siblings with mental health or learning disorders (including attention deficit hyperactivity disorder), post-traumatic stress disorder, depression, generalized anxiety disorder, substance abuse, personality or other severe psychological disorders (bipolar or schizophrenia).	_____	_____
Prenatal Exposure: Maternal distress, psychotropic medication use, alcohol or substance abuse, nicotine use, or possible exposure to environmental toxins including genetically modified foods, pesticides, petrochemicals, xenestrogens in plastics, heavy metals (lead/mercury), and fluoride, bromine, and chlorine in water.	_____	_____
Birth Complications: Forceps or vacuum delivery, oxygen loss, head injury, premature birth, difficult or prolonged labor, obstructed umbilical cord, or fetal distress.	_____	_____
Disease and High Fever: Sustained fever above 104 degrees due to bacterial infection, influenza, strep, meningitis, encephalitis, Reye's Syndrome, PANDAS, or other infections or disease processes.	_____	_____
Current Diagnosis: Of mental health, physical health, alcohol abuse, substance abuse, or learning disorder.	_____	_____

	Yes	No

Poor Diet and Inadequate Exercise: Diet high in processed food, preservatives, simple carbohydrates (sugar and flour), genetically modified foods, foods treated with herbicides, pesticides, and hormones, low daily water intake, high caffeine intake, and lack of adequate physical exercise (20 minutes, 7 times a week).

Emotionally Suppressive Psychosocial Environment: Being raised or currently living in poverty, domestic violence, physical, emotional, or sexual abuse, alcoholic or mentally unstable family environment, emotional trauma, neglect, institutionalization, and inadequate maternal emotional availability or attachment.

Mild to Severe Brain Injury: Experienced one or more blows to the head from a sports injury, fall, or auto accident (with or without loss of consciousness), or episodes of open head injury, coma, or stroke.

Prolonged Life Distress: Most commonly due to worry about money, work, economy, family responsibilities, relationships, personal safety, and/or health causing sustained periods of anxiety, irritability, anger, fatigue, lack of interest, low motivation or energy, nervousness, and/or physical aches and pains.

Stress Related Disease: Includes heart disease, kidney disease, hypertension, obesity, diabetes, stroke, hormonal, and/or immunological disorders.

Prolonged Medication Use, Substance Use or Other Addictions: Including legal or illegal drug use, substance abuse, or addiction (alcohol, drugs, nicotine, caffeine, medication, gambling, sex, spending, etc.) and overuse of screen technologies (cell phones, video games, television, computers, Internet, etc.).

Seizure Disorders: Caused by birth complications, stroke, head trauma, infection, high fever, oxygen deprivation, and/or genetic disorders and includes epilepsy, pseudo-seizures, or epileptiform seizures.

Chronic Pain: Related to accidents, injury, or a disease processes Including back pain, headache and migraine pain, neck pain, facial pain, and fibromyalgia.

	Yes	No
Surgical Anesthesia, Chemotherapy, and/or Aging: Can cause mild cognitive impairment, insomnia, and depression and be related to emotional trauma, loss and grief, chronic illness, physical decline, reduced mobility, physical, social, and emotional isolation and decreased financial security.	_____	_____
Scoring and Interpretation: Total Number of "Yes" Responses	_____	_____

In general, the greater the number of "yes" responses, the greater the risk of significant neurological dysregulation. However, even one severe "yes" response could cause significant neurological dysregulation and result in serious mental, physical, or cognitive impairment that may benefit from individually designed neurofeedback training.

CONCLUSIONS

To help readers clarify what information will be emphasized throughout our book, this chapter outlines the main focus of each of the remaining nine chapters. A simple definition of neurotherapy and neurofeedback was offered using a neuromodulation model. Hopefully, this assists readers in understanding that all neurotherapy is a type of neuromodulation. Neurofeedback is a type of neurotherapy with biofeedback for the brain, as an excellent definition. The stories and the screening at the end of the chapter illustrate the possible benefits and hope that neurofeedback may bring. The remaining chapters discuss in detail the nature, function, and capabilities of neurotherapy and neurofeedback.

REFERENCES

Bach-y-Rita, P. (1980). Brain plasticity as a basis for therapeutic procedures. In P. Bach-y-Rita (Ed.), *Recovery of function: Theoretical considerations for brain injury rehabilitation* (pp. 239–241). Berns: Hans Huber Publishers.

Bhatia, S. K., & Bhatia, S. C. (2007). Childhood and adolescent depression. *American Family Physician, 75*(1), 73–80.

Chapin, T. (2013). *Brain dysregulation risk assessment.* Peoria, IL: Resource Management Services.

Doidge, N. (2007). *The brain that changes itself.* New York: Penguin Books.

Giedd, J. N. (2004). Structural magnetic resonance imaging of the adolescent brain. *Adolescent Brain Development: Vulnerabilities and Opportunities, 1021*(6), 77–85.

Green, T., Heinemann, S., & Gusella, J. (1998). Molecular neurobiology and genetics: Investigation of neural function and dysfunction. *Neuron, 20*(3), 427–444.

Lambert, M. J., & Cattani, K. (1996). Current findings regarding the effectiveness of counseling: Implication for practice. *Journal of Counseling and Development, 74*(6), 601–608.

Landman, J. T., & Dawes, R. M. (1982). Psychotherapy outcomes: Smith and Glass's conclusions stand up under scrutiny. *American Psychologist, 37*(5), 504–516.

Legarda, S. B., McMahon, D., Othmer, S., & Othmer, S. (2011). Clinical neurofeedback: Case studies, proposed mechanisms, and implications for pediatric neurologic practice. *Journal of Child Neurology, 26*(8), 1045–1051.

Schwartz, J., & Begley, S. (2003). *The mind and the brain: Neuroplasticity and the power of mental force.* New York: HarperCollins Publishers.

Smith, M. L., & Glass, G. V. (1977). Meta-analysis of psychotherapy outcome studies. *American Psychologist, 32*(9), 752–760.

Swingle, P. G. (2010). *Biofeedback for the brain.* New Brunswick, NJ: Rutgers University Press.

Yucha, C., & Montgomery, D. (2008). *Evidenced-based practice in biofeedback and neurofeedback.* Wheat Ridge, CO: Association for Applied Psychophysiology and Biofeedback.

2

THE HISTORY OF NEUROTHERAPY

With modern parts atop old ones, the brain is like an iPod built around an eight-track cassette player.

—Sharon Begley

Types of neurotherapy and neurofeedback have a surprisingly long history of self-regulating brain work that spans thousands of years with some unexpected origins. Throughout history, humankind has experimented with different methods to help with the complexities of living. The martial arts, yoga, meditation, and prayer have been practiced for millennia. Although no one understood exactly why these exercises helped, they made us feel better and stronger. Now we know these were examples of effective brain self-regulation (Swingle, 2010). In the past, we may have not known the whys or even the hows of what made life work, but slowly people began to discover more and more information about the body. For example, in ancient Egypt, a paper papyrus was discovered with hieroglyphs demonstrating that a hit to the left side of the head would diminish vision and, specifically, a blow to the left part of the head would influence the right side of the body (Robbins, 2008). We have been trying to understand the brain and its functions from the beginning of time. With all our new advances, Ivey, Ivey, Zalaquett, and Quirk (2009) stated that the "bridge between biological and psychological processes is erasing the old distinction between mind and body, between mind and brain" (p. 44).

This chapter will explore the history of neurotherapy and the science and research behind the evolving fields of neurotherapy and neurofeedback. In an effort to better understand the power and effects of brain self-regulating techniques from biofeedback to neurotherapy to neurofeedback (NFB), this history piece will begin with chronological biographical sketches of neurotherapy pioneers and their main contributions to neurotherapy and neurofeedback. Many early experimenters will be left out of this writing, but each one helped the other to discover the power of the brain. Today, the neurotherapy and neurofeedback history is still growing, but we need to begin with the vision of one of the pioneers who discovered that the brain had electrical impulses.

NEUROTHERAPY PIONEERS

Richard Caton

Major Contributions: In 1875, Dr. Caton, a British physician, was exploring the different functions of the brain and found that the brain had electrical impulses or waves. He was working with animals and noticed that when a probe was placed in certain parts of the exposed cortices, an electrical impulse was observed. This discovery was a major beginning of the neuroscience and neurotherapy field.

Camillo Golgi

Major Contributions: Around the same time that Dr. Caton was working on electrical impulses, Dr. Golgi, an Italian anatomist, created an innovative brain stain, allowing nerve cells to be seen much more easily under a microscope. This occurred in the 1880s (Robbins, 2008).

Santiago Ramón y Cajal

Major Contributions: Using the new stain, Dr. Ramón y Cajal, a Spanish anatomist, discovered the brain cell, explaining and labeling the cell's function and structure with dendrites and axons. His work contributed to our current understanding of neuroplasticity and neurogenesis by demonstrating that cells change and grow when new learning occurs. The Nobel Prize was awarded in 1906 to Camillo Golgi and Santiago Ramón y Cajal (Robbins, 2008).

Hans Berger

Major Contributions: It took until 1924 for Hans Berger, a German psychiatrist, to discover the amplification of the brain's electrical activity from the surface of the scalp and actually record it on a type of graph paper using a reflecting galvanometer. This first was the beginning of the electroencephalogram (EEG) as we know it today, and it was Dr. Berger who coined the term EEG. Dr. Berger also was one of the first scientists to understand that a person's brain waves are different depending on the state of consciousness or attention (1929). He observed that if his subject was resting or sitting quietly with eyes closed, frequencies could be seen around 10 cycles per second (10 Hertz [Hz]). However, if the same person was concentrating on

FIGURE 2.1 Berger demonstrating his first EEG instrument.

Permission granted from Werner, 1963; photo courtesy of Dr. P. Gloor.

a difficult task such as solving a mathematical problem with eyes open, then Dr. Berger noticed that the brain wave frequencies could be counted around 15 cycles per second (15 Hz) (Masterpasqua & Healey, 2003). Eyes open and eyes closed tasks are still one method of analyzing brain waves today. Dr. Berger began the classification system for brain waves, and it, too, is still used today (see Figure 2.1).

Herbert Jasper and Charles Shagass

Major Contributions: Dr. Herbert Jasper, M.D., worked at the Department of Neurology and Neurosurgery at McGill University. Dr. Charles Shagass, M.D., was a professor of psychiatry at Temple University. They have many contributions, but the main neurofeedback emphasis of Jasper and Shagass's research (1941) was to investigate how and if alpha in the occipital lobe could be conditioned with visual and auditory responses. Their results also demonstrated that subjects could learn to voluntarily control an alpha-blocking response. It was their work that added classical conditioning to our current neurofeedback principles and models.

Joe Kamiya

Major Contributions: Dr. Kamiya earned his Ph.D. from the University of California at Berkeley in 1954. The beginning of Dr. Joe Kamiya's work was in the 1960s at the University of Chicago, studying people and teaching them to relax to promote states of deep alpha states. These low frequency brain states, alpha waves, were working around 8–12 Hz, or eight cycles per second, and Kamiya discovered that people could be trained to achieve and maintain this relaxation state through positive reinforcement (Kamiya, 1969). This state came to be known as the "felt state, the question addressed being whether the human subject is able to have any kind of awareness regarding his own alpha activity" (Othmer, 2009, p. 4). This state or alpha wave training became associated with the psychedelic movement (Myers & Young, 2012). Unfortunately, this association may have harmed the credibility of the entire movement by taking away some of the field's scientific contributions.

Maurice B. Sterman

Major Contributions: Barry Sterman earned his Ph.D. in psychology and neuroscience from the University of California at Los Angeles in 1963. Dr. Sterman intentionally focused on animals to eliminate any questions concerning felt states (Othmer, 2009). Dr. Sterman worked in the early 1960s and 1970s at UCLA and NASA, reducing the frequency of seizures in cats exposed to jet fuel. His work also included humans who had epileptic seizures conditioning to sensory motor rhythm (SMR at 12–15 Hz) and low beta waves. He used a basic reward system to teach the cats to control resting brain waves (Sterman & Friar, 1972). Because this work was for NASA, it was not published for all readers. In 1962, however, research results were published, demonstrating that "pairing a neutral auditory stimulus with electrical stimulation of the basal forebrain resulted in this auditory stimulus inducing sleep preparatory sleep behavior" (Arns, 2010, p. 291). In 1968 Wyrwicka and Sterman published another article that truly was the beginning foundation for operant conditioning of EEG activity (Wyrwicka & Sterman, 1968).

Joel Lubar

Major Contributions: Dr. Joel Lubar earned his B.S. and Ph.D. from the Division of the Biological Sciences and Department of Biopsychology at the University of Chicago. Dr. Lubar began to replicate and expand the work of

Dr. Sterman. Dr. Lubar began hypothesizing whether neurofeedback would work with children with attention deficit hyperactivity disorder (ADHD). In 1976, he and a colleague, Dr. Shouse, published the pioneering work evaluating the effect of neurofeedback on children with ADHD. At that time, it was called hyperkinetic syndrome. Dr. Lubar added another dimension to neurofeedback by setting inhibits with the intention of training to more of a normal distribution (Othmer, 2009). Dr. Lubar continued his worked at the University of Tennessee. His research reduced inattentiveness and hyperactivity in children with ADHD, focusing on theta and beta waves (Lubar, 2003).

Margaret E. Ayers

Major Contributions: Dr. Ayers earned a B.S. in microbiology and a M.A. in counseling psychology from Seattle Pacific University. She earned her D.M.A. in alternative medicine from Rio Verdi University in Provo, Utah. Dr. Ayers was known for her work with traumatic brain injuries. She was also one of the first clinicians to open a private practice focusing on neurofeedback with real-time digital EEG neurofeedback.

Siegfried and Sue Othmer

Major Contributions: Dr. Othmer received a B.S. in physics from Virginia Polytechnic Institute and State University, and he earned his Ph.D. in 1970 from Cornell University, in experimental physics with minors in theoretical physics and mathematics. Sue Othmer earned a bachelor's degree from Cornell University in 1970 in physics, magna cum laude and with distinction in all subjects.

Until the 1980s, NFB was not known to the mainstream population. Margaret Ayers, who was a strong proponent of NFB and its capabilities and who had helped treat the Othmers' son, encouraged the Othmers to develop additional NFB treatments. The Othmers have been powerful advocates for the NFB field for the past 30 years. They created their own company, EEG-Spectrum and EEG Info, and have trained countless numbers of new NFB practitioners. They are best known for Infra Low Frequency (ILF) training and use of computer graphics (Robbins, 2008).

Eugene Peniston

Major Contributions: The work of Dr. Eugene Peniston at the Veterans Administration (VAMC) in Colorado occurred in the early 1990s. Peniston and Paul Kulkosky (1989) published their work on positive results with veterans who were addicted to alcohol. Dr. Peniston also developed a neurofeedback intervention for the treatment of trauma and addiction, using alpha and theta protocols.

Thomas Budzynski

Major Contributions: Dr. Budzynski's last academic position was at the University of Washington. There are many contributions that Dr. Budzynski made to the NFB field; however, one of the major ones is his theta enhancement training. His work taught subjects to get to a twilight state where emotional learning and psychological growth occurred through biofeedback conditioning. He was also a coeditor of the popular *Introductions to Quantitative EEG and Neurofeedback* textbook (Budzynski, Budzynski, Evans, & Abarbanel, 2009).

Leslie Sherlin

Major Contributions: Dr. Leslie Sherlin earned two of his degrees at the University of Tennessee and has spent much of his career dedicated to the field of peak performance with athletes. His coauthored position paper on the efficacy of NFB with children with ADHD is widely cited (Sherlin et al., 2010). Dr. Sherlin is a NFB trainer, lecturer, writer, and researcher. He also teaches and writes on QEEG and low resolution brain electromagnetic tomography (LORETA) for diagnosis and treatment (Sherlin, 2009).

NEUROIMAGING ADVANCES

A major boon to the neurotherapy world has been the advances in the neuroimaging field. Neuroimaging offers new and additional information to correlate with neurofeedback techniques from functional magnetic imaging resonance (fMRI) to brain mapping through a 19-channel EEG. These scans provide detailed images of the functions, blood flow, metabolic rates, and structures of the brain. The scans have the capacity to validate much of the NFB research with additional data and a wealth of information that had previously not been seen or understood.

PROFESSIONAL ORGANIZATIONS

Another strong bonus to the neurotherapy, neurofeedback, and biofeedback field is the focused efforts of several professional organizations. Biofeedback Certification International Alliance offers certification for qualified professionals. Their website is www.bcia.org. The International Society for Neuronal Regulation (ISNR) and the Association for Applied Psychophysiology and Biofeedback (AAPB) both offer professional membership, national conferences, and corresponding peer-reviewed journals. The website for ISNR is www.isnr.org, and the website for AAPB is www.aapb.org. These organizations provide professionalism to the field and available resources for practitioners. Additional information about these organizations will be offered in Chapter 10.

CONCLUSIONS

This chapter provided the reader with a glimpse into the history of neurotherapy and neurofeedback, emphasizing many of the major contributors to the field. Until recently, NFB has not been widely accepted. Understanding NFB's history helps explain its steady progress into the mainstream. Recent focus in the media from *National Geographic*; *Scientific American*'s journal, *Mind*; *Wall Street Journal*; YouTube; and television coverage has also sparked additional interest. With the advances of controlled and randomized research, professional associations, and advances in neuroimaging, the field of neurofeedback is becoming more accepted as a standardized intervention for the treatment of many behavioral and psychological concerns. Dr. Frank Duffy, a Harvard professor and neurologist, summarized it best, stating,

> The literature, which lacks any negative study of substance, suggests that EEG biofeedback therapy should play a major therapeutic role in many difficult areas. In my opinion, if any medicine had demonstrated such a wide spectrum of efficacy, it would be universally accepted and widely used. (2000, v–viii)

REFERENCES

Arns, M. (2010). Historical archives: The beginning of neurofeedback. *Journal of Neurotherapy, 14*(4), 291–292.

Begley, S. (2007). In our messy reptilian brains. Newsweek Online. Retrieved May, 2013, from www.thedailybeast.com/newsweek/2007/04/08/in-our-messy-reptilian-brains.html

Berger, H. (1929). Uber das electrenenkephalogramm des menschen [On the electroencephalogram of humans]. *Archives von Pscyhiatricia Nervkrankh, 87*, 525–570.

Budzynski, T. H., Budzynski, H. K., Evans, J. R., & Abarbanel, A. (2009). Introduction to Quantitative EEG and neurofeedback: Advanced theory and applications (2nd ed.). Burlington, MA: Academic Press.

Duffy, F. H. (2000). The state of EEG biofeedback therapy in 2000: An editor's opinion. *Clinical Electroencephalography, 31*, v–viii.

Ivey, A. E., Ivey, M. B., Zalaquett, C., & Quirk, K. (2009). Counseling and neuroscience: The cutting edge of the coming decade. *Counseling Today, 52*, 44–55.

Jasper, H., & Shagass, C. (1941). Conscious time judgments related to conditioned time intervals and voluntary control of the alpha rhythm. *Journal of Experimental Psychology, 28,* 503–508.

Kamiya, J. (1969). Operant control of the EEG alpha rhythm and some of its reported effects on consciousness. In C. Tart (Ed.), *Altered states of consciousness* (pp. 489–501). New York: Wiley.

Lubar, J., & Shouse, M. N. (1976). Use of biofeedback in the treatment of seizure disorders and hyperactivity. *Advances in Clinical Child Psychology, 1,* 203–265.

Lubar, J. F. (2003). Neurofeedback for the management of attention deficit disorders. In M. S. Schwartz & F. Andrasik. (Eds.), *Biofeedback: Practitioners' guide* (pp. 409–437). New York: Guilford Press.

Masterpasqua, F., & Healey, K. N. (2003). Neurofeedback in psychological practice. *Professional Psychology: Research and Practice, 34*(6), 652–656.

Myers, J. E., & Young, S. (2012). Brain wave biofeedback: Benefits of integrating neurofeedback in counseling. *Journal of Counseling and Development, 90,* 20–28.

Othmer, S. (2009). Neuromodulation technologies: An attempt at classification. *Introduction to QEEG and Neurofeedback: Advanced theory and applications* (2nd ed.). Burlington, MA: Elsevier Inc.

Peniston, E. G., & Kulkosky, P. J. (1989). Alpha-theta brainwave training and beta endorphin levels in alcoholics. *Alcoholism, Clinical and Experimental Research, 13,* 271–279.

Robbins, J. (2008). *A symphony in the brain.* New York: Grove Press.

Sherlin, L. (2009). Diagnosing and treating brain function through the use of low resolution brain electromagnetic tomography (LORETA). In T. H. Budzynski, H. K. Budzynski, J. R. Evans, & A. Abarbanel (Eds.), *Introduction to quantitative EEG and neurofeedback: Advanced theory and applications* (2nd ed., pp. 83–102). Burlington, MA: Academic Press.

Sherlin, L., Arns, M., Lubar, J., & Sokhadze, E. (2010). A position paper on neurofeedback for the treatment of ADHD. *Journal of Neurotherapy, 14*(2), 66–78.

Sterman, M. B., & Friar, L. (1972). Suppression of seizures in epileptics following Sensorimotor EEG feedback training. *Electroencephalography and Clinical Neurophysiology, 33,* 89–95.

Swingle, P. G. (2010). Biofeedback for the brain: How neurotherapy effectively treats depression, ADHD, autism and more. New Brunswick, NJ: Rutgers University Press.

Werner, R. (1963). Jenenser EEG Symposium. Berlin, Germany.

Wyrwicka, W., & Sterman, M. B. (1968). Instrumental conditioning of sensorimotor cortex EEG spindles in the waking cat. *Physiology & Behavior, 3,* 703–707.

3

SOURCES OF BRAIN DYSREGULATION

We sit on the threshold of important new advances in neuroscience that will yield increased understanding of how the brain functions and of more effective treatments to heal brain disorders and diseases. How the brain behaves in health and disease may well be the most important question in our lifetime.

—Richard D. Broadwell

The brain's total electrical output is about 30 to 40 watts, enough to power a small household light bulb. Its electrical activity is generated by the cortex, thalamus, and the brain stem. The cortex contains 97% of the brain's 100 billion neurons and is the primary source of electrical activity measured during neurofeedback. The thalamus is the subcortical structure that controls the rhythm of neuronal firing. It's responsible for the generation of the brain-wave frequencies or bandwidths called theta, alpha, and sensory motor rhythm (SMR). Delta is generated by the deeper levels of the cortex and beta by both the cortex and the brain stem (Thompson & Thompson, 2003).

In neurofeedback, the amplitude of these brainwaves is monitored and trained in tiny measurements called microvolts, which are a millionth of a volt. Together, electrical activity and neurotransmitters, specialized brain chemicals necessary to conduct signals from one neuron to another, determine whether the neuronal transmission will be either excitatory or inhibitory (Thompson & Thompson, 2003). These in turn activate or deactivate the functions related to that area of the brain. The delicate and intricate symphony of the brain's electro-chemical processes is what determines its current state of healthy regulation. Unfortunately, many factors can disrupt the symphony and cause significant dysregulation of the brain's electrical activity.

This chapter will review several of the more significant factors involved in brainwave dysregulation. These will include genetic influences, prenatal development, environmental toxins, birth complications, disease and high fever, diet and exercise, emotionally suppressive psychosocial environments, head injury, stress, medication, substance abuse and addiction, seizure disorders and chronic pain, and cognitive decline associated with surgical anesthesia and aging. These factors are important because they have broad implications for neurotherapy assessment, treatment planning, and prevention of brainwave dysregulation.

GENETIC INFLUENCES

Genetic influences can be studied in several ways. These include familial patterns, twin studies, genome and chromosomal analysis, and epigenetic investigation. The *Diagnostic and Statistical Manual of Mental Disorders* (4th ed., Text Revision, *DSM-IV-TR*, APA, 2008) and the *Diagnostic and Statistical Manual of Mental Disorders* (5th ed., *DSM-5*, APA, 2013) provided a brief summary of familial influences on mental health disorders. More specifically, it reported transmission trends from parents to children. It noted that ADHD and post-traumatic stress disorders were more common in first-degree biological relatives. For example, depression is one and a half to three times more common among first-degree relatives, generalized anxiety followed similar trends as depression, and alcohol abuse had a 40–60% genetic risk of three to four times greater risk for first-degree relatives.

Other research has supported these conclusions. For ADHD, Amen (2001), from his clinical experience, reported that if one parent has ADHD, there was a 60% chance a child would have it. If both parents had ADHD, there was an 85–90% chance a child would be diagnosed. Levy et al. (1997), in a very large twin study, found 81% of identical twins had ADHD as compared to only 29% of fraternal twins. Morrison and Stewart (1971) investigated the parents of 59 ADHD children. They found fathers to have a significantly greater likelihood of antisocial personality disorder, mothers a higher occurrence of histrionic personality disorder, and both parents a greater likelihood of alcohol problems as compared to the parents of non-ADHD children. Finally, in a landmark study only possible since the mapping of the human genome, Comings (1995) found several chromosomal indicators of ADHD. These were specific gene sites at HLA chromosome 6, dopamine transporter gene chromosome 5, and the D4 receptor gene on chromosome 11, indicating a genetic basis for ADHD.

Heritable influences in post-traumatic stress disorder (PTSD) have been found to range from 46% in adult male and female twins (Sartor et al., 2012) to 71% among an all-female twin sample (Sartor et al., 2011). The SLC6A4 serotonin transporter gene has been found to mediate the effects of trauma. The higher the methylation (process to make new neurotransmitters) of serotonin, the more protected a person is from PTSD (Koenen et al., 2011). However, the role of genes may be limited in explaining the impact of PTSD since not all trauma survivors develop the disorder. Other risk factors likely include neuroendocrine hormonal alterations and environmental and epigenetic mechanisms (Yehuda et al., 2011). Commenting on brainwave abnormalities, Swingle (2010) noted those predisposed to PTSD may have lower posterior theta and alpha brainwaves that do not allow them to calm and recover after exposure to trauma experiences.

Sapolsky (2004) explained generalized anxiety's link to depression. He noted that genes that predispose to depression do so only in stressful environments. In other words, a genetic predisposition does not necessarily predict expression of that gene. In the case of depression, environmental stress must be encountered for the genetic predisposition to be expressed. This may also be the case in genetic influences that are transmitted across generations. Pembrey (2006), in a study of the effects of limited ancestral food supply of paternal grandparents during their mid-childhood, found that it significantly increased the mortality rates of their grandsons. This epigenetic study suggested that a single event could influence genetic phenotype for more than one generation, in a gender-specific way. He referred to it as a type of transgenerational epigenetic inheritance. The implication is that other factors such as maternal emotional duress, poverty, dislocation, or social strife resulting in stress and depression may not only impact the immediate parent–child bond but may also impact generations to come. Swingle (2010) also noted the stress–depression connection. He said those predisposed to depression likely have too much brainwave activity (high alpha or beta waves) over their left frontal lobe.

Regarding substance abuse, Bauer (2001) noted that alcoholics and their children are neurologically hardwired differently than nonalcoholics. More specifically, he found even after prolonged abstinence, they have lower levels of alpha and theta brainwaves and excessive beta brainwaves. He noted this made it more difficult for them to relax and caused them to become more reliant on the sedating effects of alcohol to make alpha and theta go up and beta go down. He suggested alcoholics and their neurologically vulnerable children are self-medicating to treat genetic brainwave pathology. Swingle (2010) also indicated that those predisposed to alcoholism have likely deficient theta and alpha waves in their occipital lobes.

Finally, exciting genome research has found further genetic influences on specific brainwave predispositions. These include strong individual alpha and alpha power in identical but not fraternal adolescent twins (Smit et al., 2006); heritability of delta, theta, alpha, and beta brainwave bands in the occipital and frontal lobes of identical versus fraternal twins (Zietsch et al., 2007); and genetic phenotype research in alcoholism, finding a relationship of the HRT3B gene to vulnerability to alcohol abuse and antisocial personality disorder (Ducci et al., 2009), and a relationship of the SGIP1 gene with low theta power and alcoholism (Hodgkinson et al., 2010).

PRENATAL DEVELOPMENT

The developing fetus is very vulnerable to many maternal and environmental influences. These include maternal stress and immune challenge, maternal psychotropic drug use, substance abuse, nicotine, and an array of environmental toxins found to be harmful to the brain and general health. Due to obvious ethical reasons, much of the research in this area is done with mice so no harm is done to human fetuses.

Environmental stress during gestation has been found to exert a major impact on the developing brain. It is during the prenatal period that neurons are being formed, migrate to their positions in the brain, and establish their proper synaptic connections. Maternal immune activation, viral infection, psychological stress, and malnutrition have been found to contribute to later development of depression, anxiety, psychotic disorders, and schizophrenia (Markham & Koenig, 2011). In a study of rats that were given tail shocks to induce stress, Bland et al. (2007) investigated the neurological building blocks of this dysregulation. They found stressed rats showed decreased basic fibroblast growth factor and decreased brain-derived neurotropic factor in the subregions of the prefrontal cortex and the hippocampus. In another pair of rat studies, prenatal viral influenza infection was found to cause significant atrophy and white brain matter thinning and thickening in specific brain areas (Fatemi et al., 2009), and prenatal immune challenge in early gestation caused adult ventricular enlargement relevant to the development of schizophrenia and autism (Li et al., 2009).

Since all drugs diffuse across the placenta and are excreted into breast milk, they can affect fetal development. The safety of psychotropic medication use during pregnancy is still unresolved. Limited information is available about the developmental outcomes of children exposed to medication. A review by Galbally et al. (2011) found a clear risk for neonatal serotonin discontinuation and withdrawal but could not conclude other health or developmental outcomes from maternal antidepressant use. More recent research, however, did find lower neuromotor performance among 6-month-olds exposed to prenatal antipsychotic medication (Johnson et al., 2012) and disturbed enteric nervous system development after prenatal antidepressant exposure (Nijenhuis et al., 2012). Overall, the benefits and risks of psychotropic medication use during pregnancy must be carefully weighed.

The affects of fetal alcohol syndrome (FAS) have been well documented (Jones et al., 1973; Clarren & Smith, 1978). These involve structural, neurological, and functional impairments. Children with FAS have microencephaly (smaller heads) and a smaller corpus callosum and cerebellum. They have impaired neurological development with disrupted prenatal brain cell migration and organization. FAS also impacts the hippocampus, responsible for memory, learning, emotions, and the processing of visual and auditory information, and the development of the central and peripheral nervous systems. Children with FAS have problems with learning disabilities, IQ, achievement, impulse control, social perception, communication, abstract reasoning, math, memory, attention, judgment, and social and adaptive skills. The research has found women who drink more than

18 drinks a week have a 30–33% chance of having a child with FAS. It is recommended that women fully abstain from alcohol use during pregnancy and while breastfeeding, since alcohol can be transported to the child through breast milk.

Functional neuroimaging studies of prenatal exposure to alcohol have found differences in the structure and functioning of the frontal, parietal, and temporal areas of the brain; the cerebellum and the basal ganglia; and cognitive areas, as well as with the white matter that connects these regions (Roussotte, Soderberg, & Sowell, 2010). This work also found prenatal exposure to cocaine and methamphetamines may be particularly toxic to dopamine-rich basal ganglia areas.

Nicotine exposure, via first- and secondhand smoke or nicotine replacement therapy, has been found to affect brain functioning and maturation during the prenatal, postnatal, and adolescent periods of life (Dwyer, McQuawn, & Leslie, 2009). Rat studies, investigating the nicotinic acetylcholine receptors that regulate critical aspects of brain maturation, found prenatal exposure to nicotine to alter the neocortex, hippocampus, and cerebellum, as well as influence later limbic system maturation during adolescence. Nicotine acts as a mild stimulant and constricts blood flow to the brain; this affects both the central and peripheral nervous system.

ENVIRONMENTAL TOXINS

Environmental toxins, present throughout life, also make their way to the developing fetus. These include rogue chemicals present in genetically modified foods; pesticides; petrochemicals; xenestrogens in plastics; heavy metals; and fluoride, bromine, and chlorine in water. Hill and Castro (2009) presented a thorough review of the impact of environmental toxins on prenatal health and development. Their work is briefly summarized below.

Citing a 2004 study by the Environmental Working Group, Hill and Castro (2009) noted over 287 chemicals in the umbilical cord blood of 10 babies at birth. Shockingly, 217 of these were known neurotoxins, 208 caused developmental disorders in animals, and 180 were known carcinogens. They said these chemicals were absorbed through respiration, direct exposure, or ingestion.

Xenestrogens, they reported, act like estrogen in the body. They are present in plastic bottles via bisphenal-A (BPA); food wrap; can lining; paint; detergents; fragrances; sunscreen; shampoo; and flame retardants in clothing, mattresses, and plastic toys. Xenestrogens have been found to increase the risk of brain, immune, and reproduction defects, and are implicated in weight gain, breast and prostate cancer, and early puberty in girls. Prenatal exposure is related to lower IQ, memory deficits, and behavioral and motor problems. Brominated flame-retardants in clothing, furniture, carpeting, car upholstery, and electronic equipment have been found to damage immune and thyroid function, and to be neurotoxic and carcinogenic.

Heavy metals including arsenic, lead, mercury, aluminum, and cadmium, as well as the nonmetal elements of fluoride, bromine, and chlorine, are also harmful to neurological functioning (Hill & Castro, 2009). Arsenic is found in pressure-treated wood that is commonly used on playgrounds, picnic tables, and decks. It is also found in groundwater, citrus fruits, cotton, and chicken feed. It can damage multiple organs, cause cancer, and decrease IQ. They stressed that lead, although removed from gas and paint, is still everywhere. It has been replaced by hydrocarbons and methanol that bring their own risks. Just a millionth of a gram of lead in a cup of blood causes learning disabilities. Mercury is also ubiquitous and can be found in the atmosphere, soil, water, and in many products we consume. It is in fish, vaccinations, fluorescent lighting, and electronics. It was once used as a fungicide in paint and in amalgam fillings for teeth. Mercury is highly neurotoxic, suppresses the immune system, inhibits hormone functioning, disrupts cell membrane permeability, dysregulates genetic signaling, and inhibits DNA repair. Aluminum is also neurotoxic and is known to produce dementia. It is found in cookware, antacids, buffered aspirin, and antiperspirants. Cadmium is found in cigarette smoke and has been found to suppress the immune system and to be toxic to the brain and liver.

Finally they noted that fluoride, bromine, and chlorine, still in common use, have been found to suppress thyroid functioning; lower body temperature; and contribute to dry skin, low energy, weight gain, constipation, elevated cholesterol, joint and muscle pain, low vital signs, cold hands and feet, and brittle fingernails. Hill and Castro (2009), questioning their continued use, pointed out fluoride is no longer used in Europe without any increase in dental decay, and Olympic swimmers will not swim in water that has been treated by bromine or chlorine. In their book, *Healing Young Brains*, they recommended environmental toxins of all types be avoided and methods be taken to detoxify the body including a healthy diet, consumption of organically grown food, elimination of petrochemically based cleaners and disinfectants, and use of food supplements to restore healthy neurological processes. Even still, absorption of some toxic chemicals may be impossible to avoid.

BIRTH COMPLICATIONS

The process of birth proceeds normally for most mothers and their babies; however, according to the National Vital Statistics Report (Hamilton, Martin, & Ventura, 2010), 11.99% of all births are premature. This puts them at significant risk for long-term physical and neurological complications. Even full-term births are not free of complications. Werner, Janevic, and Illuzzi (2011) reviewed 400,000 first-time births and investigated the neurological risks of newborns delivered with forceps, by Cesarean section (C-section), and vacuum delivery. They found of 15,000 babies delivered by forceps, 12% had seizures (an indication of oxygen loss). This compared to a 30% seizure rate for C-section or vacuum deliveries. Birth complications typically occur as a result of prematurity, oxygen loss, and head injury.

Prematurity is defined as birth before 37 weeks of gestation. Forty weeks is considered full term. According to Randis (2008), the primary complications involve low birth weight and underdevelopment of the respiratory, immunological, gastrointestinal, and neurological systems. Immature lung development results in respiratory distress and insufficient oxygenation to the brain and body. A compromised immune system causes the baby to be vulnerable to infection and sepsis, a systemic inflammatory response that can cause permanent brain damage or death. An underdeveloped gastrointestinal tract can cause necrotizing-enterocolitis and result in neuro-developmental disability or death. Regarding the neurological system, fragile, immature blood vessels in the brain can rupture from abrupt alterations in cerebral blood flow and pressure, resulting in intraventricular hemorrhaging. This can destroy cerebral tissue, leading to hydrocephalus, cognitive impairment, cerebral palsy, recurrent seizures, or death. In addition, injury to cerebral white matter due to oxygen loss and systemic inflammation can activate brain microglia that release toxins that damage, premyelinated neurons. This can cause parenchymal cysts, abnormal brain signal intensity, and reduced white and gray brain matter volume—precursors to cerebral palsy.

The long-term consequences of premature birth involve chronic lung disease; severe visual impairment; and neurological disabilities including cerebral palsy, lowered IQ, developmental delays, mental retardation, learning disabilities, impaired social skills, behavioral problems, ADHD, depression, and generalized anxiety disorder (Hack, 2006). Many factors can cause premature birth. Some of these include birthing multiple babies, poor lifestyle (drugs, alcohol, stress, nutrition, or lack of prenatal care), infection of the amniotic fluid or fetal membrane, hypertension, diabetes, anemia, problems with the uterus or placenta, physical trauma (car accident, domestic violence) or doctor-induced premature birth due to gestational diabetes or preeclampsia.

Complications in normal birth generally involve issues of oxygen loss or brain injury but can also include a long, hard labor, umbilical cord obstruction, and fetal distress (Hill & Castro, 2009). The birth process can be exhausting for both the mother and the baby. Monitoring of both their vital signs provides an indication of distress and signals the doctor as to the need for assistive measures (forceps, vacuum delivery, or C-section). As was previously noted, Werner et al. (2011) found forceps to cause fewer seizures (12%) than vacuum delivery or C-section (30%). Note that the typical cause of birth seizures is lack of oxygen to the baby's brain. Werner et al. (2011) suggested the reduced risk in forceps use may be due to the relatively reduced time involved in the forceps procedure. She also found forceps and vacuum delivery presented additional, long-term risk of neurological damage, due to possible subdural hemorrhaging (14% for forceps and 19% for vacuum delivery).

Finally, the unobstructed position of the umbilical cord is very important. Should the umbilical cord become pinched between the baby and the cervix, vital blood flow and oxygen to the baby will be cut off. If the umbilical cord is wrapped around the baby's neck, oxygen to the baby may be cut off. Depending upon the degree and length of the obstructed blood or oxygen flow, the baby may suffer hypoxia (decreased oxygen) or anoxia (no oxygen) with its associated neurological risk and impairment.

Hill and Castro (2009), in their discussion of birth complications, highlighted the function and clinical use of birth APGAR scores. They noted APGAR scores are used to assess a newborn's progress by color, heart rate, respiration, reflexes, and muscle tone. They are taken at 1 minute and at 5 minutes. If a baby has been in distress, the initial APGAR score will be low. After 5 minutes, the baby may have recovered and the second APGAR score will be normal. Clinical experience taught them not to overlook the initial APGAR score, since it may suggest more about the potential risk neurological dysregulation to the baby due to fetal distress than the second "normal" score.

DISEASE AND HIGH FEVER

High fever, in and of itself, does not appear to cause neurological damage, but it may influence brainwave dysregulation. According to Burns et al. (2013), most fevers are caused by viral or bacterial infections related to colds and influenza. A fever is one of the body's methods of killing invading microorganisms. Some fevers can cause febrile seizures in which a child can lose consciousness and have sudden jerking motions of the arms and legs. Although alarming to parents, these are usually not medically serious and rarely have long-term complications. Of greater concern is the potential of more serious underlying disease that may be causing the infection, toxic inflammation, swelling, or brain tissue damage. Four of these include meningitis, encephalitis, Reye's syndrome, and pediatric autoimmune neuropsychiatric disorders associated with streptococcus (PANDAS).

Meningitis is an inflammation of the membranes (meninges) surrounding the brain and spinal cord, usually caused by a viral infection (Reiss, 2006). It can resolve on its own or in a couple of weeks, or it can lead to a life-threatening emergency. The symptoms include a headache, fever, and stiff neck and can easily be confused with the flu (influenza). It is most common in children younger than 5 years old but can occur from 15 months to 25 years of age. Meningitis can lead to severe complications. These include hearing and vision loss, memory difficulty, loss of speech, learning disabilities, behavior problems, brain damage, paralysis, organ failure, and death.

Encephalitis involves inflammation of the brain tissue (Reiss, 2006). It is also most typically caused by a viral infection and presents with common flu-like symptoms such as fever or severe headache. Young children and older adults are at greater risk, but encephalitis from the herpes simplex virus is common in people from 20 to 30 years old. Most people have either no symptoms or mild symptoms. Encephalitis differs from meningitis in that it may be accompanied by symptoms of cognitive impairment, problems with sense or movement, and seizures. Severe cases can be life threatening or may lead to serious long-term complications. These include fatigue, mood disorders, personality changes, memory deficits, intellectual disabilities, visual and hearing defects, speech impairment, lack of coordination, paralysis, respiratory arrest, coma, or death.

In addition to serious neurological damage, high fever related to encephalitis has been found to cause an increase in ADHD and behavioral problems (Hill & Castro, 2009). During the severe influenza outbreak of 1918, there was an especially high incidence of encephalitis. Hofman (1922), in a review of the post-encephalitic behaviors in children, found a corresponding increase in ADHD and conduct disorders. This study illustrates the potential neurological dysregulation caused by high fever and disease processes.

Reye's syndrome is a rare but serious condition causing swelling in the liver and brain (Burns et al., 2013). It affects children and teenagers who have had a recent viral infection. It's been linked to an underlying metabolic disorder, previous exposure to toxins, (insecticides or paint thinner), and use of aspirin. Children with Reye's syndrome show signs 3–5 days after a viral infection (influenza or chicken pox). Symptoms typically progress from diarrhea, rapid breathing, vomiting, sleepiness, and irritable or aggressive behavior to confusion or disorientation, weakness in limbs, seizures, and decreased levels of consciousness. Hospitalization is required. Long-term complications can include motor problems, learning disabilities, and various neurological disorders. Starcko, Ray, and Dominguez's (1980) research on the relationship between aspirin use and Reye's syndrome compelled the Surgeon General to issue an advisory in 1982, warning parents not to use aspirin with young children suffering from the flu or chicken pox virus. Acetaminophen (Tylenol), ibuprofen (Advil or Motrin), or naproxen (Aleve) are preferred.

Since prolonged high fever can be potentially harmful, it should always be evaluated by a doctor (Axelrod & Diringer, 2008). General guidelines suggest younger infants, less than 3 months old, be evaluated with fevers above 100.4 degrees and older infants be evaluated with temperatures above 102.2 degrees. A high fever, considered to be a temperature above 104 degrees, should be immediately assessed by a doctor or an emergency room specialist. Finally, it is important to note that while most high fevers, even up to 107 degrees, do not result in permanent brain damage, the risk of brain dysregulation increases with high fever associated with serious underlying infection and disease.

More complicated than high fevers, a neurologically based autoimmune response can also cause neurological dysregulaton. The PANDAS describe a group of autoimmune neuropsychiatric disorders related to prepubescent childhood streptococcal infection that is associated with rapid onset obsessive-compulsive disorder (OCD) and/or tic disorders in children. In a review of 50 cases of childhood OCD, Swedo et al. (1998) found that OCD and tics, along with other symptoms including ADHD (40%), major depression (36%), overanxious disorder (28%), separation anxiety disorder (20%), and enuresis (12%), occurred shortly after exposure to a viral or bacterial infection. It was later hypothesized that an autoimmune reaction to a beta hemolytic strep-tococcal (GABHS) infection may have produced antibodies that interfere with basal ganglia and other cortical functioning, resulting in acute-onset OCD, tics and/or other symptoms noted above.

Although PANDAS have not yet been classified as a specific disease entity, in a more recent review of the research on immunological triggers for OCD, Moretti, Pasquine, Mandarelli, Tarsitani, and Biondi (2008) noted the promising results of immunomodulatory treatment for PANDAS, strength-ening the autoimmune hypothesis. They further noted the possible additional role of upper-respiratory infection in the sudden onset of OCD. Finally, since the occurrence of strep and upper-respiratory infection is very common in childhood, some perspective on the incidence of PANDAS are necessary. It has been estimated that PANDAS affect at least 200,000 persons in the United States and is therefore categorized by the National Institute of Health as a rare disease.

DIET AND EXERCISE

The American obesity epidemic accounts for 20.6% of U.S. health care costs and is on the rise. According to Crawley and Meyerhoefer (2012), in a recently published study of the medical costs of obesity, the percentage of Americans who are obese has tripled to 34% since 1960. They said for every heavyweight person who graduated into the overweight group, an overweight person graduated into the obesity group. This has resulted in an annual increase of medical spending (insurance costs and hospitalization) for men of $1,152 a year and for women, $3,613 per year. Combine the problem of obesity with declines in exercise due to elimination of physical education programs and recess in school, increase in passive electronic entertainment, and ever increasing workplace demands on the American worker, you have a perfect storm for brain dysfunction caused by nutritionally deficient diet and lack of adequate exercise.

Hill and Castro (2009) presented a critical evaluation of the American food industry and the modern American diet. They highlighted the impact of genetically modified food, overuse of herbicides and pesticides, and a diet dominated by processed foods as significantly contributing factors to nutritional deficiency, neurotoxicity, and brain dysregulation. While genetically modified (GM) food has greatly expanded the availability and reduced the cost of an abundant food supply, Pusztai (2000), working for the food industry, was alarmed to find that GM food made animals who ate them sick, infertile, and dead. He concluded that it wasn't the plant's production of the desired chemical to kill predatory insects that was the problem. Instead, it was the process of engineering itself, the way the gene was inserted, and what the gene did after its effect that made the animals, and likely humans, sick. Hill and Castro (2009) noted that the introduction of GM food and other rogue chemicals (herbicides and pesticides) into the American food supply parallels the dramatic increase in degenerative illness and disease in this country.

Also important to the discussion of food and brain dysregulation is the type of food consumed. The modern American diet is high in processed food and simple carbohydrates including sugar, soda, white bread, potatoes, pasta, and white rice. Amen (2001) described the impact of this diet on health and neurological functioning and recommended instead a diet higher in protein and lower in carbohydrates for most emotional and behavioral problems. Egger, Stolla, and McEwan (1992) investigated the effects of diet on hyperactivity. They found 116 of 185 hyperactive kids responded better to a low-allergen diet (high in protein, low in carbohydrates) plus supplements to include calcium, zinc, magnesium, and vitamins. Amen (2001) explained the consumption of carbohydrates (broken down into sugar) causes an insulin release that lowers blood sugar below normal levels. This causes a person to feel tired, spacey, confused, and inattentive. It also undermines motivation to exercise and increases craving and ingestion of more carbohydrates. This diet also effects the production of many neurotransmitters, exacerbating many emotional, learning, and behavioral problems.

The best diet, Amen (2001) advised, involves consumption of eight 8-ounce glasses of water a day to aid in brain blood flow and cell function (transport of nutrients and waste); protein at every meal to produce amino acids necessary for immune function, muscle mass, and enzymes for neurotransmitter production; complex carbohydrates from vegetables and fruit for fiber, vitamins, minerals and slower digestion; and saturated (animal, dairy, and coconut oil) and monounsaturated (omega 3 and olive oil) fats for brain and neuronal functioning. Hill and Castro (2009) further advised that these foods be organic when possible and the protein be grass-fed to avoid neural toxicity from GM, herbicides, and pesticides.

Even with this diet, not all nutritional needs are met. Amen (2001) presented a list of food supplements that improve neurotransmitter production. These will be detailed in Chapter 5, on strategies for self-regulation. For now, it is sufficient to understand that food supplements replace missing enzymes vital for restoration of neurotransmitter deficiencies. Some examples of common neurotransmitter deficiencies include dopamine for inattentive and hyperactive ADHD; serotonin for overfocused, anxiety, or compulsive problems; gama-aminobutypric acid (GABA) for temper or irritability and anger problems; and weak norepinephrine or serotonin for limbic problems or depression.

Also noteworthy is that diet alone can be used to directly affect neurotransmitter deficiencies. Fernstrom and Wurtman (1972) found that carbohydrates can increase serotonin levels, and a balanced diet of carbohydrates and protein can raise both serotonin and dopamine levels. Other relationships between diet and neurotransmitter production include eating fish, poultry, meat and eggs or legumes, dairy or tofu to increase dopamine, norepinephrine, and epinephrine so that it can boost mental alertness; eating carbohydrates such as legumes, dairy, or tofu to increase insulin because it allows tryptophan into the brain, where it can be converted to serotonin and increase relaxation; drinking orange juice or eating spinach to increase folic acid and increase serotonin to counter depression; eating Brazil nuts, tuna, swordfish, sunflower seeds, or whole grain cereals to increase selenium and improve bad moods; and eating eggs to increase choline which has been found to increase acetycholine and improve memory.

Even with a healthy diet, brain dysregulation can also be affected by lack of physical exercise. Ratey (2008), in his work on exercise and the brain, found that without 40 minutes of aerobic exercise, three times a week, the brain does not produce enough brain-derived neurotropic factor (BDNF) to assist it in full activation or synaptic plasticity. He explained how BDNF prepared the brain for optimal functioning and facilitated the growth of new brain cells. This improves the neural mechanisms involved in learning, emotional management, attention, hormonal functioning, and optimal aging. Exercise combined with a healthy diet can greatly enhance neuronal regulation.

EMOTIONALLY SUPPRESSIVE PSYCHOSOCIAL ENVIRONMENTS

Emotionally suppressive psychosocial environments can occur throughout life. They can take the form of deficient parent–child attachment in early infancy, childhood abuse, neglect, institutionalization, and adult problems with family of origin, inadequate relational attachment, or domestic violence. Schore (1997) discussed the importance of early organization of the right brain via parent–child attachment in the predisposition to psychiatric disorders. Following the theoretical work of Bowlby (1969) on secure and insecure attachment, Schore (2002) further explained that dysregulation of the right brain was the consequence of traumatic attachment and the psychogenesis of later developing post-traumatic stress disorder (PTSD). He said an infant abused in the first 2 years of life manifests a greater inability to cope with relational stress.

Frewen and Lanius (2006) detailed the neurological consequences of PTSD and the psychobiology of resulting self-dysregulation. Their research found PTSD was related to loss of activation of the prefrontal cortex, thalamus, and the anterior cingulated cortex, all necessary for emotional control and regulation. They concluded that long-term developmental and interpersonal attachment trauma can cause failure of inhibitory control over fear-induced arousal and stress, leading to reexperiencing (of trauma response) and hyper-arousal, as well as enhanced suppression of fear-induced arousal, leading to emotional numbing and dissociation.

A nationally representative study reported that 60% of men and 50% of women will experience a traumatic event at some point in their lives (Kessler et al., 1995), but not all experienced traumas will result in PTSD. The lifetime prevalence of PTSD among adults is about 6.8% (3.6% for men and 9.7% for women), and the 1-year prevalence is about 1.8% for men and 5.2% for women (Kessler et al., 2005). The primary contributing factor appears to be deficient parent–child attachment. Porges (2011), in his work on the polyvagal theory, concluded that secure early attachment was critical for the continued healthy development of the infant's autonomic nervous system. More specifically, he found that a mother's reliable response to the infant's emotional and physical needs, manifested in touch, facial expression, eye gaze, soothing voice, and nurturance, promoted the infant's development of what he termed the social engagement system. This right-brained skill set is essential for lifelong emotional regulation and interpersonal attachment. Without it, the child will be ill equipped to manage the stress and challenges of life, including trauma, and will not have the basic skills to engage in meaningful interpersonal relationships.

Other research has confirmed these findings. Thomaes et al. (2010) found that severity of child abuse was related to significant decreases in hippocampal gray matter, the anterior cingulate cortex, and the right orbital frontal cortex, all involved in emotional regulation. Fries, Shirtcliff, and Pollack (2008) found that institutionalized children had greater cortisol (stress hormone) levels in following their adopted mothers than strangers, suggesting a threat/fear response to their primary caregiver. In addition, Gerra et al. (2010) found adults, neglected as children, had increased activation of the 5-HTTSS gene, increased HPA hormones (cortisol and adrenocortiotropic hormone), and increased drug and alcohol use.

Research on insecure adult attachment has produced similar results. Whisman (1999) found that marital dissatisfaction was correlated with higher levels of PTSD and depression for women and dysthymia for men. Buchheim et al. (2005), in an fMRI study, found that adults with unresolved or disorganized attachment had greater activation of the medial temporal regions, including the amygdale and the hippocampus, related to emotional dysregulation. Quirin et al. (2010) also found that avoidant or anxious adult attachment was associated with decreased hippocampal cell density, as have other studies looking at depression and PTSD. Regarding EEG and the impact of trauma on the brain's functioning, Swingle (2010) noted that trauma is associated with decreases in the brain's posterior occipital lobe, with marked decreases in alpha and theta waves.

A report of child abuse and neglect in the United States found 3 million children, 1 in 25, had been abused or neglected (Sedlak et al., 2010). An estimate of domestic violence found 4 to 6 million adults had been victims of domestic violence, 1 in 3 involving a physical assault (Rodriguez et al., 1999). These do not take into account the unreported cases, the silent witnesses of abuse, neglect, or domestic violence. Add to this the incidence of mental health problems, substance abuse, maternal attachment injury, and other subclinical but often emotionally suppressive factors such as ongoing relational, marital, or family conflict; divorce; child custody; ineffectual parenting; and economic stress or dislocation due to work or military service, and the potential for emotionally suppressive psychosocial environments and their consequences quickly multiplies.

BRAIN INJURY

Brain injury can occur as a result of a blow to the head, as in a sports injury or fall, or by an abrupt jarring motion, such as whiplash from an automobile accident, that causes the boundary of the soft gray and white brain matter to tear, resulting in axonal shearing (Thatcher, 2000). Brain injuries can range from severe to mild. The more severe injuries are accompanied by loss of consciousness, amnesia, seizures, nausea, or coma. More mild injuries often go unnoticed. They involve dizziness, headache, changes in mood, changes in concentration level, or fatigue, and can last days, weeks, months, or years (Thatcher et al., 2001).

It is important to understand that brain injuries can be structural and/ or functional (Hill & Castro, 2009). Structural injuries involve physical damage to the brain. They can be detected with traditional magnetic resonance imaging (MRI) or computerized tomography (CT) imaging technology. Functional injuries, however, involve changes in the timing of the brain's neurological activity. These can only be detected with a quantitative electroencephalogram (QEEG) evaluation (Duff, 2004). Even normal EEG evaluations fail to identify mild functional injuries. The QEEG, however, allows the brain's electrical activity to be broken down into bandwidths so that the effects of a brain injury on the timing of specific brainwaves can be measured. Swingle (2010) noted that only 20% of brain injuries can be identified with an MRI or CT scan. He said 90% of brain injuries are identified with a QEEG.

The name given to minor brain injuries, about 10% of all brain injuries, as defined in the DSM-IV-R, is post-concussion syndrome (APA, 2008).

The symptoms of these largely unrecognized head injuries overlap with ADHD and adjustment and mood disorders. Traditional treatment for these problems will not resolve the underlying brain injury. It is therefore very important to conduct a thorough psycho-social-medical history to determine the accurate underlying cause. Also note that most people do not recall these events as significant so they often do not remember them. They will recall brain injuries that resulted in hospitalization or loss of consciousness, but the more moderate to mild injuries encountered in sports, play, and minor car accidents are often forgotten.

It has been estimated that over 2 million people a year suffer from a head injury (Wilder, 1976). Long-term problems, sometimes lasting a lifetime, can include headaches, fatigue, impaired memory, reduced concentration, attention problems, decreased information processing, depression, aggression, anxiety, irritability, sleep problems, sexual dysfunctions, personality changes (temper and self-centeredness), emotional liability, and reduced social awareness.

Ayers (1983, 1987) evaluated and treated hundreds of brain-injured clients. She reported the long-term neurological impact as involving increased low brainwave activity (3 to 5 Hertz) at the area of the injury and generalized brain slowing (5 to 7 Hertz). According to Hill and Castro (2009), the brain retreats and then parks at slow waves. Note that when injured, the percussion wave will cause the brain to impact the skull at several locations, resulting in other contusions, most often in the frontal and temporal regions (Thatcher, 2000). In addition, Sharp et al., (2011) found that brain injury also deactivates the brain's default mode network (DMN). The DMN has been described as the brain's state of wakeful rest. It is not focused on the outside world but is instead more introspective, wandering, daydreaming, creatively reflecting, retrieving memories, and gauging others' perspectives. The DMN has been implicated in several disorders including ADHD, autism, Alzheimer's disease, and schizophrenia (Buckner, Andrews-Hanna, & Schacter, 2008). Its subsystems include the parts of the temporal lobe, prefrontal cortex, posterior cingulate cortex, precuneus, and parietal cortex.

The impact of brain injury is not limited to victims of head trauma but extends to those who suffer stroke and coma. When the organic damage to brain tissue is relatively minor, the electrical activity of the surrounding area can be changed. Ayers (1995) worked with coma and stroke patients. Although the timeline for recovery from stroke is usually 18 months, 7 years later, she assisted a client in increasing his ability to walk and talk. In yet another case, she successfully assisted a patient who had been in a coma for 8 years.

A tragedy among head-injury victims is that many who fail to progress from conventional treatment or who persist in complaints, years after a brain injury, have been called malingerers and their struggles have been largely dismissed (Swingle, 2010). Long after the structural damage of brain injury has healed, the functional deficits persist. Much is being done to improve intervention for athletic concussions, to improve car and driver safety, and to protect young children with helmets while they ride bikes, but the risk of long-term brain dysregulation, even from minor injury and sports and vehicle accidents remains high.

STRESS

According to a recent national survey by the American Psychological Association (APA, 2010) most Americans are suffering from moderate to high stress, with 44% reporting their stress has increased in the last 5 years. The top causes of their stress included money, work, the economy, family responsibilities, and relationships. Their top physical symptoms included irritability or anger; fatigue; lack of interest, motivation or energy; feeling nervous or anxious; and headaches. The healthiest of the group managed their stress by exercising or walking, spending time with family or friends, reading, listening to music, or praying. Those who reported fair to poor health did not have exercise in their top five stress-management strategies. They also relied on Internet surfing and computer video games and napping as their preferred stress-management techniques. The survey also found that the children seemed to be struggling more than their parents recognized. Sixty-nine percent of parents reported their stress had slight or no impact on their kids, while only 14% of kids reported that their parents' stress doesn't bother them. Stress clearly remains a problem in this country and is a significant source of dysregulation.

Thompson and Thompson (2003) detailed the body's autonomic response to stress. Under stress, the sympathetic nervous system (SNS) responds with a flight, fight, or freeze response that enables us to fend off the stressful event. Once successful, the parasympathetic nervous system (PNS) restores us to allostatic balance. This stress response is adaptive in the short run but maladaptive in the long run (McEwen & Gianaros, 2010). Chronic functioning of the sympathetic nervous system will result in an array of physical, immunological, and emotional health problems. Sapolsky (2004) noted that the difference between the stress response of animals and humans is that animals do not ruminate about the past or worry about the future. When they encounter a stressful event, they deal with it and then return to balance. This puts humans at great risk for a variety of stress-related illnesses including heart attack, kidney diseases, stroke, and immunological disorders.

The human stress response involves a bidirectional pattern of communication between the brain and the endocrine system (hormones) and the autonomic, cardiovascular, and immune system (McEwen & Gianaros, 2010). When a state of threat is recognized, the hippocampus, amygdala, and areas of the prefrontal cortex activate the regulatory centers of the central nervous system. This stimulates the HPA or the hypothalamic-pituitary-adrenal axis to release epinephrine (adrenaline) and norepinephrine (noradrenaline) within seconds, which immediately activates the sympathetic and parasympathetic response. At the same time, a slower release of corticotrophin-releasing hormone (CRH) begins and triggers the pituitary to release ACTH or corticotrophin hormone into the bloodstream. After a few minutes, it reaches the adrenal glands near the kidney and triggers the release of glucocorticoids such as cortisol (the stress hormone). Near the same time, the pancreas is stimulated to release another hormone called glucagon. This helps raise circulating levels of sugar glucose and promotes mobilization of energy for fight or flight during times of stress. It also makes fat cells less sensitive to insulin, so under long periods of stress, the fat cells become insulin resistant.

It is the body's overexposure to stress hormones that eventually leads to conditions such as heart disease and stroke from too much cortisol and weight gain, and diabetes from too much glucose due to insulin resistance (Sapolsky, 2004). The stress response also redirects resources from the body's immune response systems to aid in fight or flight. Over time, stress also leaves the immune system depleted and the body more vulnerable to an array of immunological disorders and diseases.

Stress also affects the brain's electrical activity. Hill and Castro (2009) noted that the EEG of people under stress shows signs of increased high brainwave or beta activity (15 Hz or more). High brainwave activity is good for problem solving that decreases stress but prolonged perseveration, worry, or fixation on a problem is not good and results in increased stress. Once a problem is solved, the brain normally returns to the resting or idle state of alpha (8–12 Hz). However under prolonged stress, the brain can either feel assaulted and retreat to lower theta brainwaves (4–7 Hz) or feel stress and panic and go to even higher beta brainwaves (20–30 Hz). The decrease can be described as a trauma reaction and the increase as an anxiety disorder.

Seo and Lee (2010) investigated the relationship of EEG and salivary cortisol levels of people under chronic stress. They found a significant positive correlation between cortisol level and high beta brainwaves in both the frontal anterior cortex and the occipital lobes. Thompson and Thompson (2007) reported that the EEGs of persons under stress show decreases in both alpha (11–12 Hz) and sensorimotor rhythm (12–15 Hz) and increases in high beta (23–35 Hz) at both the anterior cingulated and frontal anterior cortex. More specifically, they noted emotional intensity or anxiety was related to 19–22 Hz activity, while active brain states were related to 23–36 Hz. Additionally, it is important to understand that after prolonged states of stress, the brain activity of the right prefrontal cortex can increase and that of the left prefrontal cortex can decrease, resulting in depression. Swingle (2010) reported that high alpha at the left prefrontal cortex can predispose a person to depression. This depression can often be indicated by low alpha or theta activity at the left prefrontal cortex.

Stress is a significant source of brain dysregulation. Sapolsky (2004) offered a brief prescription for avoiding the debilitating effects of stress. He advised to activate your stress response only for physiological threats (life or safety) but not psychological threats (past events or future worries). When stressed, use as little glucocorticoid secretion as possible to minimize its detrimental impact on the body and health. React to stress a lot at its onset, but quickly activate the recovery response. Maintain an intentional, energized calm and use calming strategies during a stressor. Use denial to decrease the impact of potential stressors. Hope for the best but prepare for the worst. Don't try to control the past or the future. Make use of small footholds and seek measured and predictable information in problem solving. Finally, seek appropriate outlets for frustration and develop meaningful social affiliations.

MEDICATION, SUBSTANCE ABUSE, AND ADDICTION

The use of prescription and illegal drugs by Americans is on the rise and with it brainwave dysregulation associated with their use and abuse. According to Gu, Dillom, and Burt (2010), the amount spent on prescription drugs has doubled since 1999 to over $234 billion a year. The most used types of prescription drugs are bronchodilators for children aged 0 to 11, central nervous system stimulants for adolescents aged 12 to 19, antidepressants for adults aged 20 to 59, and cholesterol-lowering drugs for adults aged 60 and older. The most abused types of prescription medications include opioids usually prescribed to treat pain, central nervous system depressants to treat anxiety and sleep disorders, and stimulants to treat ADHD. It's been estimated that 2.4 million Americans have used prescription drugs nonmedically.

Illegal drug use has also risen from 19.7 million in 2006 to 21.8 million in 2010 (SAMHSA, 2011). The most abused illegal drug is marijuana, with 14.6 million users, followed by cocaine, with 2.4 million users. Among high school seniors, 40% reported having smoked marijuana in the past 12 months, 25% used stimulant drugs like "speed," an amphetamine, and there has been a marked increase in experimentation with heroin.

It has been estimated that 13 million Americans have an alcohol problem, while only 2.5% have received treatment for it. In addition, over 60 million prescriptions for Valium and other tranquilizers have been written and employee use of the narcotic, Vicodin, has risen 40%, with estimates of addiction among chronic pain patients ranging from 3–40%.

Physical dependence on any substance occurs because of normal adaptation to the substance. It is often accompanied by tolerance or needing to take more of the substance to get the same effect. Abrupt cessation of the substance can produce withdrawal symptoms. Addiction is characterized by compulsive seeking and use of the drug despite sometimes severe consequences such as arrest, loss of a job, or divorce. Only a small percentage of persons with a substance abuse problem seek help. Of an estimated 23 million Americans with substance abuse problems (or 9% of the population), only about 2.6 million (or 11% of these) have sought treatment (SAMHSA, 2011).

Addiction can take many forms including compulsive gambling, sex, spending, extreme risk-taking behavior, exercise, eating, work, and use of electronic entertainment. All of these have been found to have similar behavioral and neurological consequences (Carnes, 1997) and, like substance abuse, are often associated with underlying stress or trauma (Van der Kolk, 2003).

With the ever increasing popularity of electronic entertainment, including television, video games, computers, and cell phones, children and adults who spend more than 1–2 hours a day on them are also experiencing significant levels of neurological dysregulation. Krugman (1971) found that in less than 1 minute of television viewing, brainwaves switch from the left hemisphere to right hemisphere dominance and from beta wave to low alpha wave dominance. This, he said, was caused by the radiant light produced by the cathode ray technology, flashing images many times per second. As a result, the right hemisphere became twice as active, the brain releases endorphins, cognitive and critical executive functions shut down, and the limbic system takes over, creating an unfocused, uncritical, receptive, and pleasure-seeking state. This makes television both addictive and a very powerful tool for advertisers.

Continued research also found that prolonged activity in the lower brain leads to atrophy in the higher brain regions, causing problems with concentration, irritability, and socializing with real-life people. This is particularly problematic for children with ADHD who are already prone to such difficulties. Amen (2001), a specialist in the treatment of ADHD, described television watching as "no brain" activity because the brain does not have to make new neuronal connections. He recommended limiting television viewing to 30 to 45 minutes a day. The American Academy of Pediatrics (2001) recommends no more than 2 hours of viewing per day.

Research on video game playing has also found brain dysregulation. Koepp et al. (1998) reported these games stimulate the basal ganglia to release dopamine, which causes an immediate rush of pleasure. Weber, Ritterfelf, and Mathiak (2006) found violent games caused a decrease of activity in the anterior cingulate cortex and the amygdala, potentially decreasing the ability for an emotional response to the witnessing of violent action. These studies speak to the dysregulating and potentially addicting and desensitizing effect of violent video games on the brain.

Addiction and substance abuse have been found to generally result in deficient slow-frequency brainwave (alpha and theta) dysregulation in the back of the brain at the occipital lobe (Peniston & Kulkosky, 1989). This pattern also occurs with clients suffering the effects of post-traumatic stress disorder (Peniston & Kulkosky, 1991). Over the long term, alcohol abuse results in slowing of the brainwaves so the frequency of the highest brainwave activity decreases (Swingle, 2010). In the initial stages, intoxication increases alpha waves and relieves agitation from alcoholics' usual slow wave deficiencies. Chronic alcoholism results in eventual decreases of both alpha and theta frequencies. More alcohol is needed to achieve the same relief.

Other drugs and frequently abused medications can also result in brainwave dysregulation (Swingle, 2010). Marijuana results in increased frontal alpha activity. It can also offer euphoria and relief from chronic pain, but long-term use results in high frontal alpha ADHD, which becomes permanent after 3 years of daily use. Chronic use of marijuana is associated with a slowing of peak alpha efficiency, making it more difficult to plan, exercise focused speech, and complete tasks. Cocaine and heroin also result in high alpha amplitude and alpha slowing, with severe frontal ADHD. Its characteristic conversational rambling is worse making focus much more difficult. Preexisting psychiatric conditions are also worsened by the use of cocaine or heroin. Benzodiazepines, taken for anxiety and sleep problems and similar to alcohol, also worsen slow wave deficiencies. They should be taken for only brief periods of time to avoid dependency, addiction, and rebound of symptoms. Even after several years of nonuse, the slow wave amplitude at the occipital lobe shows significant decreased activity. Central nervous system stimulants, such as Ritalin, are also increasingly abused. They have short-term beneficial effects of increasing attention and focus but have been found to have little long-term effects on reading, achievement, athletic, or social skills. Barkley (2006) reported they are effective with only 25–40% of children with ADHD. Stimulants act as a dopamine transport inhibitor, increasing dopamine in the brain, which has an internally energizing effect that externally sedates a child. Fifty percent of children experience negative side effects from stimulants, and they can lead to drug-induced behavioral disorders including psychosis, mania, drug abuse, addiction, and the very ADHD symptoms they were intended to decrease.

Less frequently abused medications include antidepressants and mood stabilizers. When overprescribed, their effects on the brain can also cause dysregulation. Saletu, Anderek, and Saletu-Zyhlarz (2006) presented their intended clinical impact on the brain. Tricyclic antidepressants have been found to increase both slow (theta) and fast (beta) wave activity and decrease alpha frequency, resulting in a sedating response. Selective serotonin reuptake inhibitors (SSRIs), produce less delta, decrease alpha, and increase beta. They cause a less sedating response. Finally, mood stabilizers or anticyclics increase theta frequency and decrease alpha. They have a calming effect on the brain.

The overuse of medication, harmful use of illegal drugs, problems with addiction, and expanding opportunities for electronic entertainment and other forms of addictive behavior are ever increasing in our society. It is alarming to think about the inattention to the underlying factors of stress and trauma that likely motivate this behavior and its effect on brainwave dysregulation.

SEIZURE DISORDERS AND CHRONIC PAIN

Over 3 million Americans suffer from a seizure disorder, with 200,000 new cases diagnosed each year (CDCP, 2011). Ten percent of the U.S. population will experience a seizure sometime in their lifetime, but only 3% will be diagnosed before the age of 80 years old. Children under 2 years old and the elderly are most vulnerable, and women experience more seizures than men. A seizure is defined as unstable electrical activity in the brain that causes involuntary changes in body movement, function, sensation, awareness, or behavior. It can involve a momentary disruption of senses, short periods of unconsciousness, staring spells, or convulsions. The cause of 70% of seizures is never determined, but stroke, head trauma, birth complications, infection (meningitis or encephalitis), and genetic disorders are the most common causes. Seizures can result in subsequent seizures, brain damage, disability, or death from injuries incurred during a seizure. Most seizure patients, near 70%, can achieve remission, being seizure-free for 5 years, while on medication, but a third continue to have seizures despite medication treatment. They have what is called drug refractory epilepsy.

Sterman (2000) reviewed 18 worldwide studies on the use of neurotherapy for drug refractory epilepsy and found that 82% reported a 30% reduction in both frequency and severity of drug refractory epilepsy. The average reduction was 50%.

Other seizure-like conditions treated with neurotherapy include absence seizures, violent behavior, tics associated with Tourette's syndrome, and pseudo-seizures. Absence seizures cannot be diagnosed with magnetic resonance imaging (MRI) which detect underlying structural problems. However, the seizures do have a very characteristic EEG signature that can be monitored with an electroencephalograph to assess the functional problems they present. Absence seizures occur when a person appears to be blank, stares "through you," has no response to verbal commands, and appears to be in a hypnotic state (Swingle, 2010). Absence seizures can occur frequently but usually last only a few seconds. Another seizure-like problem suggests underlying past brain trauma may be a contributing factor in current violent behavior. Quirk (1995) studied imprisoned violent offenders and found the same neurotherapy treatment for seizures significantly reduced expected recidivism rates from 65% to 20%. The more treatment inmates had, the lower their recidivism rate. Strohmayer (2004) also found that the same neurotherapy treatment for seizures was effective in reducing tics (involuntary verbal utterances and/or body movements) associated with Tourette's syndrome. Finally Swingle (1998) also treated pseudo-seizures, fugue states, and grand mal-like thrashing and fainting with the same neurofeedback seizure protocol.

Seizure disorders can present as severe or minor and obvious or subtle, but the problem underlying all of them is dysregulation of the brain's electrical activity that disrupts normal functioning. Sterman and Friar (1972) reported that the primary source of dysregulation involved high delta (slow brainwaves) and low sensory motor rhythm (SMR or low beta brainwaves) over the sensory motor cortex at the top of the head. Swingle (2010) suggested the coherence or relationship of different brain sites to each other was out of phase. That is, they did not fire in unison or talk to each other the way they normally would. He found that the theta/SMR or low beta ratio, at the top of the head, was higher than 2.5 for children and 2.0 for adults.

Chronic pain, like seizures, responds to the same type of neurotherapy treatment; however, its cause and EEG signature are very different. Swingle (2010) noted chronic pain is characterized by high delta (low wave) activity over the frontal area of the brain. Westmoreland (1993) and Donaldson et al. (1998) reported that the EEG signature of chronic pain involved excessive theta and alpha and deficient beta over the frontal area. In all cases, the pattern of brainwave dysregulation associated with chronic pain involved increased slow wave and decreased high wave activity, making work and interpersonal interaction very difficult and fatigue and cognitive deficiency commonplace.

Chronic pain is experienced by 100 million Americans at the cost to society of $635 billion annually, or $2,000 for every person living in the United States (NAP, 2011). Chronic pain occurs when pain signals keep firing in the nervous system for weeks, months, or even years. It is associated with injury, disease, and sometimes becomes the disease itself. The four most common types of pain are back pain (27%), headache and migraine pain (15%), neck pain (15%), and facial ache or pain (4%). Chronic pain is more frequent in women who report twice as much pain as men from headaches, face, and jaw pain. Most pain is managed with opioid pain-relieving medication or analgesics. Sales of opioid drugs quadrupled between 1999 and 2010 and abuse is a serious problem. In 2010, 12 million Americans over 12 years of age reported nonmedical use of prescription pain killers. Middle-aged adults have the highest overdose rates, and many more men than women die from overdose of prescription pain medication.

Chronic pain can have a debilitating impact on a person's life. In a survey of 303 chronic pain sufferers, over half reported they had little or no control over their pain (NAP, 2011). Sixty percent said they have breakthrough pain one or more times a day that severely impacts their lives. Seventy-seven percent reported feeling depressed. Seventy percent said they have trouble concentrating. Seventy-four percent said their pain has impacted their energy level, and 86% reported an inability to sleep well.

One particularly devastating type of chronic pain is fibromyalgia. Swingle (2010) said trauma to the front of the head is the major cause of this connective tissue disorder. Fibromyalgia is characterized by its full-body pain; chronic fatigue; and problems with mood, concentration, memory, fine motor skills, sleep, and clarity of speech. He noted that postaccident frontal fibromyalgia causes increased slow brainwave (alpha and theta) activity over the frontal part of the brain. Prolonged suffering with fibromyalgia can result in "fibrofog," causing further problems with attention, focus, and concentration. Persons with fibromyalgia have also been found to have histories of severe psychological stress, abusive relationships, serious viral infection, and autoimmune forms of arthritis. Women are more prone to developing fibromyalgia. When combined with a personality disorder, persons with fibromyalgia can become very resistant to treatment, but the brainwave dysregulation associated with fibromyalgia and other chronic pain disorders can be treated and medication reduced or eliminated.

SURGICAL ANESTHESIA AND AGING

Surgical anesthesia and the normal process of aging have both been found to affect brainwave dysregulation and increase cognitive decline. The number and length of surgeries, as well as the general health of those 65 years old or older, appear to be mediating factors. Cognitive decline related to anesthesia and aging can be enhanced with neurotherapy; however, the inevitable process of aging requires ongoing treatment to retain as much of the gain as possible.

It has been estimated that the average person will have 9.2 surgeries in their life (3.4 inpatient, 2.6 outpatient, and 3.2 no-operating room invasive procedures) (Lee, Regenbogen, & Gawande, 2008). The most common types of surgeries include coronary procedures, endoscopy, cesarean section, knee and hip replacement, and hysterectomy (CDCP, 2009). These surgeries will involve the use of anesthesia. Zhao et al. (2010) noted that the most commonly used anesthetic, isoflurane, induces widespread neurodegeneration in the mammalian brain. In a rat study designed to investigate the underlying mechanisms of this degeneration, they found isoflurane to cause death in rodent cortical and hippocampal neurons. They further noted isoflurane caused transient memory and learning problems in mice with early developmental exposure to the anesthetic.

Negative effects of anesthesia have also been found in human retrospective studies that sought to determine the cause of impairment following surgical use of anesthesia. Moller et al. (1998) reported cognitive decline in middle-aged and older patients several months after anesthesia and surgery. The degree of cognitive decline correlated with the duration of anesthesia. Studies have also found an increase in the incidence of learning disorders in children having anesthesia and surgery before the age of 4, especially affecting those with numerous surgical procedures (Kalkman et al., 2009; Wilder et al., 2009). These studies suggest the anesthetic isoflurane may induce neurotoxicity and subsequent cognitive decline.

Another, even more universal, cause of cognitive decline is aging. Current estimates of the older population indicate there are 39.6 million persons 65 years or older living in the United States. This number is expected to rise to 72.1 million by the year 2030, representing 19% of the population (FIFARS, 2010). The effects of aging on the brain include decline in short-term memory; delayed recall; and loss of sustained attention, perceptual motor skills, executive functions, problem solving, speed of performance, temporal reasoning, and verbal reasoning (Swingle, 2010).

A Canadian study investigated the frequency of cognitive impairment using a sample of 10,263 persons aged 65 years old or older (Ebly, Hogan, & Parhad 1995). It found a 28.3% rate of moderate to severe cognitive impairment and 30% mild impairment. This suggested that two-thirds of the sample had problems with cognitive impairment. Healthy persons also reported some memory loss, but their cognitive functioning was generally adequate. These numbers become even more alarming when one considers that cognitive impairment also leaves this group particularly vulnerable to physical decline and distress.

Budzynski, Budzynski, and Tang (2007) detailed the multiple, chronic, and often severe stressors involved with aging. These included pain, repeated loss and grief, chronic illness, physical decline and reduced mobility, physical and mental isolation, changes in social support system, fewer coping options, decreased financial security, nonprivate living arrangements, communication barriers, safety concerns, and societal prejudices. Neurologically, there is deterioration of neurotransmitters, decreased cerebral blood flow, and brain hypoxia, or less oxygen to the brain. Geinisman et al. (1995) noted neuroplasticity becomes compromised by neuronal loss and changes in the hippocampus during normal aging, and Garrida (2011) reviewed the likely cause of brainwave dysregulation due to stress and aging as involving glucocorticoid secretions leading to neuronal damage and problems with the hypothalamic-pituitary adrenal axis (HPA axis).

The EEG pattern of persons 65 years old and older shifts to the lower ranges. Duffy et al. (1984) found decreases in dominant alpha frequency, increases in theta, and decreases in beta. Obrist (1979), studying persons older than 75 years, found posterior frequency declines from a normal 9 to 10 Hertz to 7 to 7.5 Hertz and bi-temporal theta. In tracking their mortality, Orbist observed that those who were alive 7.3 years longer than 75 years of age had declines of 0.6 Hertz in alpha. Decline in alpha may be an indication of looming death. Keller (1988) found that those with senile dementia of the Alzheimer's type could not increase their gamma waves (involved in cognitive efficiency) while engaged in problem solving, and Duffy et al. (1995) noted a decrease in coherence (the brain's ability to talk with parts of itself) with age.

Swingle (2010) noted that delayed alpha decrease when eyes are closed is an indication of brain inefficiency related to age and reduced mental activity. He said that while age-related declines can be corrected, unlike other neurotherapy procedures that have lasting effects (barring further brain injury or dysregulation), neurotherapy for the correction of dominant alpha must be maintained with ongoing treatment. Budzynski (1996) developed such a procedure called "brain brightening." It is used to help seniors maintain a higher dominant alpha through four sessions of alpha training, four times a year. It has been found to slow down the progression of age-related effects of alpha slowing, mitigate non-Alzheimer's dementia, and delay the onset of Alzheimer's disease.

CONCLUSIONS

Sources of brain dysregulation span the lifetime. Dysregulation can occur at the hypothalamic pituitary adrenal (HPA) axis, specific brain locations, the communication patterns between brain locations, and at the chemical (neurotransmitter) and electrical (brainwave) level. The brain is vulnerable to a vast array of injury and assault from a variety of sources. These begin with genetic and epigenetic influences, prenatal development, the impact of environmental toxins, and birth complications. They continue with risk of disease and high fever, poor diet and lack of exercise, and damage caused by the trauma of emotionally suppressive environments. Life then brings further risk of head injury, debilitating stress, and damage from the consequences of extended use of medication, substance abuse, and addiction. For some individuals, the brain is even further dysregulated by seizure disorders, chronic pain, and damage done by surgical anesthesia. Finally, the normal process of aging takes its toll on the brain's cognitive functioning.

A fortunate person may only experience one or two of these injuries in his or her lifetime, with little apparent effect on their neurological functioning. Many of us, however, will be unable to avoid several of these problems, and they will impact our physical, psychological, emotional, behavioral, and cognitive health. As has been noted in this chapter, some of these threats can be prevented. We can limit exposure to environmental toxins, actively engage in good prenatal care, and avoid disease and get early treatment of any high fever. We can also eat a healthy diet and maintain a consistent exercise routine, intervene or remove ourselves from emotionally suppressive environments, and be more safety conscious, avoiding dangerous sports or wearing quality head protection. We can also minimize our use of medication and avoid problems of substance abuse or addition with healthy coping skills and strong interpersonal support systems. Seizure disorders, chronic pain, and cognitive decline from surgical anesthesia are more difficult to avoid once you become the victim of a head injury or require surgery for a health- or life-threatening problem. Finally, we are all going to get old. If we maintain our health, aging will have only minor neurological consequences, but for two-thirds of us, this will not be the case.

As clinicians, awareness and understanding of the sources of brainwave dysregulation are very important for assessment and treatment planning. While we hope clients will arrive with only a single complaint that will readily lend itself to swift treatment, it is more likely clients will have several sources of dysregulation and more complex problems that will require several types of neurotherapy intervention for successful treatment. The following chapter will present an overview of several very useful assessment procedures for effective neurotherapy treatment planning. Knowledge of the sources of brainwave dysregulation will greatly facilitate case conceptualization, clinical conclusions, and appropriate treatment options for both simple and complex cases.

REFERENCES

Amen, D. G. (2001). *Healing ADD*. New York: Putnam.

American Academy of Pediatrics (2001). Children, adolescents and television. *Pediatrics, 107*(2), 423–426.

APA (2008). *Diagnostic and statistical manual of mental disorders* (4th ed., text rev., DSM-IV-TR). Washington, DC: American Psychiatric Association.

APA (2010). *Stressed in America*. Washington DC: American Psychological Association.

APA (2013). *Diagnostic and statistical manual of mental disorders* (5th ed.). Arlington, VA: American Psychiatric Publishing.

Axelrod, Y. K., & Diringer, M. N. (2008). Temperature management in acute neurologic disorders. *Neurology Clinician, 26*(21) 585–603.

Ayers, M. E. (1983). Electroencephalographic feedback and head trauma in head and neck trauma: The latest information and perspectives on patients with a less-than-optimal recovery. *UCLA Neuropsychiatric Institute,* 244–257.

Ayers, M. E. (1987). *Electroencephalographic neurofeedback and closed head injury of 250 individuals*. Head Injury Frontiers, National Head Injury Foundations, 380-392.

Ayers, M. E. (1995). *EEG neurofeedback to bring individuals out of level two coma (Abstract)*. Proceedings of the 26th Annual Meeting of the Association for Applied Psychophysiology and Biofeedback, 9–10.

Barkley, R. (2006). *Attention deficit hyperactivity disorder: A handbook for diagnosis and treatment* (3rd ed.). New York: Guilford.

Bauer, L. O. (2001). Predicting relapse to alcohol and drug abuse via quantitative electroencephalography. *Neuropsychopharmacology, 25*(3), 332–340.

Bland, S. T., Tamlyn, J. P., Barrientos, R. M., Greenwood, B. N., Watkins, L. R., Campeau, S., Day, J. E., & Maier, S. F. (2007). Expression of fibroblast growth factor-2 and brain derived neurotrophic factor mRNA in the medial prefrontal cortex and hippocampus after uncontrollable and controllable stress. *Neuroscience, 144*(4), 1219–1228.

Bowlby, J. (1969). *Attachment and loss* (Vol. 1). New York: Basic Books.

Broadwell, R. (Ed.). (1995). *Neuroscience, memory and language* (Vol. 1). Cambridge, MA: MIT Press.

Buchheim, A., Erk, S., George, C., Kachele, H., Ruchsow, M., Spitzer, M., Kircher, T., & Walter, H. (2005). Measuring attachment representation in an fMRI environment: A pilot study. *Psychopathology, 589*(10), 1159.

Buckner, R. L., Andrews-Hanna, J. R., & Schacter, D. L. (2008). The brain's default mode network: Anatomy, function, and relevance to disease. *Annals of the New York Academy of Science, 1124,* 1–38.

Budzynski, T. H. (1996, Summer). Brain brightening. *Biofeedback,* 14–17.

Budzynski, T. H., Budzynski, H. K., & Tang, H. (2007). Brain brightening: Restoring the aging mind. In J. Evans (Ed.), *Handbook of neurofeedback* (pp. 231–266). Binghamton, NY: Haworth Press.

Burns, C. E., Dunn, A. M., Brady, M. A. Starr, M. A., & Blosser, C. G. (2013). *Pediatric primary care* (5th ed.). Philadelphia, PA: Elsevier Saunders.

Carnes, P. (1997). *The betrayal bond: Breaking free of exploitive relationships.* Center City, MN: Hazalden.

CDCP (2009). Inpatient surgery. *National hospital discharge summary: 2009.* Atlanta, GA: Centers for Disease Control and Prevention.

CDCP (2011). *Targeting epilepsy: Improving the lives of people with one of the nation's most common neurological conditions, at a glance 2011.* Atlanta, GA: Centers for Disease Control and Prevention, National Centers for Chronic Disease Prevention and Health Promotion.

Clarren, S. K., & Smith, D. W. (1978). Fetal alcohol syndrome. *New England Journal of Medicine, 298,* 1063–1067.

Comings, D. (1995). *Tourette syndrome and human behavior.* Duarte, CA: Hope.

Crawley, J., & Meyerhoefer, C. (2012). The medical costs of obesity: An instrumental variables approach. *Journal of Health Economics, 31*(1), 219–230.

Donaldson, S., Sella, G., & Mueller, H. (1998). Fibromyalgia: A retrospective study of 252 consecutive referrals. *Canadian Journal of Clinical Medicine, 5*(6), 116–127.

Ducci, F., Enoch, M. A., Yaun, Q., Shen, P. H., White, K. V., Hodgkinson, C., Albaugh, B., Virkkunen, M., & Goldman, D. (2009). HTR3B is associated with alcoholism with antisocial behavior and alpha EEG power—an intermediate phenotype for alcoholism and co-morbid behaviors. *Alcohol, 43*(1), 73–84.

Duff, J. (2004). The usefulness of quantitative EEG (QEEG) and neurotherapy in the assessment and treatment of post-concussive syndrome. *Clinical EEG and Neuroscience, 35*(4), 1–12.

Duffy, F. H., Albert, M. S., McAnulty, G., & Garvey, A. J. (1984). Age-related differences in brain electrical activity of healthy subjects. *Annals of Neurology, 16*, 430–438.

Duffy, F. H., Jones, K. J., McAnulty, G. B., & Albert, M. S. (1995). Spectral coherence in normal adults: Unrestricted principal components analysis; relation of factors to age, gender, and neuropsychological data. *Clinical Electroencephalography, 26*, 30–46.

Dwyer, J. B., McQuawn, S. C., & Leslie, F. M. (2009). The dynamics effects of nicotine on the developing brain. *Pharmacological Therapy, 122*(2), 125–139.

Ebly, E. M., Hogan, D. B., & Parhad, I. M. (1995). Canadian impairment in the nondemented elderly. Results from the Canadian study of health and aging. *Archives of Neurology, 52*(6), 612–619.

Egger, J., Stolla, A., & McEwen, L. (1992). Controlled trial of hyposensitization in children with food induced hyperkinetic syndrome. *Lancet, 339*, 1150.

Fatemi, S. H., Folsom, T. D., Reutiman, T. J., Abu-Odeh, D., Mori, S., Huang, H., & Oishi, K. (2009). Abnormal expression of myelination genes and white matter volume abnormalities following prenatal viral influenza infection at E16 in mice. *Schizophrenia Research, 112*(1–3), 46–53.

Fernstrom, J., & Wurtman, R. (1972). Brain serotonin content: Physiological regulation by plasma neutral amino acids. *Science, 178*(4059), 414–416.

FIFARS (2010). Federal interagency forum on aging-related statistics. *Older Americans 2010: Key indicators of well being.* Washington, DC: US Government Printing Office.

Frewen, P. A., & Lanius, R. A. (2006). Toward a psychobiology of post-traumatic self-dysregulation: Reexperiencing, hyperarousal, dissociation and emotional numbing. *New York Academy of Sciences, 1071*, 110–124.

Fries, A. B., Shirtcliff, E. A., & Pollack, S. D. (2008). Neuroendocrine dysregulation following early social deprivation in children. *Developmental Psychobiology, 50*(6), 588–599.

Galbally, M., Snellen, M., & Lewis, A. J. (2011). A review of the use of psychotropic medication in pregnancy. *Current Opinions in Obstetric Gynecology, 23*(6), 408–414.

Garrida, P. (2011). Aging and stress: Past hypotheses, present approaches and perspectives. *Aging and Disease, 2*(1), 80–99.

Geinisman, Y., Detoledo-Morrell, L., Morrell, F., & Heller, R. E. (1995). Hippocampal markers of age-related memory dysfunction: Behavioral, electrophysiological, and morphological perspectives. *Progress in Neurobiology, 45*(3), 223–252.

Gerra, G., Zaimovic, A., Castaldini, L., Garofano, L., Manfredini, M., Somaini, L., Leonardi, C., Gerra, M. L., & Donnini, C. (2010). Relevance of perceived childhood neglect, 5-HTT gene variants and hypothalamus-pituitary-adrenal axis dysregulation to substance abuse susceptibility. *American Journal of Medical Genet B Neuropsychiatric Genet, 153B*(3), 715–722.

Gu, Q., Dillom, C. F., & Burt, V. L. (2010). Prescription drug use continues to increase: US prescription drug data for 2007–2008. *NCHS Data Brief, No. 42.* Hyattsville, MD: National Center for Health Statistics.

Hack, M. (2006). Young adult outcomes of very-low-birth-weight children. *Seminar Fetal Neonatal Medicine, 11*(2), 127–137.

Hamilton, B. E., Martin, J. A., & Ventura, S. J. (2010). Births: Preliminary data for 2010. *National Vital Statistic Reports, 60*(2), 1–19.

Hill, R. W., & Castro, E. (2009). *Healing young brains.* Charlottesville, VA: Hampton Roads.

Hodgkinson, C. A., Enoch, M. A., Srivastava, V., Cummins-Oman, J. S., Ferrier, C., Iarikova, P., . . . Goldman, D. (2010). Genome-wide association identifies candidate genes that influence the human electroencephalogram. *Proceedings of the National Academy of Sciences, 107*(19), 8695–7000.

Hofman, L. B. (1922). Post-encephalitic behavior in children. *Johns Hopkins Hospital Bulletin, 33,* 372–375.

Johnson, K. C., Laprairie, J. L., Brennan, P. A., Stowe, Z. N., & Newport, D. J. (2012). Prenatal antipsychotic exposure and neuromotor performance during infancy. *Archives of General Psychiatry, 69*(8), 787–794.

Jones, K. L., Smith, D. W., Ulleland, C. N., & Streissguth, A. P. (1973). Patterns of malformation in offspring of chronic alcoholic mothers. *Lancet, 1,* 1267–1271.

Kalkman, C. J., Peelen, L., Moons, K. G., Veenhuizen, M., Bruens, M., Sinnema, G., & de Jong, P. T. (2009). Behavior and development in children and age at the time of first anesthetic exposure. *Anesthesiology, 110,* 805–812.

Keller, W. J. (1988). *Forty hertz EEG in elderly patients with mild dementia and Alzheimer's type.* Paper presented at the 16th Annual Meeting of the International Neuropsychological Society, New Orleans, LA.

Kessler, D. C., Sonnega, A., Bromet, E., Hughes, M., & Nelson, C. B. (1995). Posttraumatic stress disorder in the national comorbidity survey. *Archives of General Psychiatry, 52,* 1048–1060.

Kessler, D. C., Berglund, P., Demler, O., Jin, R., Merikangas, K. R., & Walters, E. E. (2005). Lifetime prevalence and age-of-onset distribution of DSM-IV disorders in the National Comorbidity Survey Replication. *Archives of General Psychiatry, 62*(6), 593–602.

Koenen, K. C., Uddin, M., Chang, S. C., Aiello, A. E., Woldman, D. E., Goldman, E., & Galea, S. (2011). SLC6A4 methylation modifies the effect of the number of traumatic events on risk for posttraumatic stress disorder. *Depressions and Anxiety, 28*(8), 639–647.

Koepp, M. J., Gunn, R. N., Lawrence, A. D., Cunningham, V. J., Dagher, A., Jones, T., Brooks, D. J., Bench, C. J., & Grasby, P. M. (1998). Evidence for striatal dopamine release during a video game. *Nature, 339,* 266–268.

Krugman, H .E. (1971). Brain wave measures of media involvement. *Journal of Advertising Research, 11*(1), 3–9.

Lee, P., Regenbogen, S., & Gawande, A. A. (2008). *How many surgical procedures will Americans experience in an average lifetime? Evidence from three states.* Program abstract of 55th Annual Meeting of the Massachusetts Chapter of the American College of Surgeons, Boston, MA.

Levy, F., Hay, D., McStephen, M., Wood, C., & Waldman, I. (1997). Attention deficit hyperactivity disorder: A category or continuum? A genetic analysis of a large scale twin study. *Journal of American Academy of Child and Adolescent Psychiatry, 36,* 737–744.

Li, Q., Cheung, C., Wei, R., Hui, E. S., Feldon, J., Meyer, U., . . . McAlonan, G. M. (2009). A prenatal immune challenge is an environmental risk factor for brain and behavior change relevant to schizophrenia: Evidence from MRI in a mouse model. *Plos One, 4*(7), e6354.

Markham, J. A., & Koenig, J. I. (2011). Prenatal stress: Role in psychotic and depressive diseases. *Psychopharmacology, 214*(1), 89–106.

McEwen, B. S., & Gianaros, P. J. (2010). Central role of the brain in stress and adaptation: Links to socioeconomic status, health and disease. *Annals of New York Academy of Sciences, 1136,* 190–222.

Moller, J. T., Cluitman, P., Rasmussen, L. S., Houx, P., Rasmussen, H., Canet, J., . . . Gravenstein, J. J. (1998). Long-term postoperative cognitive dysfunction in the elderly ISPOCD1 study ISPOCD investigators. International Study of Post-Operative Cognitive Dysfunction. *Lancet, 351,* 857–861.

Moretti, G., Pasquine, M., Mandarelli, G., Tarsitani, L. & Biondi, M. (2008). What every psychiatrist should know about PANDAS: A review. *Clinical Practice & Epidemiology in Mental Health, 4*(13). doi: 10.1186/1745-0179-4-13

Morrison, J. R., & Stewart, R. A. (1971). A family study of the hyperactive child syndrome. *Biological Psychiatry, 3,* 189–195.

NAP (2011). *Institute of Medicine report from the committee on advancing pain research care and education: Relieving pain in America, a blueprint for transforming prevention, care, education and research.* Washington DC: The National Academies Press.

Nijenhuis, C. M., ter Horst, P. G., van Rein, N., Wilffert, B., & de Jong-van den Berg, L. T. (2012). Disturbed development of the enteric nervous system after in utero exposure of selective serotonin re-uptake inhibitors and tricyclic antidepressants. Part 2: Testing the hypothesis. *British Journal of Clinical Pharmacology, 73*(1), 126–134.

Obrist, W. D. (1979). Electroencephalographic changes in normal aging and dementia. *Brain Function in Old Age, 7,* 102–111.

Pembrey, M. (2006). Epigenetics: Sins of the fathers, and their fathers. *European Journal of Human Genetics, 14,* 131–132.

Peniston, E. G, & Kulkosky, P. J. (1989). Alpha-theta brainwave training and beta endorphin levels in alcoholics. *Alcoholism, Clinical and Experimental Research, 13,* 271–279.

Peniston, E. G., & Kulkosky, P. J. (1991). Alpha-theta brainwave neurofeedback therapy for Vietnam veterans with combat-related post traumatic stress disorder. *Medical Psychotherapy: An International Journal, 4,* 47–60.

Porges, S. W. (2011). *The polyvagal theory: Neurophysiological foundations of emotions, attachment, communication and self-regulation.* New York: Norton.

Pusztai, A. (2000). The need for rigorous risk assessment. *Chemistry and Industry, 8,* 230.

Quirin, M., Pruessner, J. C., Gillath, O., & Eggert, L. D. (2010). Adult attachment insecurity and hippocampal cell density. *Social Cognitive Affective Neuroscience, 5*(1), 39–47.

Quirk, D. A. (1995). Composite biofeedback conditioning and dangerous offenders: III. *Journal of Neurotherapy, 1,* 44–54.

Randis, T. M. (2008). Complications associated with premature birth. *Virtual Mentor, 10*(10), 647–650.

Ratey, J. J. (2008). *Spark: The revolutionary new science of exercise and the brain.* New York: Little Brown.

Reiss, C. S. (2006). *Neurotropic viral infections.* New York: Cambridge University.

Rodriguez, M., Bauer, H., McLoughlin, E., & Grumback, K. (1999). Screening and intervention for intimate partner abuse: Practices and attitudes of primary care physicians. *Journal of the American Medical Association, 9*(3), 97–110.

Roussotte, F., Soderberg, L., & Sowell, E. (2010). Structural, metabolic and functional brain abnormalities as a result of prenatal exposure to drugs of abuse: Evidence from neuroimaging. *Neuropsychology Review, 20*(4), 376–397.

Saletu, B., Anderek, P., & Saletu-Zyhlarz, G. M. (2006). EEG topography and tomography (LORETA) in the classification and evaluation of the pharmacodynamics of psychotropic drugs. *Clinical Electroencephalography and Neuroscience, 37,* 66–80.

SAMHSA (2011). *Results from the 2010 national survey on drug use and health: Summary of national findings, NSDUH series H-41, HHS publication No. (SMA) 11–44658.* Rockville, MD: Substance Abuse and Mental Health Services Administration.

Sapolsky, R. M. (2004). *Why zebras don't get ulcers.* New York: Holt.

Sartor, C. E., Grant, J. D., Lynskey, M. T., McCutcheon, V. V., Waldron, M., Statham, D. J., . . . Nelson, E. C. (2012). Common heritable contributions to low-risk trauma, high risk trauma, posttraumatic stress disorder, and major depression. *Archives of General Psychiatry, 69*(3), 293–299.

Sartor, C. E., McCutcheon, V. V., Pommer, N. E., Nelson, E. C., Grant, J. D., Duncan, A. E., . . . Heath, A. C. (2011). Common genetic and environmental contributions to post-traumatic stress disorder and alcohol dependence in young women. *Psychological Medicine, 41*(7), 1497–1505.

Schore, A. N. (1997). Early organization of the nonlinear right brain and development of a predisposition to psychiatric disorders. *Development and Psychopathology, 9,* 595–631.

Schore, A. N. (2002). Dysregulation of the right brain: A fundamental mechanism of traumatic attachment and the psychogenesis of posttraumatic stress disorder. *Australian and New Zealand Journal of Psychiatry, 36,* 9–30.

Sedlak, A. J., Mettenburg, J., Basena, M., Petta, I., McPherson, K., Greene, A., & Li, S. (2010). *Fourth national incidence study of child abuse and neglect (NIS-4): Report to Congress executive summary.* Washington, DC: U.S. Department of Health and Human Services, Administration for Children and Families.

Seo, S. H., & Lee, J. T. (2010). Stress and EEG. In M. Crisan (Ed.), *Convergence and hybrid information technologies* (pp. 413–426). In Tech, Croatia.

Sharp, D. J., Beckman, C. F., Greenwood, R., Kinninen, K. M., Bonnelle, V., De Boissezon, X., Leech, R. (2011). Default mode network functional and structural connectivity after traumatic brain injury. *Brain, 134*(8), 2233–2247.

Smit, C. M., Wright, M. J., Hansell, N. K., Geffen, G. M., & Martin, N. G. (2006). Genetic variation of individual alpha frequency (IAF) and alpha power in a large adolescent twin sample. *International Journal of Psychophysiology, 61*(2), 235–243.

Starko, K. M., Ray, C. G., & Dominguez, L. B. (1980). Reye's syndrome and salicylate use. *Pediatrics, 66,* 859–864.

Sterman, M. B. (2000). Basic concepts and clinical findings in the treatment of seizure disorders with EEG operant conditioning. *Clinical Electroencephalography, 31,* 45–54.

Sterman, M. B., & Friar, L. (1972). Suppression of seizures in epileptics following sensorimotor EEG feedback training. *Electroencephalography and Clinical Neurophysiology, 33,* 89–95.

Strohmayer, A. (2004). *SMR neurofeedback efficiency in the treatment of Tourette's Syndrome.* Paper presented at the meeting of the International Society for Neuronal regulation, Ft. Lauderdale, FL.

Swedo, S. E., Leonard, H. L., Garvey, M., Mittleman, D., Allen, A. J., Perimutter, S., . . . & Dubbert, B. K. (1998). Pediatric autoimmune neuropsychiatric disorders associated with streptococcal infections: Clinical descriptions of the first 50 cases. *American Journal of Psychiatry, 155,* 264–271.

Swingle, P. G. (1998). Neurofeedback treatment of pseudoseizure disorders. *Biological Psychiatry, 44,* 1196–1199.

Swingle, P. G. (2010). *Biofeedback for the brain*. New Brunswick, NJ: Rutgers University Press.

Thatcher, R. W. (2000). EEG operant conditioning (biofeedback) and traumatic brain injury. *Clinical Electroencephalography, 31*(1), 38–44.

Thatcher, R. W., North, D. M., Curtin, R. T., Walker, B. S., Biver, C. J., Gomez, J. F., & Salazar, A. M. (2001). An EEG severity index of traumatic brain injury. *Journal of Neuropsychiatry and Clinical Neuroscience, 13*(1), 77–87.

Thomaes, K., Dorrepaal, E., Draijer, N., de Ruiter, M. B., van Balkom, A. J., Smit, J. H., & Veltman, D. J. (2010). Reduced anterior cingulate and orbitofrontal volumes in child abuse-related complex PTSD. *Journal of Clinical Psychiatry, 71*(12), 1636–1644.

Thompson, M., & Thompson, L. (2003). *The neurotherapy book*. Wheat Ridge, CO: Association for Applied Psychophysiology and Biofeedback.

Thompson, M., & Thompson, L. (2007). Neurofeedback for stress management. In P. M. Lehrer, R. L. Woolfolk, & E. Wesley (Eds.), *Principles and practice of stress management* (pp. 249–287). New York: Guilford.

Van der Kolk, B. (2003). Post traumatic stress disorder and the nature of trauma. In M. Solomon & D. Siegel (Eds.), *Healing, trauma attachment, mind, body and brain*. New York: Norton.

Weber, R., Ritterfelf, U., & Mathiak, K. (2006). Does playing violent video games induce aggression? Empirical evidence of a functional magnetic resonance imaging study. *Media Psychology, 8*(1), 39–60.

Werner, E. F., Janevic, T. M., & Illuzzi, J. (2011). Mode of delivery in nulliparous women and neonatal intracranial injury. *Obstetrical Gynecology, 118*, 1239–1246.

Westmoreland, B. F. (1993). The EEG in cerebral inflammatory processes. In E. E. Niedermeyer & F. L. DaSilva (Eds.), *Electroencephalography: Basic principles, clinical applications and related fields* (3rd ed., pp. 291–304). Baltimore, MD: Urban Schwartzenberg.

Whisman, M. A. (1999). Marital dissatisfaction and psychiatric disorders: Results from the national morbidity survey. *Journal of Abnormal Psychology, 108*(4), 701–706.

Wilder, C. S. (1976). *Health interview survey*. Rockville, MD: National Center for Health Statistics, US Department of Health, Education and Welfare.

Wilder, R. T., Flick, R. P., Sprung, J., Katusic, S. K., Barbaresi, W. J., Mickelson, C., . . . & Warner, D. O. (2009). Early exposure in anesthesia and learning disabilities in a population-based birth cohort. *Anesthesiology, 110*, 796–804.

Yehuda, R., Koenen, K. C, Galea, S., & Flory, J. D. (2011). The roles of genes in defining a molecular biology of PTSD. *Dis Markers, 30*(2–3), 67–76.

Zhao, Y., Liang, G., Chen, Q., Joseph, D. J., Meng, Q., Eckenhoff, R. G., . . . & Wei, H. (2010). Anesthetic-induced neurodegeneration mediated via inositol 1,4,5-trisphosphate receptors. *Journal of Pharmacology and Experimental Therapeutics, 333*(1), 12–22.

Zietsch, B. P., Hansen, J. L., Hansell, N. K., Geffen, G. M., Martin, N. G., & Wright, M. J. (2007). Common and specific genetic influences on EEG power bands delta, theta, alpha and beta. *Biological Psychiatry, 75*(2), 154–163.

4

THE NEUROPHYSIOLOGY OF SELF-REGULATION

Perhaps most excitingly, we are uncovering the brain basis of our behaviors—normal, abnormal and in-between. We are mapping a neurobiology of what makes us.
—Robert Sapolsky

The human brain is the master organ controlling every function of our body. It contains over 100 billion neurons; weighs only about two and a half to three pounds; and receives 20% of our cardiac output, 25% of our oxygen, and uses 25% of all the glucose available to our body. Its consistency is that of a soft-boiled egg, and it is precariously housed in a hard, protective skull, often making it vulnerable to damage as in the case of concussion or closed head injuries. The brain is responsible for our behavior, affect, perception, cognition, and personality. It controls how our body responds to stress and disease. It's responsible for our body's physiological and emotional functioning, daily maintenance, decline, repair, and recovery. When all is going well, our breathing, heart rate, body temperature, digestion, and affect promote health and a sense of well-being. When distressed, our breathing and heart rate increase, peripheral body temperature decreases, digestion slows, and affect becomes tense and reactive.

When properly functioning, our brain is self-regulating. It helps us navigate the demands of life, allowing us to cycle as needed between states of calmness and alert. However, prolonged exposure to distress or other sources of dysregulation can cause neurological instability, resulting in impaired self-regulation. More specifically, the electrochemical functioning of our neurons can become imbalanced and our bodies can't function as designed. As a result, we develop a variety of behavioral and emotional health problems related to the underfunctioning and overfunctioning of specific parts of our brain. For example, when we can't shut off the distressed response, we may develop an overfunctioning anxiety disorder. When we become exhausted, we may develop an underfunctioning depressive disorder. In addition, dysregulation can also occur when the normal communication pathways between neurons and brain structures or regions become disrupted.

The purpose of this chapter is to explore the brain's essential self-regulating capacity and its implications for neurotherapy. This will be done by first reviewing the major structures of the brain, their general purpose and function, and basic neuroanatomy. The chapter will then look at the earliest experiences of life and the critical role attachment plays in the development of the central nervous system. Finally a brief review of the autonomic nervous system will also be presented along with a discussion of the polyvagal theory and the vital role of the social engagement system in mediating the impact of stress.

THE BRAIN AND NEUROANATOMY

Thompson and Thompson (2003) in *The Neurofeedback Book* and Kershaw and Wade (2011) in *Brain Change Therapy* offered a descriptive but brief review of the brain and basic neuroanatomy. The following material summarizes their work. It is not meant to provide a full anatomical description but rather to highlight the brain's major structures and functions. Of special interest for our discussion are both an understanding of healthy brain functioning and the kinds of problems that can occur when the brain fails to maintain efficient self-regulation.

Generally speaking, the brain can be divided into three major regions: the forebrain, the midbrain, and the hindbrain. The forebrain is the seat of higher reasoning or our executive functions. It is also referred to as the neocortex. The midbrain is responsible for emotion and motivation and involves the limbic system. The hindbrain, known as the reptilian brain, is where our survival instinct and autonomic functions originate. This three-part model is called the triune (three-in-one) brain.

The hindbrain consists of the brainstem, the cerebellum, the medulla oblongata or upper spinal cord, and the pons. It is responsible for innervation to the face and neck, heart and lung regulation, skeletal muscle tone, coordination and precise motor performance, working memory, sleep, and arousal. It is also important in maintaining consciousness.

The midbrain, or limbic system, consists of the amygdala, the thalamus, and the hippocampus. The amygdala connects all areas of emotion, the autonomic nervous system, the endocrine system, and unconscious memory. It can be stimulated by a triggering event and is related to post-traumatic stress disorder. The thalamus routes all sensory information except smell through the respective visual, auditory, somatosensory, and motor cortexes. It is also important in EEG (electrical) rhythms and provides a feedback loop with the cortex. The hippocampus also has connections to areas related to emotion, the autonomic nervous system, and the endocrine system. It is involved with consciousness, laying down of memory, and recall. It allows us to compare present situations with past memories.

The forebrain consists of the thalamus, hypothalamus, and cerebrum. The cerebrum includes the cerebral cortex and basal ganglia and connects to the limbic system. It is the largest part of the brain and is responsible for communication between the midbrain and the cerebral cortex. It is the hypothalamus along with the pituitary gland that controls the endocrine (hormonal) activity in the body. This maintains homeostasis (heart rate, vasoconstriction, temperature, blood pressure, digestion, body weight, etc.). The forebrain also manages such complex behaviors as social interaction, learning, working memory, speech, language, and habit control.

The cerebral cortex or the outer portion of the brain, integrates information from the sense organs, manages emotions, retains memory, and mediates thinking and emotional expression. It is divided into two hemispheres, the right and left, and is connected by the corpus callosum, or neuronal fibers allowing communication between the hemispheres. Short fibers act as major roads connecting areas of the right and left hemisphere, and long fibers act as superhighways allowing fast connection between areas. Surrounding the corpus callosum is the cingulate gyrus. It is active in cognitive tasks, maintaining focus, and problem solving. Problems with the cingulate gyrus involve obsessive thinking and compulsive behavior.

The right hemisphere is generally involved with social interaction, spontaneity, and aesthetic appreciation. More specifically, the right hemisphere helps to regulate attention, inhibit old habits, and sense the gestalt of an experience. It involves parallel processing, spatial relationships, the understanding of geometric forms, orientation in space, and holistic perception. It also plays a vital role in the emotional aspects of language through the processing of verbal intonation. Right hemisphere dominance is noted by distractibility, stimulus seeking, novelty, change, emotional involvement, extroversion, and an external locus of control. It is also related to histrionic tendencies, impulsiveness, and mania. It relies on an accommodating, fast, and simultaneous style of information processing. Its dominant neurotransmitters are noradrenaline (speeding up action) and serotonin (slowing down action). Right hemisphere dominance is what we use for emotional processing and can be a source of problems with impulsivity, aggression, disinhibition, anxiety, and social interaction.

The left hemisphere is involved with language, writing, math, logical reasoning, and analytical, sequential processing. More specifically, it is the center for speech and syntax, writing, auditory verbal representation, object naming, word recall, visual imaging by auditory input, letter and word perception and recognition, abstract verbal formation, and perception of complex relationships. It also regulates attention, aids in inhibiting action and switching our responses, and is the source of inner dialogue used to regulate behavior. Left hemisphere dominance is noted by a lack of emotions, introversion, goal-directed thinking and action, and an internal locus of control. It relies on an assimilative, slower style of serial processing. Its dominant neurotransmitter is dopamine (responsible for reward-driven behavior). Left hemisphere dominance is what is typically measured on an intelligence test and can be the source of problems with language, dyslexia, learning disorders, negative internal dialogue, and depression.

Each hemisphere is divided into four lobes. These are the frontal, temporal, parietal, and occipital lobes. The frontal lobes are responsible for our so-called executive functions. They help us plan for the future, anticipate consequences, analyze choices, learn and express language (Broca's area), and inhibit inappropriate or unwanted behavior. They also hold our personality, sense of self-confidence, independent judgment, willingness to take risks, and our extroverted or introverted nature. Persons with attention deficit hyperactivity disorder often have problems with their frontal lobes. Problems with the right frontal lobe often result in anxiety. Problems with the left result in depression.

The temporal lobes assist with auditory processing, short-term or working memory, comprehension of word meaning (Wernicke area) and integration of new information, retrieval of words, and the emotional valance of thoughts and behavior including temper control. They also organize our sense of hearing and smell. Problems with the left temporal lobe can involve aggression, violent thoughts, sensitivity to provocation, paranoia, decreased verbal memory, and emotional instability. Problems with the right temporal lobe can involve perception of melodies, meaning of verbal tone, social cues, and facial expression. It also involves social difficulty, problems processing music, distortion in visual and auditory memory, a sense of déjà vu, and religious or moral preoccupation.

The parietal lobes are involved in integrating raw sensory information, perception of the physical body, and motor functions including touch, pressure, temperature, taste, pain, spatial relations, and navigation. Problems with the parietal lobes include difficulty processing information and understanding directions, sensory sensitivity, physiological arousal, problems with attention, and hyper-vigilance.

The occipital lobe is responsible for visual processing, image construction, visual memory, and pattern recognition. Problems with the occipital lobe can involve impaired vision and difficulty dreaming. The occipital lobe has also been implicated in problems with post-traumatic stress disorder.

NEUROANATOMY

The brain's 100 billion neurons receive and send information through electrochemical communication. Every neuron is composed of a nucleus, axons, and dendrites. The synaptic space between dendrites and other neurons is filled with neurotransmitters. Neurotransmitters facilitate neuronal communication. A process called methylation is responsible for "turning on" or "turning off" specific neurotransmitter production. Food supplements such as Niacin and folic acid are sometimes used to increase or decrease the methylation process of targeted neurotransmitters. Communication between neurons occurs when chemical ions in one axon generate a chemical charge that is sent to the dendrites of another. This either increases or decreases the likelihood that the receiving neuron will produce its own electrical impulse across the synaptic gap junction. As sequences of neurons fire or stop firing across the synaptic gap, the function related to that part of the brain is activated or inhibited. Learning occurs when a specific circuit reacts in a certain pattern. This allows a memory to form or an action to be reexperienced.

A neuron's resting electrical potential is roughly 70 millivolts. This is a measure of the difference of the charge of the ions inside the cell and those outside it when the neuron is not firing (Fisch, 1999). To fire, a neuron must become depolarized at about −55 millivolts, creating an action potential or release of neurotransmitters and electrical activity. When polarized, no firing occurs. When hyperpolarized, the neurons become dull and less responsive to other cells. Millions of neurons firing together produce patterns of electrical activity called brainwaves. Steriade et al. (1990) suggested that scalp potentials or brain waves are cortically generated and regulated by the thalamus; together they generate specific brainwave patterns. The major brainwave patterns are delta, theta, alpha, beta, and gamma.

Delta is 1–4 Hertz (Hz) or cycles per minute and is related to hypothalamic function and deep, dreamless sleep. Persons with ADHD have higher delta waves when awake. These waves are also related to dementia and head injury. Theta is 4–7 Hz and is produced in the limbic system and related to twilight states of drowsiness, meditation, hypnosis, past memory, and symbolic imagery. Those with ADHD have been found to have intrusive theta waves when trying to concentrate. Theta waves are also important in healing and recovery. Alpha is 8–12 Hz and is related to thalamic function and focused relaxation. Alpha is thought to be the brain's idling rhythm. Strong alpha waves are important to health, a key to weight management and focus of peak sports performance. As we age, alpha tends to decrease. It is also interesting to note that alpha is not present in up to 10% of healthy individuals (Stern & Engel, 2005). Beta is 12–40 Hz. Lower beta brainwaves are active in concentration, sequential thinking, and problem solving. Higher beta waves are related to anxiety, irritability, and negative internal chatter. Lower beta waves are related to depression. Gamma waves range from 25–100 Hz but are usually thought to be around 40 Hz. They are related to cognitive efficiency, rapid eye movement in sleep, and deep states of meditative compassion. Persons with learning disabilities have lower gamma waves.

EEG Frequency Band Ranges, Description and Morphology

All EEG samples are filtered at .16–45 Hz. Gain = 70uV. Time = 2 seconds.

Electroencephalo-graphy 0.16–45.0 Hz	The EEG is composed of many electrical frequencies produced by the cortex and driving mechanisms. The EEG is most commonly measured from 0.16–45.0 Hz or similar range of frequencies.	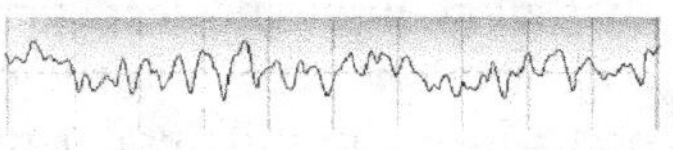
Delta 0.5–3.5 Hz	The Delta frequencies are predominant during sleep and recovery in healthy adults.	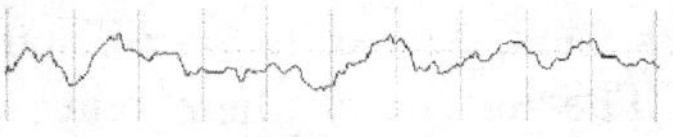
Theta 4.0–7.7 Hz	The Theta frequencies are predominant during drowsing or are associated with creative states.	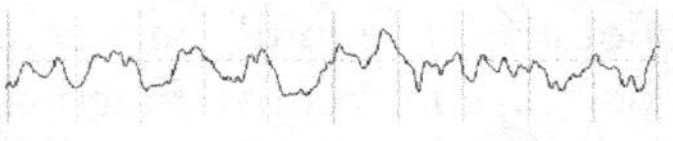
Alpha 8.0–12.0 Hz	The Alpha frequencies are predominant during an awake and alert state yet not during cortical arousal. They are often referred to the idle rhythm.	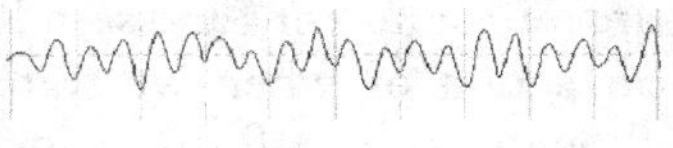
Low Beta 13.0–21.0 Hz	The lower Beta frequencies are present during times of focus and engagement.	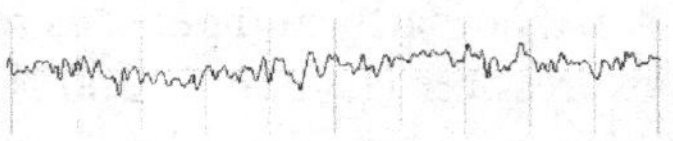
High Beta 22.0–35.0 Hz	The higher Beta frequencies are predominant during concentration and higher levels of cortical activation.	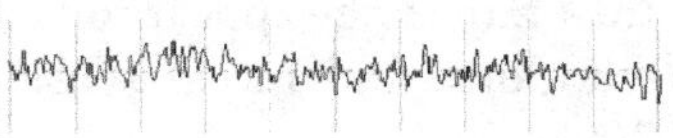
Gamma 35.0–45.0 Hz	The Gamma frequencies represent higher levels of cognition and are often representative of learning processes.	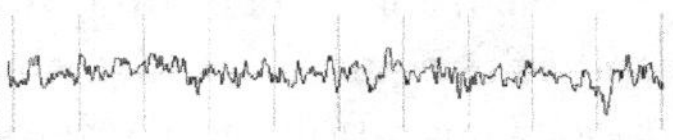

FIGURE 4.1 Brain wave chart

Permission granted. ©Leslie H. Sherlin

The electrical activity of the brain is very important and because it is related to various psychological and behavioral problems, its healthy regulation is essential. There are many factors that can cause dysregulation of the brain's electrical activity. Some have been mentioned above and others were detailed in Chapter 3, *Sources of Brain Dysregulation*. Neurofeedback, biofeedback for the brain, offers an effective intervention for reregulation of the brain's electrical activity.

The brain's neuronal communication occurs in discernible patterns based upon the connections between structures and the type of gray or white matter found in the cerebral cortex. Gray matter refers to neuronal cell bodies that have unmyelinated axons, dendrites, and glial cells. Glial cells provide nutritional and structural support for the brain's blood–brain barrier. Unmyelinated neurons are slower moving. White matter refers to areas that contain mainly myelinated or fiber sheath protected axons. Myelination gives this matter its white color. The less dense, myelinated axons, create the "superhighways" that allow high-speed transmission of signals from one structure to another and from one region of the brain to another. These communication patterns occur in many different patterns, from front to back, hemisphere to hemisphere, and within hemispheres. Myelination is greater in the right hemisphere, due to its long-distance, emotional-based communication functions. The left hemisphere relies on more sequential organization and has less myelination. It is important to note that the myelination of the neurons is not complete until the second decade of life. This is why teenagers have less developed executive functions.

Two types of neurons are important for emotional well-being. They are mirror neurons and spindle neurons. Mirror neurons fire when we perform an action or when we watch someone else perform an action. They are thought to be a form of imitative learning and are important in interpersonal empathy and perhaps the transmission of cultural values and emotional expression (Iacoboni, 2008). Spindle neurons are unusually large neurons with only one dendrite that transmits signals from region to region across the brain. They appear to be important for emotional communication, social emotions, and moral sense (Allman, Atiya, Erwin, Nimchinsky, & Hof, 2001).

Neuronal functioning directly affects the brain's ability to communicate and self-regulate. Problems with neurotransmitters have been found to affect mood, cognition, and interpersonal interaction. Mirror neurons have been implicated in autism spectrum disorders and spindle neurons in psychotic disorders.

Medication treatment, developed to help restore the brain's healthy self-regulation, has been found to have limited efficacy and unwanted side effects. This has motivated many clients and therapists to search for alternative strategies. Neurofeedback, focusing on the brain's electrical activity, is one such option.

ATTACHMENT THEORY

Attachment theory was initially proposed in the clinical context by Mary Ainsworth et al. (1978) and John Bowlby (1988). By assessing infants' responses to separation from their mothers, characteristics of secure, ambivalent, and avoidant attachment were defined. Securely attached children feel distress when separated from their caretaker but feel secure that the parent will return. Ambivalently attached children become very distressed when a caretaker leaves because they have learned that they cannot depend on their mother to be there when they need her. Their mothers have been physically or emotionally unavailable. Children with avoidant attachment show no preference between their caretaker and a complete stranger. These children have likely felt punished by a neglectful or abusive caretaker and have learned to avoid seeking their help.

The causes of insecure attachment are many. They include a young or inexperienced mother, or a mother who is unavailable due to addiction, depression, trauma, or other mental health problems. Inconsistency of care due to frequent moves or placements in foster care or a mother's struggle with illness, hospitalization, divorce, or death can also affect attachment, as can the child's struggle with its own illness, surgery, or hospitalization as well. In more severe cases, insecure attachment is related to problems with emotional or physical neglect or abuse including poor nutrition, insufficient exercise, lack of medical care, poor attention, poor empathy for the child's feelings, verbal abuse, or physical harm or injury.

The effects of insecure attachment extend through childhood into adulthood. These children have been found to have a higher incidence of oppositional defiance and conduct disorders, as well as a greater frequency of post-traumatic stress disorder and reactive attachment disorder. As adults, they may be mistrustful and avoid closeness or emotional connection. They may be more rigid, intolerant, critical, and controlling. Many will be anxious, chaotic, and insensitive to others' needs. Some will not be able to establish or maintain meaningful and healthy adult relationships. As parents themselves, they may perpetuate insecure attachment, having difficulty being consistently present for their children.

Today we know that these clinical findings also have a basis in early infant neurological development. Neurological research has established that infants' spinal motor pathways are immature at birth and take several years to develop (Schore, 1994, 2001), and their healthy development is directly related to the reciprocal attachment and behavioral interaction between the mother and the infant. Porges (2011) has found that these factors go far beyond an infant's response to separation from its mother. They involve a much more subtle behavioral dance, which he described as the social engagement system.

THE SOCIAL ENGAGEMENT SYSTEM

The social engagement system is potentiated by the infant's normal corticobulbar pathways, sufficiently developed at birth, allowing it to signal its caregiver through vocalizations and facial grimaces, to engage social gaze and smile, as well as to perform nutrient seeking or sucking behavior. Porges's research found that muscles of the face and head influence the receptivity of social cues. These include facial expressions, eye gaze, vocalization, head orientation, and modulation of the middle ear muscles to improve the extraction of the human voice from background sounds. This reduces psychological distance and acts as a filter that can influence the engagement behaviors of others, especially available caregivers.

Of even further interest is that the responsive interaction of an engaged caregiver, who instinctively rocks an infant while feeding, stimulates the infant's visceral states. This activates the muscles of mastication, promotes digestion, and calms the myelinated vagus nerve of the autonomic nervous system. As a result, the limbic system's fight, flight, or freeze response is dampened and the infant feels safe, secure, and attached to its caregiver. Moreover, this securely attached infant feels safe and secure in the world, allowing it to be optimally prepared to face the normal demands and developmental challenges of life. This establishes a strong pathway for healthy self-regulation. Without secure attachment, the maturing child and developing adult will be neurologically vulnerable to states of physical, emotional, and neurological dysregulation.

THE AUTONOMIC NERVOUS SYSTEM

The human nervous system is composed of two major parts. These are the central nervous system (CNS), which consists of the brain and spinal cord, and the peripheral nervous system (PNS), which includes the other nerves of the body, connecting organs and limbs to the CNS. The PNS has two parts: the somatic nervous system (SNS) and the autonomic nervous system (ANS). The SNS is responsible for conscious behavior such as walking, talking, or scratching your head. The ANS is responsible for what is generally thought of as involuntary behavior such as breathing, skin temperature, and muscle tension. However, we now understand through biofeedback that these previously involuntary functions can come under voluntary control.

The ANS is primarily responsible for the body's homeostatic function and is further divided into two major parts, the sympathetic and parasympathetic nervous systems. These have opposite and complimentary purposes. The sympathetic system is excitatory and the parasympathetic is inhibitory. Under threat, the sympathetic system prepares us for a fight or flight response. Energy is rerouted from less necessary bodily functions, such as digestion or reproduction, to respiration, heart rate, and motor readiness. Once the threat has diminished, the parasympathetic system returns us to baseline, nonthreat functioning, where we can rest and recover.

The ANS controls the activity of smooth muscles, cardiac muscles, and glands. It controls the muscles of the digestive system, the sphincter, the gall bladder, urinary tract, eyes, blood vessels, and the respiratory system. It controls adrenal, salivary, lacrimal, and sweat glands and influences the pancreas and reproductive systems. It has also been found to innervate the muscle spindles in the skeletal muscle system. Overactivation of the sympathetic response can result in difficulties with relaxation, digestion, and sleep. Other common ANS problems include hypertension, migraine headaches, panic disorder, generalized anxiety, and obesity.

In his book *Why Zebras Don't Get Ulcers*, Robert Sapolsky (2004) reviewed the work of Hans Selye (1979), which he conducted in the 1930s. While investigating the effects of injecting an ovarian extract in rats, Selye discovered that it was the stress the rats experienced, not the injected ovarian extract, that caused them to develop peptic ulcers, greatly enlarged adrenal glands (the source of two important stress hormones) and shrunken immune tissues. He had discovered the physiological processes involved in the development of stress-related disease. He made two important conclusions. First, the body has a consistent set of responses to a broad array of stressors, and second, if the stressors go on too long, they make you sick. Selye called his discovery the general adaptation syndrome, but today it's called the stress response.

The stress response (Thompson & Thompson, 2003) is anatomically controlled by amygdala-hypothalamus-pituitary-adrenal axis or the AHPA. A dysregulated AHPA is responsible for a number of disorders. When understimulated, these include anxiety, fibromyalgia, and chronic pain. When overstimulated, depression can occur. Under normal response to stress, the AHPA releases norepinephrine to stimulate the sympathetic nervous system, which causes the release of corticotrophin-releasing hormone (CRH) and argentine vasopressin, an antidiuretic hormone involved in cardiac performance. Serotonin can also increase CRH activity. This in turn stimulates the adrenal glands to produce glucocorticoids (GC) to down-regulate the CRH. Cortisol counteracts the effects of both increased norepinephrine and epinephrine. In situations of chronic stress, CRH levels remain very high despite high levels of GC. This causes more norepinephrine and higher CRH levels, eventually depleting serotonin and resulting in symptoms of chronic anxiety and depression. Other affective and physiological responses the stress response include fear, constricted affect, stereotypical thinking, rumination, decline in cognitive performance, impaired sleep, and dampened immune system response.

Of particular interest to the human condition is Sapolsky's (2004) observation that animals and people differ in their response to stress. Animals can't get stressed about events far in the future nor do they worry about anticipated danger. They simply go about their business until an immediate threat dictates they mobilize a stress response to escape the danger. People, on the other hand, are capable of worrying about anything, fretting about the past, anxiously anticipating the future, or becoming upset over things they can't do anything about. Disaster, as in stress-related disease, occurs when the stress response is chronically provoked. This results in problems we describe as anxiety, neurosis, paranoia, or hostility.

Sapolsky (2004) defined a stressor as anything that knocks you out of homeostatic balance and the stress response as what your body does to reestablish homeostasis. He also refined the idea of homeostasis, replacing it with the term allostasis. He felt the term homeostasis implied an optimal level or set point in functioning, like an ideal blood pressure, and a local or single regulatory mechanism, like reducing muscle tension with medication. He said allostasis was about the brain coordinating body-wide changes, along with a variety of changes in behavior. For the problem of high blood pressure, these could include changes in breathing, heart rate, muscle tension, diet, exercise, and sleep.

The autonomic nervous system is a marvelously designed mechanism of self-regulation. When properly functioning, it allows us to respond to threat and danger and to return to states of rest and recovery, but as human beings we are vulnerable to dysregulation of our ANS. Our ability of abstract reasoning; depth of memory; susceptibility to trauma, injury, or illness; and ability to anticipate and perseverate on past, future, or uncontrollable events leave us at precarious risk.

THE POLYVAGAL THEORY

The polyvagal theory extends our understanding of the adaptive reactions of the autonomic nervous system (Porges, 2008). It proposed a phylogenetic shift in the evolution of reptiles to mammals involving the vagal pathway regulating the heart. More specifically, it outlined three stages in the development of the mammal's autonomic nervous system (ANS).

The first and oldest is called immobilization and involved feigning death and behavioral shutdown to avoid death or catastrophic trauma. It relies on the unmyelinated portion of the vagus nerve called the dorsal motor nucleus. The second and next in evolution, is the familiar fight-or-flight response used to escape an immediate risk of harm. It is dependent on the sympathetic nervous system (SNS) and the spinal cord and involves an increase in metabolic activity and cardiac output. The third and most recently evolved is the social engagement system involved in attachment and self-regulation of stress. It relies on the myelinated portion of the vagus nerve that originates in the area of the brain stem called the nucleus ambiguous. It utilizes facial expression, vocalization, and listening as a means to inhibit the influence of the SNS and thus allow healthy bonding and attachment.

Porges (2008) also presented a concept he called neuroception to describe our continuous evaluation of environmental risk to assess safety, danger, or life threat. Independent of our conscious awareness, neuroception of safety is important before social engagement behavior can occur. Once perceived safe, we can inhibit the more primitive limbic structures that control fight, flight, or freeze, and engage the social behaviors associated with nursing, attachment, social bonding, and reproduction. As previously noted, these are mediated by the muscles of the face, middle ear, and head, allowing for mastication, recognition of familiar vocal tone, and head turning. Oxytocin, a neuropeptide involved in the formation of social bonds, is released and makes immobilization without fear possible in healthy relationships.

The polyvagal theory and the concept of neuroception hold many implications for self-regulation and mental health. If neuroception is faulty or impaired, a baby or individual adult will be unable to accurately detect whether the environment is safe or another person is trustworthy. While defensive measures can be taken, even by a baby, they are certain to be psychologically costly (Porges, 2011). Research has found a link between areas of the temporal cortex that fail to inhibit fight, flight, or freeze in people with autism and schizophrenia. People with anxiety and depression also have compromised social behavior, and many institutionalized children suffer from reactive attachment disorder. Porges (2011) is working on a biologically based intervention involving acoustic stimulation of the neural circuits that regulate the muscles of the inner ear, face, and head to exercise the neural pathways involved in listening and social engagement.

CONCLUSIONS

The brain is the master organ of our body and exerts specialized control over both physiological and psychological functions. Neuroanatomy informs us that our neurons operate both chemically and electrically. When these systems are healthy, our body operates like a finely tuned orchestra. When dysregulated, they cause serious illness and disease. Early life experiences are also important in healthy self-regulation. The clinical principles of attachment theory have been validated by research in neurological development. Healthy childhood attachment not only sets the stage for healthy adult relationships but also provides the neurological platform for effective stress management and physical and mental health. Lack of secure attachment has been connected to many mental and behavioral health problems. The autonomic nervous system functions to maintain homeostatic balance and is our primary source of protection from stress and threat. When overtaxed, illness and disease follow. Anxiety disorders and depression are the consequences of an overactivated and exhausted sympathetic nervous system. Allostasis offers us a broader view of homeostatic possibility by widening the potential self-regulatory changes of our body and the variety of behavioral interventions available to restore healthy functioning. Finally, the polyvagal theory extends our understanding of the autonomic nervous system by highlighting the importance of the social engagement system and neuroception in the establishment of healthy attachment and trusting adult relationships for stress regulation and mental health. In the next chapter, we will review several strategies to restore healthy self-regulation.

REFERENCES

Ainsworth, M., Blehar, M., Waters, E., & Wall, S. (1978). *Patterns of attachment: A psychological study of the strange situation.* Hillsdale, NJ: Erlbaum.

Allman, J., Atiya, H., Erwin, E., Nimchinsky, P., & Hof, A. (2001). Anterior cingulated cortex: The evolution of an interface between emotion and cognition. *Annals of the New York Academy of Sciences, 935,* 107–117.

Bowlby, J. (1988). *A secure base: Parent-child attachment and healthy human development.* New York: Basic Books.

Fisch, B. J. (1999). *Fisch and Spelhmann's EEG primer: Basic principles of digital and analog EEG.* Philadelphia, PA: Elsevier.

Iacoboni, M. (2008). *Mirroring people: The new science of how we connect with others.* New York: Farrar, Straus & Giroux.

Kershaw, C. J., & Wade, J. W. (2011). *Brain change therapy.* New York: Norton.

Porges, S. W. (2008). The polyvagal theory: New insights into adaptive reactions of the autonomic nervous system. *Cleveland Clinic Journal of Medicine, 75*(10), 1–5.

Porges, S. W. (2011). *The polyvagal theory: Neurological foundations of emotions, attachment, communication & self-regulation.* New York: Norton.

Sapolsky. R. M. (2004). Your personal pathology. *Scientific American Mind, 14*(1), 95.

Sapolsky, R. M. (2004). *Why zebras don't get ulcers.* New York: Holt.

Schore, A. N. (1994). *Regulation and origin of the self: Neurobiology of emotional development.* Hillsdale, NJ: Erlbaum.

Schore, A. N. (2001). Effects of a secure attachment relationship on right brain development, affect regulation, and infant mental health. *Infant Mental Health Journal, 22*(1–2), 17–66.

Selye, H. (1979). *The stress of my life.* New York: Van Nostrand.

Stern, J. M. & Engel, J. (2005). *Atlas of EEG patterns.* Philadelphia, PA: Lippincott Williams & Wilkins.

Steriade, M., Gloor, P., Llinas, R. R., Lopes de Silva, F. H., & Mesulam, M. M. (1990). Basic mechanisms of cerebral rhythmic activities: Report of the IFCN Committee on Basic Mechanisms. *Electroencephalography and clinical neurophysiology, 76,* 481–508.

Thompson, M., & Thompson, L. (2003). *The neurofeedback book: An introduction to basic concepts in applied psychophysiology.* Wheat Ridge, CO: The Association for Applied Psychophysiology and Biofeedback.

5

STRATEGIES FOR
SELF-REGULATION

The brain is a coincidence detector. When something wiggles inside the brain and something wiggles in the outside world at the same time, it is the brain's job to take notice.

—Douglas Dailey

S elf-regulation as a general concept describes the body's and mind's ability to assess itself and the situation and decide what physiological or behavioral changes are needed to maintain homeostasis (Criswell, 1995). More accurately referred to as allostasis, Sapolsky (2004) noted this multifaceted process is very intricate, likely nonlinear, and can be affected by various internal changes and/or external behavioral adjustments. Self-regulation via allostasis requires assessment of the current state of the varied neurological, somatic, and autonomic systems; a survey of the immediate and anticipated environmental demands and stressors; and application of various internal and behavioral strategies for returning to a state of balance. Understanding the allostatic process assists in knowing there are many adaptive methods available in achieving homeostasis.

The purpose of this chapter is to review several strategies for optimal self-regulation. These will include interpersonal connection, the use of dietary supplements, exercise, skin temperature training, diaphragmatic breathing, heart rate variability, mental imagery and hypnosis, therapeutic harmonics, audio-visual entrainment, transcranial DC stimulation, and neurofeedback. While this list is long, it is by no means exhaustive. Many other interventions have also been found to facilitate self-regulation. Some of these include biofeedback for muscle tension and galvanic skin response, meditation, massage therapy, selective use of medication, sleep hygiene, healthy diet, acupuncture, cognitive therapy, and spirituality. These are beyond the scope of this chapter but well within Sapolsky's (2004) allostatic range of possibilities.

INTERPERSONAL CONNECTION

Although most of the strategies reviewed in this chapter involve a set of prescriptions, procedures, devices, and instrumentation that lend themselves to a more mechanistic view of self-regulation, it would be a mistake to presume interpersonal connection is unimportant to the endeavor. As previously cited, early attachment sets the stage for the still-developing central nervous system. In addition, research informs us that social interaction and extroversion throughout life have been found to increase resilience and reduce stress. Further, healthy marriage, meaningful intimate relationships, and religious involvement can also promote positive self-regulation. Finally, psychotherapy and counseling and its reliance on an empathetic therapeutic relationship can, in time, heal the injury of insecure attachment and support a variety of efforts at restoration of healthy self-regulation.

From an early age we rely on secure attachment with our mothers to promote the continuing development of our autonomic nervous system. This reciprocal dance of need and attention, otherwise called the social engagement system (Porges, 2011), played out through eye glance, facial expression, familiar voice, head tilt, and nurturing behavior, creates for the infant trust in its mother and confidence that the world is a safe place. It creates a buffer against the stress and challenge of life, establishes healthy emotional development, and sets up a responsive ability to facilitate other social connections (Schore, 1994).

Throughout life we use social engagement skills to manage stress and to establish meaningful social relationships, support systems, intimate relationships, marriages, and membership in religious communities. As Sapolsky (2004) wrote, these make stressors much less stressful, but they depend on getting support from the right person, the right network of friends, the right community, and a caring and loving spouse. Overall, the fewer social relationships a person has, the shorter his or her life and the worse the impact of infectious diseases. After controlling for age, gender, and health, people with the fewest social connections are about two and a half times more likely to die as those with the most social connections (House, Landis, & Umberson, 1988), and factors such as divorce, marital discord, and isolation are associated with immune suppression (Robles & Keicolt-Glasser, 2003). More controversially, the research also seems to indicate that religiosity in and of itself does not improve health but regular attendance at religious services is reasonably predictive of decreased mortality and of decreased cardiovascular disease and depression (Sloan & Bagiella, 2002). The skills to develop meaningful interpersonal relationships are very important throughout our life. They affect our health and shape our mortality.

The hallmark of effective psychotherapy and counseling is the establishment of an empathetic therapeutic relationship. This has been true since the days of psychoanalysis and client-centered therapy and remains true today. Current research on counseling effectiveness has found that the specific theoretical approach or type of professional training is much less important than the quality of the therapeutic relationship and customized (individualized) treatment (Ahn & Wampold, 2001; Wampold, 2002). Work in affective neuroscience, human development, and clinical practice has reaffirmed the role of interpersonal connection and emotion in both self-regulation and clinical practice (Fosha, Siegel, & Solomon, 2009). Within an empathetic therapeutic relationship, clients can feel safe to explore their feelings and more encouraged to face and change the impact of stress in their lives.

Although neurotherapy strategies for self-regulation utilize structured procedures, treatment protocols, and various devices and equipment, trust and rapport between the client and the neurotherapist are still important to the treatment process. Without trust it is difficult to get a full clinical picture from a psychosocial medical history or honest updates of therapeutic change as clients report progress, decline, or no change. Without rapport, clients may feel less willing to try suggested interventions, failing to benefit from what may seem to be secondary or tertiary strategies that could make a significant difference. Without social connection, the neurotherapy process would only be a set of procedures and not a truly joint effort toward health and improved self-regulation.

DIETARY SUPPLEMENTS

There is a vast array of dietary supplements that can help improve self-regulation. While nothing substitutes for a healthy diet, careful use of dietary supplements can promote improved neurological and immunological functioning (Balch, 2010). The strongest research evidence suggests omega 3s found in fish oil, Vitamin D and N-acetylcysteine are especially important (Hill & Castro, 2009). Omega 3 fatty acids with DHA (docosahexaenoic acid) and EPA (eicosapentaenoic acid) have been found to improve cardiac function and problems with depression, anger, postpartum depression, schizophrenia, and bipolar disorder. Omega 3s have been found to support healthy heart and brain functioning, vision, and the maintenance of normal blood pressure. The typical dose is 3,000 mg a day.

Vitamin D, normally acquired when the skin is exposed to the sun's ultraviolet rays, has been found to be very important in normal antibiotic production of the immune system, building strong bones and teeth, supporting colon and pancreatic health, reducing cancer risk, and decreasing mental health problems. The typical dose is 5,000 IU a day.

N-acetylcysteine (NAC) is very important in neuronal functioning. It has been found to stabilize the protein structures that aid in the formation of glutathione, which modulates glutamatergic, neurotropic, and inflammatory pathways. It has been shown to be beneficial in the treatment of addictions (marijuana dependence, nicotine and cocaine addiction, and gambling), obsessive-compulsive disorders, trichotillomania (grooming disorder), schizophrenia, and bipolar disorders (Dean, Giorlando, & Berk, 2011). It has also been used with some efficacy in patients with Alzheimer's disease. Most recently, it has been found to ease irritability and repetitive behaviors in children with autism (Hardan et al., 2012). Persons with a family and/or personal history of these conditions would benefit from NAC's neurologically stabilizing influence. The usual dose is 1,200 mg a day.

Other dietary supplements have been effectively used in the treatment of ADHD. Amen (2001), in his book *Healing ADD*, listed several supplements that he has found effective in treating six subtypes of ADD. Each subtype is associated with a specific brain region and characteristic behavioral and emotional symptoms. He recommended L-tyrosine for classic, prefrontal lobe, hyperactive and inattentive ADD. For anterior cingulate or overfocused ADD, he suggested St. John's Wort and L-tyrosine, 5 HTP, or L-tryptophan. He suggested 5 HTP was better than L-tryptophan because it allowed 70% versus 3% brain absorption. For temporal lobe ADD, an unstable and volatile type of the disorder, he recommended GABA to calm the neuronal activity. He noted GABA acts like an anticonvulsant or anti-anxiety agent. For limbic or depressed ADD, he suggested DLPA, a precursor to norepinephrine, L-tyrosine, and S-Adenosyle-Methionine (SAMe), which increases cell membrane fluidity and affects the neurotransmitters involved in depression. For the sixth type of ADD, called the "Ring of Fire" because of its widespread brain dysregulation, he suggested GABA and fish oil with no stimulating agent. For more specific information on evaluation and proper dosages for adults and children, refer to Amen's (2001) original recommendations. Also note that in that same work, Amen provided a detailed guide for the use of neurofeedback in the treatment of each of the six subtypes of ADD.

Still other dietary supplements have been found useful for brain and immunological functioning, general health, memory, and sleep. The supplement DHEA is often taken to slow the aging process, enhance exercise performance, prevent Alzheimer's disease, improve libido, fight fatigue, soothe menopausal symptoms, treat erectile dysfunction, enhance the health of persons with HIV/aids, and to stimulate the immune system. Niacin is an essential B vitamin that helps break down carbohydrates, fats, and proteins into energy. It supports digestion and healthy nervous system functioning. Alpha Lipoic acid, a metabolite antioxidant, converts glucose (blood sugar) into energy. It is used to treat peripheral neuropathy by protecting the nerve cells from damage and preventing free radical damage in the brain. Vitamin C is also an antioxidant and helps the body fight off cellular injury, illness, and disease. Turmeric is derived from the herb curcuma and supports the body's healthy inflammatory response, aiding in the prevention of cancer, atherosclerosis (artery blockage), and symptoms of osteoarthritis.

Phosphotidyl Serine, Gingko biloba, Vitamin E, and ibuprofen are good for improving memory and cognitive functioning (Amen, 2001). Melatonin, a hormone that helps regulate sleep, has been found to help with jet lag, shift work, sleep onset, insomnia, quality of sleep, and sleep problems in children with neuro-psychiatric disorders such as ADHD, autism, and epilepsy.

Before taking any dietary supplement, it is important to consult your physician or a homeopathic specialist. Supplements can have unwanted side effects, interact with other medications, and reach levels of toxicity if overused. For more details about the use of dietary supplements refer to Balch's (2010) book, *Prescription for Nutritional Healing*.

EXERCISE

One of the simplest, least expensive and most effective strategies for self-regulation is exercise. We all appreciate the physical and long-term health benefits of a regular exercise program, but we may not appreciate its neurological, cognitive, and mental health benefits.

Ratey (2008), in his book *Spark: The Revolutionary New Science of Exercise and the Brain*, wrote about the benefits of exercise for learning, stress, anxiety, depression, attention disorders, addiction, hormonal change, and aging. He concluded that a minimum of 40 minutes of aerobic exercise, three times a week, stimulates the brain to produce brain-derived neurotropic actors (BDNF). BDNF is important for energy metabolism and synaptic plasticity. It is activated by glutamate, increases antioxidant production, and actually grows new brain cells. Ratey (2008) described BDNF as "Miracle Gro" for the brain. He said stress from exercise sparks brain growth if it isn't too severe and fortifies the infrastructure of nerve cells against damage and disease.

The best exercise routine involved 6 hours a week or 45 minutes to an hour a day of interval training, bringing your heart rate up very high for short periods of time and then returning to a lower rate for longer periods. Four days a week should be dedicated to longer, moderate intensity exercise such as weight training, yoga, or tai chi, and 2 days a week to shorter, high intensity exercise such as cycling, walking, jogging, running, or swimming. Ratey concluded that physical activity is the natural way to prevent the negative consequences of stress, and everyone can give 6 hours a week to their brain.

In a study on the effects of exercise on depression, Blumenthal et al. (1999) found exercise to be as effective as antidepressant medication in reducing the symptoms of depression among older patients with major depression. In his landmark study, he assigned 156 men and women, age 50 and older, diagnosed with major depression, into three groups. One group received Zoloft, another exercise, and a third Zoloft and exercise. At the end of 16 weeks, he found 52% of the Zoloft group, 55% of the Zoloft and exercise group, and only 30% of the exercise-alone group, were still depressed. Six months later, he found 38% of the exercise and medication group had relapsed, compared to only 8% of the exercise-alone group. Blumenthal concluded that although antidepressants may facilitate a more rapid therapeutic response than exercise, after 16 weeks, exercise was equally effective in reducing depression.

Exercise has also been found to prevent diabetes and high blood pressure, lessen the impact of ADHD on learning performance, slow cognitive decline in aging, alter blood hormone (cortisol) levels, decrease the impact of anxiety disorders, and improve the outcomes of addiction treatment programs (Ratey, 2008). While modern conveniences, electronic entertainment, sedentary lifestyles, and processed food have jeopardized our health, exercise is one strategy available to everyone to improve their healthy self-regulation.

SKIN TEMPERATURE TRAINING

One of the most direct forms of biofeedback, a group of self-regulation techniques that rely on operant conditioning of the autonomic nervous system, involves the voluntary control of peripheral skin temperature (Schwartz & Andrasik, 2003). When stressed, the smooth muscles surrounding blood vessels become constricted, rerouting blood to internal organs and large muscle groups in preparation for a flight-or-fight response. This is called the vasomotor response. Once constricted, the amount of blood flow to the periphery is reduced, and the surface skin temperature decreases (Criswell, 1995). Normal peripheral skin temperature is 86 plus or minus two degrees for women and 88 plus or minus two degrees for men. Less than these amounts suggests a stress reaction and more suggests a relaxation response.

Skin temperature training is used to treat asthma, hypertension, migraine headaches, and Raynaud's disease. Raynaud's disease is noted by cold hands and cold feet associated with circulatory problems, such as in diabetes, resulting in difficulty healing, gangrene, and sometimes amputation. Clinical criteria for resolution of migraines and hypertension involves maintaining peripheral skin temperature of 94 to 95 degrees. The relaxation response is indicated by temperatures above 90 degrees. Demos (2005) noted that most neurotherapists employ skin temperature training because it is the fastest and easiest way to introduce clients to neuroregulation (self-regulation) skills. It has also been found to facilitate the effectiveness of neurofeedback.

The procedure for skin temperature training is as follows:

1. Acquire an inexpensive digital or hand held temperature thermometer. A digital unit can be purchased for around $20 and handheld thermometers for less than a dollar each. See www.cliving.org for details on skin temperature equipment.

2. Hold the thermometer or attach the digital sensor with gauze tape to palm side, large finger of your nondominant hand.

3. Sit normally until the reading stabilizes. This is your prebaseline peripheral skin temperature. If your hands are cold from outdoors, let them first adjust to the room temperature.

4. Then close your eyes and focus on "letting go" and replacing anxious thoughts with calming thoughts. Imagine a relaxing place. Repeat to yourself, "I am . . . calm. I am . . . relaxed. I am . . . warm. My arms . . . are calm. My arms . . . are relaxed. My arms . . . are warm. My hands . . . are calm. My hands . . . are relaxed. My hands . . . are warm."

5. Take time to allow your imagination to recreate all the beautiful aspects of your relaxing place. Notice what you see, hear, feel, smell, and/or taste. Let the picture in your mind become a movie and enjoy it as it plays out in your mind's theater.

6. If the temperature decreases, you may be trying too hard. Take a few deep breaths. Remind yourself to let go and allow the imagery to unfold. If you are still having problems, it may be more helpful to follow along with a guided relaxation exercise.

7. Sometimes it is also helpful to have the client use imagery when learning biofeedback. Imagine the smooth muscles of the blood vessels beginning to relax, the blood flowing more easily through your arms, hands, and fingers, and your skin beginning to feel warmer.

8. Now open your eyes and notice your temperature reading. This is your treatment-induced reading. Congratulations on learning how to increase your peripheral skin temperature.

9. Next, return to normal nonimagery activity and after a few minutes notice your postbaseline peripheral skin temperature. This is a measure of how much your training has generalized to your usual state.

10. Practice skin temperature training for 5–8 days in a row so it becomes your normal state of arousal.

DIAPHRAGMATIC BREATHING

Another very useful and easily learned self-regulation skill is diaphragmatic breathing. Most of us do not breathe from our diaphragms. We take shorter breaths from our chest. If you were fortunate to be a trained singer, wind instrument player, or highly trained athlete, you might have been taught to use your diaphragm because it greatly improves your performance.

Since the brain needs both glucose (blood sugar) and oxygen to survive, improved oxygenation will improve its performance. Normal breath rates are between 12 and 15 breaths per minute. Children 2 to 5 years old breathe more often, about 25 to 30 breaths per minute, kids 5 to 12, 20 to 25 times per minute, and older than 12, 15 to 20 times per minute (Schwartz & Andrasik, 2003). The relaxation response is breathing between four and six breaths per minute. A very inexpensive breathing pacer software tool is available over the Internet as a way to get you started (See www.bfe.org for details on the EZ-Air Plus breathing pacer).

Diaphragmatic breathing can be applied to many health problems. These include hypertension, asthma, heart disease, anxiety and panic disorders, depression, sleep problems, chronic pain, circulatory problems, substance abuse, learning, and anger management. Like skin temperature training, diaphragmatic breathing has also been found to enhance the effectiveness of neurofeedback (Demos, 2005).

The procedure for diaphragmatic breathing is as follows:

1. First put one hand on your chest and one on your stomach or diaphragm, just below your rib cage. Notice which hand is moving the most. If it is your chest, you are a reverse, shallow, or chest breather and are probably not getting enough oxygen to your lungs, heart, and brain, unknowingly triggering a stress response. If your diaphragm is moving the most, you are likely a healthy breather but may want to reduce the number of breaths you take each minute.
2. Count the number of breaths you take each minute by watching a second hand and count the number of times you breathe in and out in one minute. Fifteen to 25 is too many, 12 to 15 average, and four to eight, optimum. Make a note of your prebaseline breath rate.
3. Keeping one hand on your chest and the other on your diaphragm, breathe in and allow the air to expand your diaphragm, moving the hand you placed there, while keeping the hand on your chest relatively still. When full, hold your muscles slightly before you exhale.
4. Now exhale, pushing the hand on your diaphragm inward until all the air is out of your lungs. Try to talk. If you can still talk then air remains in your lungs and you need to exhale a little more. Again, pause, hold your muscles slightly before you begin to inhale.
5. If you are having trouble, try standing sideways in front a mirror and watch your body movement as you inhale and exhale. You could also ask a friend to put their arms around you and gently apply pressure to your back and stomach while you are exhaling, letting air in while you inhale. Finally, you could try using the mantra "belly in . . . belly out."
6. Practice diaphragmatic breathing 15 minutes a day during daylight, active hours. Don't wait to practice at night while you are already relaxing.
7. Use small circular stickers strategically placed throughout your environment to remind you to breathe diaphragmatically. Put one on your bathroom mirror, at your desk, on the refrigerator, the car dashboard, your briefcase, the phone, etc.

HEART RATE VARIABILITY

Heart rate variability (HRV) is a highly researched and very effective biofeedback technique that utilizes heart rhythm feedback (beat to beat changes in heart rate) to promote improved self-regulation. HRV is derived from the electrocardiogram (ECG). Research by the Institute of HeartMath (McCarthy, Atkinson, & Tomasino, 2001) has found that an optimal level of beat to beat variability is key to an organism's inherent flexibility, adaptability, and healthy functioning. Negative emotion, on the other hand, leads to increased disorder in the heart's rhythm, which adversely affects the autonomic nervous system, physiological functioning, and psychological health.

Introducing the concept of the "heart brain," Armour (1991) noted that the heart has a complex intrinsic nervous system sufficiently sophisticated to qualify as a "little brain." He found that the heart has a network of several types of neurotransmitters, proteins, and support cells. Like the brain but capable of independent action, its circuitry of over 40,000 sensory neurites allow it to detect circulating hormones and neurochemicals and to sense heart rate and pressure. This information is constantly sent to the brain; processed by the higher centers that influence perception, decisions making, and other cognitive processes; and relayed back to the body through the autonomic nervous system.

When two or more of the body's oscillatory systems such as respiration and heart rhythm become synchronized, the field of physiology describes it as a state of coherence (Childre & Cryer, 2008). The concept of coherence is borrowed from the field of physic and the concept of entrainment. Entrainment describes two or more waves that are in phase. Think of a flock of birds acting as one, flying together, making the same turns, and altering course as one body. Think of multiple light sources coming together to create the in-phase power of a laser. In HRV, respiration, heart rate, and brain activity can be thought of as entrained. When negatively entrained or desynchronized, as in the stress response, the nervous system, emotional and cognitive states, and associated bodily functions will become taxed. When positively entrained, synchronized, or in a state of coherence, there is increased parasympathetic activity (calmness and recovery); efficient and harmonious functioning of the cardiovascular, nervous, hormonal, and immune systems; sustained positive emotion; and constructive integration of the cognitive system. In other words, we think, feel, and function in a balanced, healthy, and self-regulated manner.

In neurofeedback work, HRV is used to strengthen self-regulatory functioning before beginning neurofeedback training. The Emwave software package designed by the Institute of HeartMath, uses a plethysmograph attached to the big finger of the nondominant hand or an ear sensor clip to measure heart rate variability (HRV). (See www.heartmath.com for details on the Emwave system.) As HRV is measured, it is fed back to the client through various visual and auditory feedback signals including bells and gongs, graphs, colored performance indicators, trace lines of heart rate and respiration, and progression through several video graphic presentations. The process involves three steps. The first is to focus on the area of your heart. The second is to do heart-focused breathing or imagining breathing in and out of your heart. The third is making an emotional shift by thinking of a positive feeling such as care or appreciation or by recalling an uplifting experience that will help you recreate a positive feeling. Over the course of four sessions, clients can enhance their HRV from low to medium, high, and very high levels of challenge. Finally, it is interesting to note that most biofeedback treatment plans begin with four sessions of HRV work because it sets the self-regulatory baseline for more specific biofeedback interventions such as muscle tension and galvanic skin response.

MENTAL IMAGERY AND HYPNOSIS

In their book *Brain Change Therapy*, Kershaw and Wade (2011) make a strong case that clients must engage in neurological repatterning to learn how to manage state changes toward more efficient self-regulation. In their approach, they identified the neurological states that must be activated for change to occur. These included beta activation for clients who are depressed, alpha activation for clients who need calm energy to resolve anxiety, and alpha theta activation for clients who need deeper reflection and recovery for problems involving addiction and emotional trauma. The authors suggested that metaphor, mental imagery, and hypnosis combined with neurotherapy and traditional cognitive therapy can promote access to these states.

According to Cormier, Nurius, and Osborn (2009), when clients verbalize their problems, become aware of their underlying self-defeating or irrational beliefs, and learn how to challenge them, substituting more rational, positive internal scripts, they are working at the beta brainwave level. When they close their eyes, engage in relaxation exercises, follow a suggested metaphor, or a structured mental imagery script (Naparstek, 1994), they are accessing alpha states and thus able to feel a calm focus that had previously eluded them. When they engage in hypnosis (Erickson & Rossi, 1981) and deeper trance, clients access alpha theta states and become able to benefit from deeper reflection, symbolic meaning, and emotional and physical recovery.

Kershaw and Wades's (2011) description of brainwave state flexibility and state flow suggest that clients could improve their self-regulation by developing skills at all three brainwave levels, being able to move up and down as their symptoms direct. These skills could be learned through the use of prepared relaxation, mental imagery, and self-hypnosis scripts or prerecorded materials, or by engaging the skills of a professional hypnotist or cognitive behavior therapist. (See www.chapinandrussell.com for details on a Deep State Mental Imagery Resource).

THERAPEUTIC HARMONICS

Another strategy for self-regulation that relies on the principles of entrainment is therapeutic harmonics. Swingle (2010), in a brief summary of his work on the clinical use of therapeutic harmonics, described them as subliminal sound presented below the threshold of hearing that affects mood, thoughts, and physiological functions including brainwave activity. The essential feature of his harmonics is that they are embedded in filtered pink noise that sound somewhat like running water and are played at a very low volume so that they do not interfere with whatever activity the client may be engaged, from studying to sleep.

The original research in acoustic brainwave entrainment was conducted by Oster (1973) in which he demonstrated that binaural beats, two separate tones, tuned slightly differently than each other, would cause the brain to entrain and alter its state of consciousness or brainwave activity. Binaural beats have also been found to synchronize the two hemispheres of the brain because both ears send neural signals to the sound processing centers (olivary nuclei) in both hemispheres of the brain. For over 20 years Swingle's (1992, 2008) research has expanded this knowledge to investigate the use of blended subliminal harmonics as a supplementary and potentiating treatment in neurotherapy (Swingle, 2008). He has developed several therapeutic harmonic CDs for specialized clinical applications. Some of these include the Alert CD for ADHD that decreases theta wave activity, the Serene CD for anxiety that reduces fast beta wave activity and increases slow theta wave activity, the Sweep CD for trauma that increases theta and alpha wave activity, and the Harmonic Sleep CD for insomnia that increases slow theta and delta wave activity. (See www.ToolsforWellness.com for details on therapeutic harmonics.) Swingle found that the typical length of neurofeedback treatment could be significantly reduced from 40 or 60 sessions to 15 or 20 with the use of therapeutic harmonics. Other neurotherapy practitioners recommend that clients use therapeutic harmonics after completing neurofeedback treatment, as an at-home method to strengthen the gains made in treatment.

Also available directly to consumers on the commercial market are harmonic CDs developed by Dr. Jeffrey Thompson, Ph.D., of the Center for Neuroacoustic Research. His harmonics are different than Swingle's in that the brainwave audio processes are embedded into lush, multilayered, ambient musical soundtracks. After listening for only a few minutes, the brain becomes entrained to the intended brainwave for the selected application. Some of his 90 CDs include delta for sleep and rejuvenation; theta for insight and intuition; alpha–theta for an awakened mind (deep meditation);

alpha for relaxation and quiet meditation; beta for energy and focus; and gamma for enhanced perception, openness to compassion, insight, and personal transformation. Thompson's (2007) CDs are designed for personal, at-home use and can help enrich and strengthen one's access to the various brainwave states. (See www.neuroacoustic.com for details on harmonic CDs.)

AUDIO-VISUAL ENTRAINMENT

Audio-visual entrainment (AVE) utilizes alternating sound (binaural beats) and flashing lights to access various brainwave states for improved self-regulation. Siever (2000) suggested that AVE is effective because of several simultaneously occurring factors. It may stimulate the generation of dendrites and neurons as found in electrically stimulated rat brain tissue. Neurotransmitter production is affected, increasing endorphin and serotonin levels and decreasing melatonin, and cerebral blood flow is increased within the auditory and visual cortex (29–50%) with a whole-brain oxygen increase of 5%. Interestingly, photic stimulation is greatest at 7.8 Hz, the Schumann Resonance frequency, the frequency at which electromagnetic radiation circles the Earth, and the frequency of deep meditation. AVEs also create a sense of dissociation and stabilization necessary for clearing the mind and silencing anxious thoughts and mental chatter. Finally, hypnotic trance and meditative states are facilitated, which are useful for accessing and healing trauma, deep relaxation, and brain synchrony.

AVE has been used to treat many problems including ADHD, autism, behavioral disorders, cognitive decline in the elderly, insomnia, chronic pain, fibromyalgia, anxiety, depression, seasonal affective disorder, brain injury (stroke and aneurism), performance enhancement, jet lag, and chronic fatigue (Siever, 2006). Although AVE equipment can be obtained for home use, persons who have a history of epilepsy, seizure disorder, migraine headaches, head injury, mental illness, or who are currently using substances should not use it unless under the supervision of a trained health care professional.

One of the most popular types of AVE equipment is the David Pal Device (Siever, 2006). It consists of the AVE unit, about the size of a deck of cards, headphones, and a wraparound eye set with blue-tinted white LEDs. It is preprogrammed to run 18 different protocols utilizing delta, theta, alpha, SMR (sensory-motor rhythm), and beta brainwaves. It cannot store session-by-session data but can be programmed by a therapist for a client's home use to potentiate neurofeedback training. (See www.mindalive.com for details on the David PAL.)

Another type of AVE equipment utilizing only visual stimulation with clear LED glasses is called the Spectra (Swingle, 2010). It too is used as an adjunct to neurofeedback. The Spectra has three settings. SpectraSweep functions to balance the frontal region, for improved emotional regulation.

SpectraAlert improves cognitive efficiency for students with learning problems and the elderly wanting to retain cognitive sharpness. SpectraSerene helps to resolve mood disorders and to treat seasonal affective disorder. As with other visual stimulation devices, persons with epilepsy, migraines, or seizure disorders should not use Spectra without professional supervision. (See www .ToolsforWellness.com for details on the Spectra.)

TRANSCRANIAL DC STIMULATION

Only two strategies for self-regulation involve direct electrical stimulation. They are cranial electrical stimulation (CES) and transcranial DC stimulation (TDCS). A precursor to TDCS, CES utilizes battery-driven, cranial micro-amperage stimulation. It produces very low amperage, less than one milliampere, on the surface of the scalp. It has been found to be safe and effective, activating a range of .3–100 Hz of brainwave electrical stimulation to promote self-regulation. In CES, electrodes are placed at various locations on the head or more typically with clips on the earlobes. The level of stimulation is barely felt. At most, it is experienced as a tingling or itching sensation. Sessions typically run from 20 minutes to an hour.

CES was originally developed to treat sleep problems. It has since been found effective in treating anxiety, depression, pain, and substance abuse. Side effects of its use are rare, mild, and self-limiting, occurring only at the highest settings and amounting to slight skin irritation at the electrode sites. Smith (2001), studying 2,500 CES users, found 93% of the sample reported 25% reduction in pain of all types, 90% reported decreased depression, 93% improved sleep, 94% less chronic fatigue, and 90% reported at least 25% less anxiety. Gilula and Kirsch (2005) found that CES has equal or greater efficacy for the treatment of depression, with fewer side effects, as compared to antidepressant medication. CES has been found to increase alpha (calming anxiety) and slow frequency theta (calming the central nervous system) in the back of the brains of alcoholics, helping them maintain sobriety.

Transcranial direct current stimulation (TDCS) delivers a small electrical current to the nervous tissue of the brain. The current is delivered by a battery and flows in one direction. It reaches the brain through small wet sponges that attach to the skull. Dailey (2011) has documented the explosive growth of research studies on TDCS, suggesting a tripling of studies every 3 years. Today's TDCS units have been primarily used in iontophoresis, a method of drug delivery utilizing charged electrical particles and electrical current to more precisely deliver dosages of dexamethason (a steroid) and magnesium. A TDCS unit delivers one to two milliamperes of current, allowing a stronger stimulating effect than traditional CES. It is also capable of generating a more precise current flow, adjusting to client scalp resistance due to sweat and sponge conditions (drying during treatment).

TDCS was originally used to increase or decrease the excitability of neurons in various parts of the cortex and to study the effects of neurophysiology, cognition, and performance. Dailey (2011) has cited over 40 clinical applications, from addiction to vision problems, with some of the strongest effects noted in the resolution of depression in four sessions.

In the United States, both CES and TDCS are now listed as FDA-approved medical devices and can be purchased only by a licensed health care provider. (See www.mindalive.com for David PAL with CES capability and www.mind@growing.com for TDCS devices.) In Canada, CES devices can be purchased over the counter and are suitable for home use.

NEUROFEEDBACK

Neurofeedback is significantly different than the previously noted strategies of self-regulation. Its primary focus is on changing the electrical activity of the brain, the foundation of the body's emotional and behavioral functions. Referred to as EEG biofeedback or brainwave biofeedback, neurofeedback combines the capability of the electroencephalogram (EEG) with advances in computer technology and operant conditioning (Swingle, 2010). This enables near real-time monitoring of EEG, allowing the brain to recognize itself, and change or self-regulate its electrical activity as guided by specific treatment protocols that either reward (strengthen) or inhibit (weaken) targeted brainwave patterns. Neurofeedback can teach clients how to interrupt dysfunctional neurological patterns and establish more stable ones.

Neurofeedback is based upon two major tenets (Thompson & Thompson, 2003). The first is that the EEG reliably reflects measurable mental states. The second is that these states can be trained. It has been well established that the EEG measures various brainwave states (delta, theta, alpha, beta, and gamma) related to consistent mental states (sleep, deep relaxation, calm focus, problem solving, and cognitive efficiency). The word "training" is used instead of "treatment" because training requires active engagement and repeated effort in strengthening a response, while treatment implies a passive intervention where something is done to a client without his or her active involvement.

There are two major goals in neurofeedback training (Thompson & Thompson, 2003). The first is to increase or decrease a particular brainwave frequency in a selected area of the brain that has been found to be related to a client's presenting emotional or behavioral problem. For example, with ADHD clients, neurofeedback can increase the sensory motor rhythm (low beta) and decrease theta and high beta at the center of the sensory motor strip on the top of the head. The second goal is to improve the overall stability and communication of neuronal networks across the brain and between or within its hemispheres. For example, with trauma clients,

FIGURE 5.1 Russell-Chapin setting up for an NFB session

Permission granted by Duane Zehr of Bradley University

neurofeedback can increase the synchrony or coherence (simultaneous firing) of alpha and theta across the cingulate (middle part of the brain). Neurofeedback restores brain function, rhythm, timing, frequency, and synchronization that allow the brain to better orchestrate perception, motor action, and conscious experience (Farmer, 2002).

During neurofeedback, a client sits in a comfortable chair and watches a monitor that plays a video game, music, or movie. On the client's head and ears are attached three to five sensors. The sensors are attached with conductive paste or self-adhesive gauze. One or two sensors are located at targeted brain locations. Two to three other sensors are attached to the ears or chest and act as a referent and/or ground for the active sensors. The sensors are hardwired and attached to an EEG amplifier. There are many amplifiers on the market. They vary in price, flexibility, and comprehensiveness of biofeedback capability (EEG, skin temperature, muscle tension, heart rate variability, etc.). Nexus, sold by the Sten's Corporation, is one of the more comprehensive devices and allows customization of training screens. (See www.stens-biofeedback.com for more details on the Nexus.) (see Figure 5.1).

The EEG amplifier then sends the EEG information, via wireless Bluetooth technology, to a computer where a specialized software program allows the neurotherapist to select, monitor, and interact with a specific training protocol. The Nexus software program is called Biotrace. As a client focuses on the desired brainwave, the video game, music, or movie will play. When the client wanders away from the targeted brainwave, the game, music, or movie will stop. The brain wants to be stimulated, so it is naturally motivated to relocate the targeted brainwave. In addition, unique tones such as a bird chirping, a bleep alert, or a horn sound can inform a client when he or she is becoming too anxious or too drowsy. This signals him or her to refocus and better remain at the targeted brainwave. Training sessions usually last between 30 and 45 minutes. It can take from 10 to 60 sessions to achieve a desired result. The usual number of sessions is 20 to 40.

Change in neurofeedback is very subtle, often too subtle to be felt by a client. Outside reports from parents, friends, or physicians of significant behavioral or attitudinal changes are more likely to be observed over time. Swingle (2010) wrote that change in neurofeedback is like the stock market or a baseball game. Even during a prosperous time, the market may go up or down from day to day, week to week, or month to month, but the overall trend is up. In baseball, a team might score 10 runs one night, five the next, two the third, but still be winning each game. To help clients recognize and assess progress during training, they may complete behavioral checklists noting problems that have improved, stayed the same, or become worse.

Neurofeedback has been found to be helpful with ADHD, seizure disorders, anxiety, depression, trauma, addiction, insomnia, immune functioning, and autism spectrum disorders. It has also been used for peak performance in sports, business, and the creative arts.

Although a neurologically based strategy for self-regulation, neurofeedback does have some limitations. These include slight side effects such as dizziness from focus while training and minor irritability at the sensor site due to cleansing of the site with an alcohol pad before sensor placement. Of more concern is the potential for abreaction or emotional experiences after some training protocols and in some cases developing an aversive reaction to a substance of abuse. Most experienced therapists understand these as positive outcomes, but some clients may be alarmed in their return of dreams, breadth of emotional expressivity, and new intolerance of alcohol or drugs. Finally, neurofeedback requires the ability to sit relatively still, to focus, and to tolerate sensors and wires being attached to the head. Continued delivery methods are being developed. Some procedures have used a vibrating stuffed animal as feedback for younger children, and sounds have been successfully used with clients in a fugue or coma-like state.

The clinical impact of neurofeedback to improve the self-regulation of brainwave activity related to emotional and behavioral problems is very intriguing. Swingle (2010) suggested it side-steps defenses and dysfunctional belief patterns, loosens perceptions, and helps clients make better use of therapy. Kershaw and Wade (2011) noted that in therapy, clients talk about it and feel better. In neurofeedback, clients feel better and are then able to talk about it. In the authors' experience, neurofeedback seems to potentiate the neurological platform, allowing clients who had previously been unable to implement counseling goals to put them into action and be successful. It has also helped clients with moderate to severe problems, often managed by medication, make meaningful change and in some cases reduce and even eliminate their need for medication. Neurofeedback offers clients an effective alternative when counseling and medication are not sufficient in helping them resolve their concerns.

CONCLUSIONS

Self-regulation describes the body's and mind's ability to assess the situation and decide what physiological or behavioral changes are needed to maintain homeostasis. Allostatsis informs us there are many internal and external changes or strategies to improve self-regulation. This chapter reviewed 10 of these strategies including interpersonal connection, dietary supplements, exercise, skin temperature training, heart rate variability, mental imagery and hypnosis, therapeutic harmonics, audio-visual entrainment, transcranial DC stimulation, and neurofeedback. Significantly different and central to the body's functioning, neurofeedback focuses on changing the brain's electrical activity. Using EEG biofeedback, advanced computer technology, and principles of operant conditioning, neurofeedback allows clients to learn how to change and self-regulate dysregulated brainwave patterns related to many emotional and behavioral problems.

REFERENCES

Ahn, H., & Wampold, B. E. (2001). Where oh where are the specific ingredients? A meta-analysis of component studies in counseling and psychotherapy. *Journal of Counseling and Psychotherapy, 3*(48), 251–257.

Amen, D. (2001). *Healing ADD.* New York: Putnam.

Armour, J. A. (1991). Anatomy and function of the intrathoricic neurons regulating the mammalian heart. In I. H. Zucker & J. P. Gilmore (Eds.), *Reflex control of the circulation* (pp. 1–37). Boca Raton, FL: CRC.

Balch, P. A. (2010). *Prescription for nutritional healing* (5th ed.). New York: Avery.

Blumenthal, J. A., Babyak, M. A., Moore, K. A., Craighead, W. E., Herman, S., Khatri, P., . . . Ranga Krishnan, K. (1999). Effects of exercise training on older patients with major depression. *Archives of Internal Medicine 19*(159), 2349–2356.

Childre, D., & Cryer, B. (2008). *From chaos to coherence: The power to change performance.* Boulder Creek, CA: Institute of HeartMath.

Cormier, S., Nurius, P., & Osborn (2009). *Interviewing and change strategies for helpers: Fundamental skills and cognitive behavioral interventions* (6th ed.). Belmont, CA: Brooks/Cole.

Criswell, E. (1995). *Biofeedback and somatics.* Cotati, CA: Free Person.

Dailey, D. (2011). *TDCS protocols and resources.* Santa Clara, CA: MindGrowing.

Dean, O., Giorlando, F., & Berk, M. (2011). N-acetylcysteine in psychiatry: Current therapeutic evidence and potential mechanism of action. *Journal of Psychiatry and Neuroscience, 2*(36), 78–86.

Demos, J. N. (2005). *Getting started with neurofeedback.* New York: Norton.

Erickson, M., & Rossi, E. (1981). *Experiencing hypnosis: Therapeutic approaches to altered states.* New York: Irvington.

Farmer, S. (2002). Neural rhythms in Parkinson's disease. *Brain Journal of Neurology, 125*(6), 1176–1176.

Fosha, D., Siegel, D. J., & Solomon, M. F. (Eds.) (2009). *The healing power of emotion: Affective neuroscience development & clinical practice.* New York: Norton.

Gilula, M. F., & Kirsch, D. L. (2005). Cranial electrotherapy stimulation review: A safer alternative to psychopharmaceuticals in the treatment of depression. *Journal of Neurotherapy, 9*(2), 7–26.

Hardan, A. Y., Fung, L. K., Libove, R. A., Obukhanych, T. V., Nair, S., Herzenberg, L. A., . . . Tirouvanzian, R. (2012). A randomized controlled pilot trial of oral N-acetylcysteine in children with autism. *Journal of Biological Psychiatry, 71,* 956–961.

Hill, R. W., & Castro, E. (2009). *Healing young brains: The neurofeedback solution.* Charlottesville, VA: Hampton Roads.

House, J., Landis, K., & Umberson, D. (1988). Social relationships and health. *Science, 241,* 540.

Kershaw, C. J., & Wade, J. W. (2011). *Brain change therapy.* New York: Norton.

McCarthy, R., Atkinson, M., & Tomasino, D. (2001). *Science of the heart: Exploring the role of the heart in human performance.* Boulder Creek, CA: Institute of HeartMath.

Naparstek, B. (1994). *Staying well with guided imagery.* New York: Warner.

Oster, G. (1973). Auditory beats in the brain. *Scientific American, 229,* 94–102.

Porges, S. W. (2011). *The polyvagal theory.* New York: Norton.

Ratey, J. J. (2008). *Spark: The revolutionary new science of exercise and the brain.* New York: Little Brown.

Robles, T., & Keicolt-Glasser, J. (2003). The physiology of marriage pathways to health. *Physiology and Behavior, 79,* 409.

Sapolsky, R. M. (2004). *Why zebras don't get ulcers.* New York: Holt.

Schore, A. N. (1994). *Affect regulation and the origin of the self: The neurobiology of emotional development.* Hillsdale, NJ: Erlbaum.

Schwartz, M. S., & Andrasik, F. (2003). *Biofeedback: A practitioner's guide* (3rd ed.). New York: Guilford.

Siever, D. (2000). *The rediscovery of audio-visual entrainment technology.* Edmonton, Alberta, Canada: Comtronic Devices.

Siever, D. (2006). *The AVE session & protocol guide for professionals.* Edmonton, Alberta, Canada: Mind Alive.

Sloan, R., & Bagiella, E. (2002). Claims about religious involvement and health outcomes. *Annals of Behavioral Medicine, 24*, 14–21.

Smith, R. (2001). Is microcurrent stimulation effective in pain management? An additional perspective. *Journal of Pain Management, 11*(2), 62–66.

Swingle, P. G. (1992). *Subliminal treatment procedures: A clinician's guide.* Sarasota, FL: Professional Resource.

Swingle, P. G. (2008). *Basic neurotherapy: The clinician's guide.* Vancouver, British Columbia, Canada: Author.

Swingle, P. G. (2010). *Biofeedback for the brain: How neurotherapy effectively treats depression, ADHD, autism and more.* Piscataway, NJ: Rutgers University.

Thompson, J. (2007). *The brainwave suite.* Retrieved from www.TheRelaxation Company.com

Thompson, M., & Thompson, L. (2003). *The neurofeedback book.* Wheat Ridge, CO: Association for Applied Psychophysiology and Biofeedback.

Wampold, B. E. (2002). *The great psychotherapy debate.* Mahwah, NJ: Erlbaum.

6

BASIC CONCEPTS AND PRINCIPLES IN NEUROFEEDBACK

All that we know, all that we are, comes from the way our neurons are connected.
—Tim Berners-Lee and Mark Fischetti

Neurofeedback as a clinical approach to the resolution of psychological and behavioral problems has its origins in the study of the brain's electrical activity and behavioral psychology. The development of the human electroencephalogram (EEG) combined with the application of principles of learning, knowledge of the brain's neuroplasticity, and principles of biofeedback and self-regulation have made it possible to detect, monitor, and change the brain's electrical activity related to many emotional and physiological disorders. More recent advances in computer and electronic technology have allowed these research discoveries to be readily applied to the clinical setting. This chapter will present several of the basic concepts and principles that underlie the current practice of neurofeedback. Included will be a discussion of the importance of the electroencephalogram as a method to reliably assess and monitor the brain's electrical activity. It will also review the principles of operant and classical conditioning as well as the contributions of biofeedback and self-regulation, as these provide the means and methods to change neurological functioning. In addition, this chapter will discuss the role of electronics and computer technology and software in creating a clinical platform from which to observe and direct neurofeedback intervention.

At its core, the effective practice of neurofeedback is about understanding and changing the brain's electrical activity related to clients' psychological and behavioral problems. This requires in-depth knowledge of the function of specific brainwaves or the rhythms of the brain and their behavioral correlates. Therefore, this chapter will also present a detailed description of the primary brainwaves targeted for change. Finally, the chapter will conclude with a discussion of the basic principles of neurofeedback training and address such concepts as sensor location and training protocols, the use of rewards and inhibits, and the role of thresholds in changing the brain's electrical activity associated with client's psychological and behavioral problems.

MEASURING THE BRAIN'S ELECTRICAL ACTIVITY

Much of what we know about the electroencephalogram (EEG) can be attributed to the efforts of the German psychiatrist Hans Berger between 1929 and 1938 (Millett, 2001). He published 14 reports on the EEG and its relationship to cognitive and neurological disturbance. Of particular importance is his study of a phenomenon called "alpha blocking." Alpha waves are thought to reflect the brain's "idling" status, a readiness to respond to stimuli. Alpha blocking involves an abrupt cessation of alpha brainwaves when an individual opens his or her eyes and pays attention to objects in the environment (Berger, 1929). Initially thought to be an all-or-nothing response, alpha blocking was later subjected to quantitative analysis and found to occur as a matter of degree. The concept of desynchronization (or phase synchronization) was later used to reflect this gradient (Pfurtscheller, 1986). However, it is important to note that the alpha-blocking phenomenon allowed calibration of cognitive and attentional states and became the basis for the development of the quantitative EEG (Kaiser, 2005).

Traditionally, as used in neurological and sleep studies, the EEG is analyzed qualitatively to identify categories of abnormal characteristics that may be related to seizure activity or sleep disturbance. However, the EEG can also be analyzed quantitatively, subjected to mathematical and statistical analyses that yield measures such as frequency (brainwave type), amplitude (brainwave strength), and phase relations (brainwave synchronicity) (Kaiser, 2005). These then led to the development of normative databases that allowed comparison of individual EEG profiles to the norm. Without quantitative EEG analysis, neurofeedback could not reliably assess current brainwave characteristics nor document their change due to neurofeedback training.

Measuring the brain's electrical activity is very difficult. In the early days, a wire was placed directly into the brain of animals or under the skin of humans. Today we use sensors that are attached to the head with special conductive paste. Kaiser (2005) noted that the brainwave activity at the scalp is very faint. It is measured in the millionths of a volt or a unit of measurement called a "microvolt." Measurement of the EEG can be distorted by many things including the thickness of the skull, skin characteristics, blood pulse, muscle tension, and eye movement. Some of these influences can be controlled by cleaning the skin or relocating the sensors. Others can be managed with simple directions to the client to relax his or her jaw or by artifacting the data before analyzing it. Artifacting is a mathematical filtering process that can minimize the effects of the distortions on the final EEG.

Kaiser (2005) explained that sensors used to detect the brain's electrical activity read about a billion cortical neurons. Since many of the negative and positive potentials of these neurons cancel each other out, the EEG detects only what is left over, just a small fraction of the electrical activity under the sensor. Further, he said, it is the difference in the electrical potential between two sensors (one called an active and the other the referent) that is measured by an EEG amplifier. This information is then compressed and represented in many forms. These include the customary single trace line graphic form for each International 10–20 System (Jasper, 1958) brain site location, a two-dimensional topographical chart of the brain, or a three-dimensional tomographical representation of the internal brain structure. Color codes are typically provided for the two- and three-dimensional displays to indicate any variations in the standard deviations of the brain's electrical activity as compared to the norm.

An EEG can be conducted by simply taking one recording from a single brain site, such as Cz at the top of the head, with a basic neurofeedback EEG amplifier and manufacturer's software (Demos, 2005) and comparing the results to the normative distribution for both eyes opened and eyes closed states (Montgomery et al., 1998). For example, you may recall that alpha at eyes open will be blocked or significantly less than alpha at eyes closed. The

Neurofeedback General Hemispheric Functions

Left Hemishphere	Right Hemishphere

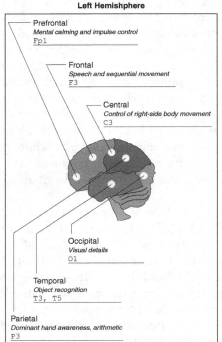
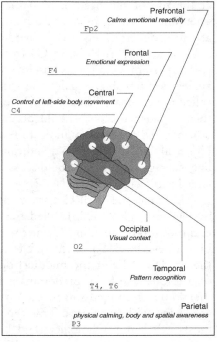

Left Hemishphere:
Prefrontal — *Mental calming and impulse control* — Fp1
Frontal — *Speech and sequential movement* — F3
Central — *Control of right-side body movement* — C3
Occipital — *Visual details* — O1
Temporal — *Object recognition* — T3, T5
Parietal — *Dominant hand awareness, arithmetic* — P3

Right Hemishphere:
Prefrontal — *Calms emotional reactivity* — Fp2
Frontal — *Emotional expression* — F4
Central — *Control of left-side body movement* — C4
Occipital — *Visual context* — O2
Temporal — *Pattern recognition* — T4, T6
Parietal — *physical calming, body and spatial awareness* — P3

FIGURE 6.1 Hemispheric map

Permission granted by © Biofeedback Tutor, adapted by John Balven and Fisch normative brainwave distribution for alpha (8–12 Hz) at Cz, eyes closed (ec), is 16.6 mV as compared to eyes opened (eo) at 9.3 mV. The other normative distributions at Cz include theta (4–8 Hz) at 12.4 mV (ec) and 10.7 mV (eo), SMR-sensory motor rhythm (12–15 Hz) at 5.1 mV (ec) and 4.4 mV (eo), beta (13–21 Hz) at 8.1 mV (ec) and 6.4 mV (eo), and the theta to beta ratio at 1.6 to 1 (ec) and 1.8 to 1 (eo). More details on the normative distribution of the brainwaves will be presented later in this chapter.

An EEG can also be conducted by inspecting the compressed spectral array at Cz, C3, or C4 (Demos, 2005). Most neurofeedback amplifiers and software will generate a three-dimensional spectral array of the EEG frequency bands from a single site. A three-dimensional spectral array presents sequentially repeated EEG samples or epochs, approximately one per second, in a visual graphic form that generate what appears to be a three-dimensional representation of the EEG. It is color coded and indicates elevations and valleys to represent high and low amplitudes (brainwave strength) across the brainwave bandwidths. This type of EEG allows assessment of the proportions between frequency bands. In other words, it allows observation of any gross abnormalities, asymmetries, or uneven frequency bandwidths. In general, the lower bandwidths (delta and theta) should show higher amplitudes than the higher bandwidths (alpha, SMR, beta, and gamma). For example, at Cz at the top of the head, a high theta compared to beta indicates possible attention deficit disorder, and a high beta to alpha or theta indicates possible attention deficit hyperactivity disorder, obsessive compulsive disorder, depression, or anxiety. If alpha at C3 (top left hemisphere) is high and alpha at C4 (top right hemisphere) is low, then problems with depression and/or anxiety are possible. Finally, the spectral array can also help assess what is called peak alpha efficiency or where alpha seems to have the highest amplitude. A normal alpha should occur at about 10 Hz. A lower peak alpha efficiency (8 to 10) may indicate learning problems or cognitive decline. A higher alpha (10 to 12) may indicate cognitive efficiency or increased intelligence. Again, more will be discussed about normal brainwave distributions later in this chapter.

Another type of EEG assessment is a five-channel assessment developed by Paul Swingle (2008b) called the Quick Q. The Quick Q evaluates five brain locations including Cz at the top of the head, O1 at the back of the head at eye level, F3 at the left front of the head, F4 at the right front of the head, and Fz at the middle front of the head. It provides information on the quality of the predominant brainwaves in each of these locations, their ratio or comparison to each other, and the typical types of problems associated with each area. This type of EEG provides information on the most prevalent psychological and behavioral disorders including attention deficit hyperactivity disorder, cognitive efficiency, trauma, sleep, pain, depression, anxiety, and obsessive-compulsive disorder. It can be done in less than 20 minutes; assesses eyes open, eyes closed, and a cognitive challenge (reading or math task); has a normative base; and generates a narrative report with brainwave amplitudes, ratios, and neurofeedback training guidelines.

The final type of EEG assessment is the 19-channel full quantitative EEG. This is usually administered when there is suspicion or report of serious head injury or significant neurological dysregulation due to a more pervasive insult to the brain from such problems as oxygen deprivation, high fever, stroke, or an organic disease process. This presumes that the other types of EEG will not be sufficient in guiding the development of an effective treatment plan. Only suitably trained professionals should administer and analyze a 19-channel EEG. Like the Quick Q, a 19-channel EEG will sample eyes open, eyes closed, and a cognitive challenge (reading or math). Unlike the Quick Q, a quantitative EEG can utilize one of several normative data bases, such as Neuroguide by Robert Thatcher et al. (1989, 2003), and its reports will include two- and/or three-dimensional topologic or tomographic representations of the brain's current neurological functioning across all 19 brain locations. It also provides information on brainwave amplitudes, ratios, and phase relationships and will detail comprehensive, 19-channel treatment guidelines toward the restoration of healthier neurological functioning. Please note that neurofeedback can never repair structural brain damage. It can only help improve the functioning of structurally sound areas of the brain.

Hughes and John (1999) described how a QEEG is particularly well suited to identifying and aiding in differential psychiatric diagnosis. They reviewed the EEG and QEEG literature and concluded that the QEEG was especially useful in distinguishing between delirium or dementia and depression, schizophrenia, and mood disorders; assessing cognitive, attentional, or developmental disorders; distinguishing between environmentally induced and endogenously mediated behavioral disorders; evaluating alcohol or substance abuse; and evaluating postconcussive syndrome. As Kaiser (2005) concluded, the QEEG allows us to eavesdrop on neuronal communication, understand psychiatric and neurological disorders by their EEG footprint, and offers neurotherapists the opportunity to train clients to alter abnormal patterns of neuronal electrical activity associated with emotional, cognitive, and behavioral problems. As the discipline continues to mature, he stated that the QEEG will likely emerge as a mainstay of neurology, sleep medicine, psychiatry, psychology, and counseling.

LEARNING AND NEUROPLASTICITY

There are two learning paradigms involved in neurofeedback. These are operant and classical conditioning (Thompson & Thompson, 2003). In operant conditioning, voluntary behavior is rewarded to increase the likelihood of its reoccurrence (Skinner, 1938). In classical conditioning, involuntary or autonomic nervous system behavior is paired with a conditioned stimulus.

After a sufficient number of pairings, the conditioned stimulus elicits the involuntary response (Watson, 1913). In neurofeedback, operant conditioning occurs when a client is rewarded for finding a targeted brainwave state with a visual or auditory reward. The reward may be in the form of progress on a video game, enjoyment of one's favorite music or movie, or satisfaction of a reinforcing sound or visual display. It is important to note that the brain is inherently motivated to seek stimulation and although initial attempts at finding the desired brainwave state may be awkward and sometimes frustrating, with continued effort the brain will succeed and the new brainwave response will be strengthened until it becomes automatic. Most neurotherapists want their clients to succeed 70–80% of the time. This keeps the client motivated with sufficient positive reinforcement to persist at the task even as the level of challenge is increased. By increasing the level of challenge or the threshold required to receive the positive reward, the desired brainwave state response becomes strengthened.

Classical conditioning in neurofeedback occurs when the desired brainwave state is paired with another behavior such as calm focus during an athletic performance or cognitive activation during an academic task. By pairing the desired brainwave response with a specific behavior, the client is better able to optimize his or her performance. Another form of classical conditioning used in neurofeedback is called associative learning. It involves using an inhibit signal, presented as an annoying sound or visual indicator, to alert the client to discontinue an undesired behavior. For example, neurofeedback training frequently involves decreasing slow brainwave activity that can interfere with attention and decreasing fast wave activity that can cause anxiety. By pairing an aversive or annoying sound or visual inhibit to these mental states, the likelihood of their reoccurrence is decreased.

Other forms of learning used in neurofeedback include secondary reinforcement, generalization, and extinction (Thompson & Thompson, 2003). Examples of secondary reinforcement include verbal encouragement and prizes for completing a neurofeedback session. These can increase client motivation, especially for the apprehensive client or reluctant child, who may appreciate more immediate human feedback or a tangible reward for his or her effort. Children greatly enjoy selecting an item from a treasure chest filled with foreign coins, fossils, polished stones, arrowheads, or seashells after completing a neurofeedback session. Generalization involves applying what has been learned in the office to the outside world at home, work, or school. This can be done by reminding clients to take a moment before engaging a task at home, work, or school to mentally warm up, deeply breathe, or focus their attention. Extinction occurs when a conditioned stimulus is no longer paired with the unconditioned stimulus or when a behavior is no longer reinforced. In neurofeedback, this tendency is diminished by overtraining and refresher training. Overtraining involves the continuation of neurofeedback after the initial changes have occurred to strengthen the brain's ability to access and hold the new brainwave state. The stronger the new neuropathways, the more benefit neurofeedback will provide. Refresher training is used to keep the new skills strong. If the new skills are not practiced or reinforced by better home, work, or school performance, their strength may decrease. Also, future life events such as emotional trauma, anesthesia from surgery, illness, head injury, or aging may result in further neuronal dysregulation. Refresher training can keep the newly acquired skills sharp.

As Thompson and Thompson (2003) noted, learning theory alone does not explain why neurofeedback results seem to last. They suggested that structural changes in the brain that affect the production of neurotransmitters and the functioning of brain synapses also occur. Others have described this phenomenon as neuroplasticity. Swingle (2008a) defined neuroplasticity as the brain's capacity to be modified by learning. As examples, he noted the old scientific belief that intelligence and brain damage were permanent and that the brain could not regenerate itself. Today an ever-growing body of research suggests this is not true. Swingle (2008a) said the brain is capable of astounding regeneration, growth, and change, and that the potential for recovery and growth is not biologically predetermined. He cited the work of Thompson and Thompson (2003) who reported improvement in intelligence of 10 to 12 points after neurofeedback training and the work of Hoffman, Stockdale, and Hicks (1995) and Walker, Norman, and Weber (2002), who used neurofeedback with clients suffering from traumatic brain injury. Their results found improvement on computerized tests of mental abilities from 20–60% and self-report improvements of activity and successful return to work of greater than 50% in over 80% of patients. Swingle (2008a) concluded that if the nerve cells are destroyed and there is no electrical signal to be measured or trained, then improvement with neurofeedback cannot be expected, but if there is intact brain structure and a few neurons still firing, then function can be restored. Learning he said, including neurofeedback, changes the brain's cellular structure via the branching of neuronal axons and new synaptic growth, the primary mechanisms of cell communication (LeDoux, 2002).

Neurofeedback's focus on the restoration of neuronal functioning represents a dramatic advancement in our understanding of the brain's capacity for regeneration, neurogenesis, and neuroplasticity. It is cause for increased optimism in the treatment of many psychological, cognitive, and neurologically based disorders. As perspective, Swingle (2008a) noted that conventional qualitative EEG and magnetic resonance imaging (MRI) focus primarily on the assessment of "structural" abnormalities and correctly identify only 20% of the cases of traumatic brain injury (Walker et al., 2002). Quantitative EEG and neurofeedback, however, with their focus on neuronal "functioning," have been found to identify 90% of traumatic brain injury patients (Thorton & Carmody, 2005). This greatly expands the opportunity to identify and treat those previously untreated persons struggling with the many consequences of traumatic head injury including problems with mood, anger, memory, agitation, anxiety, fatigue, comprehension, perseveration, motivation reasoning, problem solving, rate of activity, and concentration. It also portends the value of neurofeedback in identifying and treating many others who are struggling with an even wider array of other functionally based psychological, behavioral, and physiological problems. Neurofeedback and neuroplasticity greatly expand our clinical value to clients.

BIOFEEDBACK AND SELF-REGULATION

Although sometimes overlooked, neurofeedback is a form of biofeedback. In general, biofeedback involves treatment of the peripheral nervous system including heart rate, breathing, muscle tension, skin temperature, and galvanic skin response. Neurofeedback involves treatment of the central nervous system or neuronal functioning. They both use similar self-regulatory mechanisms for change but are focused on different physiological functions. In many respects, neurofeedback can trace its clinical roots to advances in biofeedback.

Biofeedback has been described as a physiological control technique that uses monitoring devices to feed back information about the bodily functions of the autonomic nervous system, not normally under conscious control. Schwartz and Andrasik (2003), in a fuller definition, emphasized that biofeedback is a process that enables an individual to learn how to change physiological activity for the purpose of improving health and performance. Swingle (2008a) pointed out that before the 1960s, such physiological systems were thought to be homeostatic in nature and not under conscious control. However, research by DiCara and Miller (1969) found that both animals and humans could learn to control or self-regulate the activities of the autonomic nervous system and create states of "body quiet" with autonomic biofeedback. This established that physiological systems could become self-regulated and biofeedback could be used as a clinical tool to improve health.

Earlier research on alpha brainwaves by Adrian and Matthews (1934) found that they could be stimulated by an optical photic driving technique. Many years later, Kamiya (1969), also working with alpha brainwaves, used a simple reward system to increase alpha brainwave production and create deep states of "mental quiet." Wyrwicka and Sterman (1968), working with cats, found that a food reward could be used to motivate cats to increase the production of the SMR (sensory motor rhythm) brainwave and improve their resistance to seizures caused by exposure to a compound found in rocket fuel. His work was later extended to reducing seizures in people (Sterman, 2000). These studies established biofeedback's utility as a clinical tool for improving self-regulation of human brainwave activity.

Today, both traditional biofeedback and EEG biofeedback techniques are used in the effective treatment of clients' psychological and behavioral problems. Demos (2005) noted that performance in neurofeedback training can be greatly enhanced if clients first learn to regulate their peripheral skin temperature and diaphragmatic breathing. Mastering these skills before neurofeedback training gives clients the kinesthetic understanding and confidence to know they can regulate their body's physiological functioning. This is important both because of the primary benefit of improved physiological self-regulation on their health and the secondary benefit of being able to control their body's physiological response during neurofeedback training. For example, when a client struggles with a high-anxiety auditory alert signal during training, he or she will know how to relax his or her muscles and breathe deeply to quiet the alert signal. As a consequence, the client may also feel more confident in being able to regulate his or her brainwaves as he or she reacts to the auditory and visual reinforcements and inhibits involved in neurofeedback training.

Peripheral biofeedback measures can also be helpful in monitoring clients' physiological responses during training. For example, many neurofeedback treatment screens will automatically monitor clients' muscle tension or EMG, as this may interfere with effective training. Should a high EMG response be noted, the clinician can verbally alert the client and offer some corrective action such as, "Relax your jaw." Other peripheral monitors can also be utilized. These include breathing rate, skin temperature, and ectodermal or galvanic skin response to monitor clients' emotional reactivity. Finally, biofeedback and self-regulation techniques can also play an important role as part of a total treatment plan and be the preferred intervention for issues involving specific muscle tension, emotional reactivity, and skin temperature, as these may relate to problems with pain, headaches, anxiety, or circulation.

The concepts of biofeedback and self-regulation are central to the effective practice of neurofeedback. They provide clinical access to the peripheral and central nervous system. They also empower clients with the knowledge and skills to alter the course of their debilitating disorders toward the restoration of their physiological health and emotional well-being.

ADVANCEMENTS IN COMPUTER AND ELECTRONIC TECHNOLOGY

The advent of advanced computer and electronic technology has allowed neurofeedback to evolve from the laboratory setting to widespread clinical application. No longer does a practitioner need huge stacks of bulky and expensive electronics and computer equipment to monitor EEG and other physiological indicators. This equipment has been consolidated into a small multifunction EEG amplifier that can fit into the palm of your hand and laptop computers with vast memory, processing speed, and graphics capability, making neurofeedback technology practical and readily available for clinical use. It has been estimated that today there are between 10,000 and 20,000 neurofeedback practitioners in the United States and half as many more worldwide (Crane, 2009).

The heart of neurofeedback training lies in the capacity of the EEG amplifier and the computer software designed to interface with it. Thompson and Thompson (2003) explained how an EEG amplifier works. As previously noted, the brain produces only tiny microvolts (millionths of a volt) of alternating electrical current. The EEG amplifier amplifies these microvolts by more than 100,000 times. Since other environmental sources of electrical energy such as static electricity and 60 Hz activity from fluorescent lighting, electrical wiring, radio signals, or electrical office equipment can interfere with EEG, the amplifier only amplifies the electrical activity from the brain. Then the amplifier changes the alternating analog current to the digital form that a computer can work with. This is called sampling. The rate of sampling is very important in the quality and accuracy of the EEG to be observed. A smaller sampling rate of 128 samples per second only allows you to clearly observe up to 32 Hz of brain electrical activity. The sampling rates of today's EEG amplifiers can range from 256 Hz per second, up to 2,000 and even 8,192 samples per second, allowing a wide range and very accurate observation of the brain's electrical activity. Finally, the EEG amplifier takes the digital signal and filters it, minimizing distortions, organizing it, and displaying it in a manner that can be easily read and interpreted by the clinician. There are several different types of filters. High pass filters filter the brainwaves below its cutoff. Low pass filters filter the waves above its cutoff. Notch filters filter a narrow band (for example, 60 Hz activity) to monitor its possible interference in the EEG reading. Finally, there are band pass filters, which organize the electrical activity into the familiar brainwave bandwidths of delta, theta, alpha, SMR, beta, and gamma.

Even though much technology has gone into collecting and organizing the brain's electrical activity into an accurate and observable form, the clinician must still guard against artifact interference of the EEG. Artifacts are defined as any outside source of interference with an accurate reading of the EEG (Thompson & Thompson, 2003). As previously noted, these can include 60 Hz interference from other sources of electricity in the office but can also include such factors as the client's neck or jaw muscle tension, eye movement, static electricity, or poor sensor or EEG cable connections. Even clients' metal jewelry or active cell phone operation could cause electrical interference. In the case of cell phones, many amplifiers employ Bluetooth wireless communication with the computer. This means that an incoming call or email message could interrupt the Bluetooth communication and disrupt the neurofeedback session. A skilled neurofeedback practitioner will be aware of these sources of possible artifact interference and be prepared with measures to counteract their influence. These might include instructions to the client to relax or unclench the jaw, location of the neurofeedback equipment in an office relatively free from 60 Hz activity, double checking sensor and cable connections or replacing worn sensors or cables, and the removal of jewelry or the shutting down of cell phones. While today's differential amplifiers screen out much of this artifact activity, they cannot screen it all. Therefore, many manufacturers have included computerized artifacting tools in the supporting EEG software. These allow the clinician the opportunity to identify and remove artifact distortion from the EEG before analyzing the data it has generated.

High-quality EEG amplifiers also incorporate the capacity for peripheral biofeedback. These may include but are not limited to such functions as skin temperature, muscle tension, electrodermal activity, breathing rate, and blood oxygenation. As previously noted, some conditions may be more effectively treated with traditional biofeedback methods such as pain, headache, blood circulation, breathing, and emotional reactivity. In addition, it may be useful to monitor some physiological reactions while doing neurofeedback, such as muscle tension, to minimize its effect on the EEG.

All neurofeedback amplifiers also come with supportive computer software. Demos (2005) has detailed a list of considerations in selecting an effective neurofeedback training system. These include those that are supported by a Windows operating system; allow multiple channel wideband neurofeedback training, EEG assessment, and training; support multiple mode peripheral biofeedback; have easy artifacting capability; support use of dual monitors; and have flexibility in selection training screens and different types of auditory and visual reinforcement. Some available neurofeedback software systems also allow practitioners to create and design their own training screens and to add on other software or peripherals for other types of training such as hemoencephalography (cerebral blood flow), heart rate variability, low frequency, or alpha theta synchrony neurofeedback training.

When selecting a laptop computer and operating system, be sure it has the necessary memory, processing speed, and sound and graphics capability. The neurofeedback system's manufacturer can assist you with these specifications. Also be sure the neurofeedback system permits you to do both single-channel and two-channel training. This will allow you to do both single-site amplitude and dual-site synchrony or coherence training. More will be presented about neurofeedback training protocols later in this book. In order to preserve the greatest flexibility, also be sure that the training system allows you to work with a wide bandwidth of brainwaves, multiple biofeedback functions, and a wide variety of training screens and types of visual and auditory reinforcement so that you can address the varied needs and preferences of your clients. Some may need certain types of training and others not. Some may prefer certain screens and dislike others. Some may respond better to certain types of reinforcement and others not. As in any form of therapy, maintaining rapport and client motivation is very important for effective treatment.

In addition, some neurotherapists prefer training systems that allow for dual monitors, creation of their own training screens, and the addition of other software. Dual monitors allow the client to view a training screen while the clinician views an administration screen. This is a seamless way of conducting neurofeedback that allows the client to focus on the source of auditory and visual reinforcement and the clinician to monitor the client's performance and adjust reward and inhibit thresholds (levels of challenge) without distracting or interrupting the client's training. While not necessary, some neurotherapists prefer to design or create their own training screens. Most systems come with many suitable training screens, but they are not individualized to a particular client or for a specialized training application. The ability to design and create your own training screens streamlines individualized training and does not restrict the neurotherapist to prepackaged training protocols. Finally, some neurotherapists prefer to have the flexibility to add new peripheral biofeedback applications or neurofeedback training protocols as they become available. This allows the neurotherapist the opportunity to respond to a wider range of clients' treatment needs and apply the latest in neurofeedback training approaches.

Other equipment important in providing effective neurofeedback training includes EEG cables, sensors, conductive paste, abrasive skin gel, alcohol pads, handheld thermometers, selections of music and videos, and a children's treasure chest of interesting giveaways. EEG cables are usually included in most neurofeedback training systems. Having an extra set of cables is very useful when one may wear out or fail. Sensors and conductive material vary by manufacturer. Some use special metal clips or flat sensors with a plastic surround. Some use saline solution and sponges or a conductive paste to promote good electrical connections from the scalp to the sensor. Sometimes the scalp requires special preparation to promote good connections. An abrasive gel can loosen dead skin or skin leathered by the sun, and alcohol pads can remove body or hair oils that could interfere with good connections. A handheld thermometer can be used to inexpensively teach peripheral skin temperature warming. Once taught, clients can practice at home. You may recall that skin temperature warming and diaphragmatic breathing have been found to facilitate neurofeedback training. A handout for home practice of both can be given to clients to assist them in learning these skills. Music and videos are very strong reinforcers, especially when they are meaningful to clients. Most neurofeedback systems come with some music and video capability, but developing your own library or asking clients to bring in their favorite music or movies can assure their reinforcing value. Finally, a children's treasure chest of interesting items can provide secondary motivation and reward for children who can benefit from additional motivation and reinforcement for participating in neurofeedback training. The course of training can be long, 20 to 40 sessions, over 10 to 20 weeks. The small giveaways of foreign coins, seashells, fossils, arrowheads, or polished stones can provide something tangible for children's efforts.

Neurofeedback equipment as a medical device has been reviewed by the Federal Drug Administration (FDA). The FDA has the obligation to protect the public from unsafe medical equipment and medical practices. Swingle (2008a) noted that the FDA found neurofeedback equipment to be safe and effective for relaxation and muscle reeducation but nothing more. The FDA restricts manufacturers from making statements about the effectiveness of any medical equipment or practice that has not been approved. Therefore, neurotherapists are cautioned not to say the FDA has approved neurofeedback for any specific problem and instead describe how it works and its benefits (Demos, 2005). Demos (2005) went on to encourage neurofeedback practitioners to develop and use a release form for clients to read and sign, acknowledging this understanding. Please note that although the FDA has not approved neurofeedback for any specific problem, much efficacy research exists to document its varied effectiveness with a wide range of emotional and behavioral disorders (Yucha & Montgomery, 2008). Also note that commercial-grade biofeedback and neurofeedback systems cannot be made available to the public for medical applications. However, a layperson may possess a system if a licensed health care provider monitors its application. Some neurotherapists do make equipment available to clients for home use but only under their direct clinical supervision. Finally, the safety of neurofeedback equipment has been assured by some manufacturers by designing it to be battery powered and not powered by line voltage. However, not all neurofeedback equipment is battery powered. Battery-powered equipment assures that clients are at no risk of electric shock in its use. Please note some clients confuse neurofeedback with direct cranial electrical stimulation and believe that an electric current is being transmitted to their scalp. In neurofeedback training, the sensors only conduct or read the electrical activity of the brain. They do not transmit electrical stimulation. This can also be made clear in a thorough informed consent or treatment release form.

THE RHYTHMS OF THE BRAIN: THE PRIMARY BRAINWAVES

The clinical practice of neurofeedback is made possible due to advancements in computer and electronic technology that have allowed us to monitor, amplify, and filter the raw electroactivity of the brain or EEG (electroencephalogram) into several clinically useful frequency bandwidths. These primary bandwidths include delta, theta, alpha, sensory motor rhythm (SMR), beta, and gamma. Each of these bandwidths has specific characteristics including a waveform, wave strength, wave symmetry, and corresponding physical and mental states (Swingle, 2008a). The waveform or frequency varies from very slow electrical activity, less than one cycle per second, to very fast activity, several hundred cycles per second, measured in Hertz (Hz). It is typically illustrated as the number of up and down waves in a one-second span of time or epoch. The wave strength or its amplitude is measured in millionths of a volt or microvolt (mV). It is typically illustrated as the height of the wave at a given time. Wave symmetry indicates its rhythmic (synchronized) or arrhythmic (desynchronized) nature. It is illustrated respectively as either a balanced, symmetrical repeating wave or an unbalanced, asymmetrical, unevenly repeating wave. Wave symmetry informs the clinician about the brain's coherence or how well various areas of the brain connect or communicate with each other.

Thompson and Thompson (2003) noted that the dominant EEG frequency varies by age. The dominant adult eyes closed frequency is in the alpha range between 9–10 Hz, with more intelligent people having alpha at 11 Hz. Delta is dominant in the frontal and central regions of children from ages 3 to 5. As children become older, ages 6 to 8 to adolescence, low alpha gradually increases to about 10 Hz. As adults age, alpha begins to decline until near death, when it disappears. See Thompson and Thompson (2003) for a fuller description of these and other brainwave characteristics.

Of particular interest to the neurotherapist is the specific brainwave bandwidths, or the rhythms of the brain and their corresponding behavioral correlates. It is important to note that different neurotherapists define the frequency bandwidths differently; however, they all use the typical bandwidth labels noted above. The following descriptions follow the work of Swingle (2008a), Demos (2005), and Thompson and Thompson (2003).

Delta Waves

Delta waves are .5–2 Hz (Swingle, 2008a), 1–4 Hz or 1–3.5 Hz (Demos, 2005), or .5–3 Hz (Thompson & Thompson, 2003). They are related to slow brain activity or stage 4, dreamless sleep. When they occur in the waking state, they reflect generalized brain inefficiency or a low pain threshold. They are predominant in infants. Arrhythmic delta has been found in college students with difficulty in problem solving. Kershaw and Wade (2011) suggested delta waves were related to hypothalamic function and human growth hormone release in stage 3 and 4 sleep, needed for healing and regeneration. Swingle (2008a) reported high frontal delta to be related to chronic pain such as fibromyalgia and Lyme disease and high central delta to attention and learning problems. High delta waves anywhere are often related to traumatic brain injury.

Theta Waves

Theta waves are 3–7 Hz (Swingle, 2008a); 4–7, 4–7.5, or 4–8 Hz (Demos, 2005); and 3–7, 4–7, or 4–8 Hz (Thompson & Thompson, 2003). At the high end, they are related to reduced activity and involved in global thinking, spontaneity, daydreams, inattention, absence of directed thought, hypnotic states, and meditation; and at the lower end, depression, anxiety, and drowsiness. Swingle (2008a) noted that theta involves the mind's ability to quiet itself, and low amounts or amplitudes of theta in the back of the head or the occipital lobe was related to sleep disturbance, low stress tolerance, predisposition to addiction, inability to shut off the brain, and anxiety related disorders. These are also consistent with persons suffering from post-traumatic stress disorder. He also noted that theta is higher at sources of traumatic brain injury. Kershaw and Wade (2011) suggested theta waves were related to the limbic system and twilight or hypnogogic (going down) and hypnopomic (coming up) states of consciousness. They noted these allow access to past memories, universal symbols, and archetypal imagery of the hippocampus, and thus aid in the discharge of traumatic memories.

Alpha Waves

Alpha waves are 8–12 Hz (Swingle, 2008a), 8–12 or 8–13 Hz (Demos, 2005), or 8–12 Hz (Thompson & Thompson, 2003). They are related to relaxed focus, inner calm, peacefulness, or calm attention, and have been described as the brain's "idling rhythm." Swingle (2008a) noted that alpha waves are very important to help the brain operate more efficiently and to get in and out of "park" when needing to access the other brainwave states for other purposes. Alpha waves are also related to cognitive efficiency (alpha efficiency) and intellectual performance (peak alpha frequency). The speed of alpha wave change or alpha efficiency has been found to diminish as we age and with reduced mental activity. When alpha waves disappear, death is imminent. Slow alpha efficiency can result in cognitive sluggishness and memory problems. Medications typically taken by seniors can also cause slow alpha efficiency. Alpha efficiency can be restored, but this is temporary and must be repeatedly trained, four times a year, to be maintained. Peak alpha frequency, with amounts or amplitudes greater than 10 Hz, is related to higher intellectual performance. Lower alpha frequency, below 10 Hz, is related to lower intellectual performance. This can be restored with neurofeedback and has been found to result in up to a 10-point increase in intelligence test scores (Thompson & Thompson, 2003). Excessive alpha in the front of the brain can cause attention problems; difficulty planning, organizing, sequencing, and following through; hyper-verbosity; and sleep disturbance (Swingle, 2008a). Left frontal alpha imbalance can cause depression. These can also be treated with neurofeedback. Increased alpha amplitudes have also been found to be related to visualization skills, visual memory, emotional trauma, and artistic skill or interests. Alpha frequency can be trained for peak performance with athletes, musicians, actors, and artists. It can also be used with businesspeople to increase efficient decision making. Kershaw and Wade (2011) suggested alpha waves were related to the thalamus and when increased, also suppress a sense of hunger, making them very useful for weight control work.

Sensory Motor Rhythm, or SMR Waves

Sensory motor rhythm (SMR) waves are 13–15 Hz (Swingle, 2008a), 12–15 or 12–16 Hz (Demos, 2005), or 13–15 Hz (Thompson & Thompson, 2003). They are related to physiological and perceptual quieting, body stillness or reduction in muscle tone, an alert mind, and a state of internal orientation. They are not considered part of the traditional EEG bandwidth. They actually fall between the high alpha and low beta range and are considered another kind of "resting state." Swingle (2008a) noted they are related to muscular problems, headaches, chronic pain, body tension, dystonia (movement disorders), tics or trembling, and seizure disorders that have a motor component such as epilepsy and "pseudo-seizures" including fugue states, fainting, thrashing, freezing and hypnotic-type trances, and stroke (Swingle, 1998). Neurofeedback training of SMR waves has been found especially helpful with drug refractory patients who don't experience adequate seizure control with medication. Sterman (2000) found 82% of patients had a 30% reduction in frequency and severity of seizures, with an average reduction being 50%. They have also been used to reduce the recidivism rate of violent offenders from a typical 65% to 20% (Quirk, 1995). Finally, neurofeedback training of the SMR waves is also involved in the reduction of impulsivity and hyperactivity related to attention deficit hyperactivity disorder (Lubar et al., 1995). This work has provided some of the strongest evidence of neurofeedback's efficacy (Yucha & Montgomery, 2008).

Beta Waves

Beta waves are 16–25 Hz and 28–40 Hz (Swingle, 2008a), 13–21 Hz (Demos, 2005), and 16–36 Hz (Thompson & Thompson, 2003). They are typically broken down into low beta (lobeta) and high beta ranges. Swingle (2008a) described beta waves as "fast waves" related to information processing and problem solving. They use a lot of energy, so it is important to be able to increase them when needed and decrease them to rest. They have also been described as the brainwaves associated with focus, analysis, relaxed thinking, and external orientation (Demos, 2005). Low amounts or amplitudes of beta at the front of the head are related to hypoactivity, inattention, comprehension difficulties, learning problems, and depression. High amplitudes of beta at the back of the head are related to anxiety, low stress tolerance, sleep problems, and depression. Beta spindling, or marked spikes in the beta range on the EEG, is an indication of anxiety. If beta is too high for too long, chronic fatigue or emotional volatility can result. Too little beta as compared to theta, in the central part of the brain, can lead to hyperactivity due to understimulation. Stimulant medication can temporarily provide this stimulation until neurofeedback training can reactivate this area. Then medication can be slowly reduced. Too much beta throughout the brain can be related to a traumatic brain injury, stroke, or general anxiety disorder. High beta in the front middle part of the brain (anterior cingulate) is related to obsessive-compulsive disorder. Swingle (2008a) added that children with autism often have a "hot midline" and said this can cause them to become stuck on the negative, incessantly repeat phrases, have obsessive concern of an event, or display compulsive repetition of behaviors. Thompson and Thompson (2003) noted that beta elevations between 19–21 or 20–23 Hz are related to anxiety, emotional intensity, obsessive thoughts, and passivity, while beta elevations from 24–36 Hz are related to worry, rumination, fretting, hypervigilance, and feeling "stressed out." They also noted elevations in the mid-20s can act as a marker for alcohol or substance abuse, causing persons to use them as a means to control anxiety. Kershaw and Wade (2011) described those with low to moderate beta brainwaves as more action oriented and "movers and shakers." When beta becomes too excessive, they suggested this could cause symptoms of anxiety, stress, paranoia, irritability, and negative internal chatter. When beta is too low, risk is increased for depression, insomnia, and attention deficit hyperactivity disorder. Neurofeedback has been found very effective for treating a variety of beta-related disorders.

Gamma Waves

Gamma waves are 40 Hz (Swingle, 2008a), 40 Hz (Demos, 2005), and 28–42 Hz (Thompson & Thompson, 2003). They are related to sharp focus, language comprehension, insight, memory retention, and learning. When used with other types of neurofeedback training, they are thought to consolidate the resulting learning or neurological change. They have also been used in peak performance to increase focus, energy, creativity, and insight. Gamma waves are found throughout the brain. They occur in synchronous bursts during adult problem solving, help organize the brain, and promote mental sharpness. They are decreased in persons with learning disorders or those who have other cognitive deficits and increased in persons with higher cognitive functioning. They act to consolidate learning and optimize integration of new information. Kershaw and Wade (2011) noted that they are continuously present during rapid eye movement sleep and have been found in monks who've spent 10,000 to 50,000 hours meditating on compassion (Lutz et al., 2004). Gamma waves appear to involve a higher level of neurological functioning that has benefit for the entire brain.

NEUROFEEDBACK TRAINING

Although much more will be said about neurofeedback training in the later chapters of this book, it is important to understand the influence of two other brainwave bandwidths on the EEG and some basic principles of training in neurofeedback. The two bandwidths are called 50 or 60 Hz ambient electrical activity and 60 Hz or EMG (electromyogram) interference (Thompson & Thompson, 2003). The basic training principles include sensor placement; single-channel training of focal neurological problems; two-channel training of coherence or neurological network communication problems; and setting of rewards, inhibits, and thresholds.

The monitoring and control of interfering sources of electrical activity is less about the brain's inherent electrical activity and more about maintaining the effectiveness of neurofeedback training. As previously noted, outside sources of electrical activity such as fluorescent lighting and office equipment can interfere with accurate EEG monitoring. Ambient 50 Hz and 60 Hz electrical activity refers to the nature of the electrical power used in Europe, Israel, and Australia (50 Hz) and North America (60 Hz). These are monitored during neurofeedback training so that their interference on the EEG can be minimized by altering sources of interference in the training environment. EMG or 60 Hz interference with the EEG is also monitored during training because it too can distort or overwhelm the neurofeedback instrument's filters and cause inaccurate EEG readings. Its influence can be minimized by coaching the client to use deep breathing techniques or to relax muscle groups causing the EMG interference. Once these factors are reasonably controlled, effective training can begin.

Neurofeedback training requires a wide range of knowledge including but not limited to neuroanatomy, the relationship of mental health and disorders to the electroencephalogram, neurofeedback protocols, sensor placement, and training procedures. While many of these topics will be presented in this book, like any other clinical endeavor, certification training in neurofeedback, supervision, and experience are the best teachers.

Sensor placement and protocol selection go hand in hand. The International 10–20 System (Jasper, 1958) provides a topographical map of the various possible training site locations. These, however, are determined by the client's presenting symptoms and the corresponding EEG assessment results that indicate areas of high or low brainwave functioning and/or problems with coherence or communication between two areas of the brain. In general, single-channel training protocols are selected to train a localized or single brain site. They may allow training of several brainwaves at one time. Usually, one brainwave is targeted to be increased (rewarded) and the others to be decreased (inhibited). In two-channel training protocols, two brain sites are selected to be trained at the same time. This allows training of the coherence or communication between these sites. This type of training may also address several brainwaves at the same time and allow for increasing (rewarding) and decreasing (inhibiting) the targeted brainwaves. Selection of a specific protocol is made with knowledge of the client's symptoms and the research surrounding the protocol's efficacy for that problem (Yucha & Montgomery, 2008).

After the neurofeedback training protocol has been selected, the neurotherapist must set the proper reward and inhibits for the targeted brainwaves. A reward is designed to increase the amplitude of the desired brainwave by allowing the client to progress in a video game, listen to desired music, watch a video, or receive any other type of reinforcing auditory and/or visual stimulation. An inhibit is designed to decrease the amplitude of the targeted brainwave by giving the client an alert, such as a bird chirping or a "bleep" sound, or sometimes involving an annoying auditory signal such as a horn, pink noise, "gong" sound, or "uh-oh" warning. A threshold is set for both rewards and inhibits and establishes a cut-off point where the reward and/or inhibit will be triggered. When the client's brainwave amplitude is above the reward inhibit, the stimulation will be provided. When it is below, it will cease. When the client's brainwave amplitude is above the inhibit threshold, the auditory warning will sound until the client decreases that brainwave. Thus during a neurofeedback session and across repeated sessions, the brainwave targeted for increase will be strengthened and the brainwaves targeted for decrease will be reduced, increasing and decreasing the symptomatic behavior corresponding with each brainwave. In the case of two-channel training, two brainwaves may be simultaneously rewarded and others inhibited. By simultaneously rewarding two brainwaves, their coherence (synchrony) or communication will be improved.

In general, during neurofeedback training, low brainwaves such as delta and low theta and high brainwaves such as high beta are inhibited, while moderate brainwaves such as high theta, alpha, SMR, and lobeta are rewarded. As previously noted, the high brainwave of gamma is also typically rewarded. Treatment plans and training protocols can sometimes become very complicated and involve several brain locations and multiple protocols. Quality clinical supervision is vitally important, as is frequent reevaluation of client progress. As with any clinical intervention, even though neurofeedback offers clients an exciting option for significant symptom reduction, sometimes even beyond the benefits of counseling and medication, it is not a standalone treatment and is best used in conjunction with other medical, behavioral, and psychotherapeutic interventions.

CONCLUSIONS

Neurofeedback training begins with a thorough assessment of the brain's electrical activity as it relates to the client's presenting concerns. This is done by conducting a quantitative electroencephalogram (QEEG), which compares the client's current neurological functioning to a normative database. There are both very simple and complicated ways of assessing a client's EEG. Most neurotherapists will use a single-site assessment at middle of the head (Cz), inspect the resulting spectral array, or use Swingle's (2008b) Quick Q to more fully evaluate the most common clinical problems presented for treatment. However, clients with more complex or organically caused dysregulation, such as traumatic brain injury, will benefit from a full 19-channel QEEG to help identify other areas of dysregulation needing treatment.

Once evaluated, neurofeedback then employs the principles of learning, new knowledge of the brain's neuroplasticity, mechanisms of biofeedback and self-regulation, and recent advances in computer and electronic technology to change the brain's neurological functioning. Principles of operant and classical conditioning permit the gradual reinforcement of new responses. The brain's own capacity for neuroplasticity allows it to alter its electrical activity and form new neuronal pathways conducive to healthier behavior. Mechanisms of biofeedback and self-regulation access, display, and harness the client's physiological functioning so they can learn how to control and regulate previously unconscious and dysregulated physiological functions including skin temperature, breathing rate, muscle tension, and brain electrical activity. New computer and electrical technology then provides the neurotherapist with the ability to monitor, in near real time, the brain's electrical activity, filter the raw EEG into specific brainwaves, and control which brainwaves are altered toward more effective self-regulation.

Finally, the rhythms of the brain (delta, theta, alpha, SMR, beta, and gamma), their ratios to one another, and coherence or communication between sites is reviewed. Then specific brain sites and training protocols can be selected for neurofeedback training. Each type of brainwave corresponds to specific types of normal emotional, behavioral, or cognitive functioning or dysregulation. This information, along with client's report of symptoms, directs the type of training needed. By identifying the problem brain site location using the International 10–20 System (Jasper, 1958) and the results of the QEEG analysis, the neurotherapist can train a specific location or the coherence between two locations toward restoration of optimal functioning. This involves employing the principles of neurofeedback training that can either increase (reward) healthy brainwave functioning or decrease (inhibit) less healthy brain wave functioning. Neurofeedback training continues until the targeted brainwaves are altered in the desired direction and the client reports sufficient symptom reduction. Neurofeedback is not only applied to clinical problems but can also be used to improve optimal or peak performance in athletics, the creative arts, and business. While neurofeedback promises change beyond what may have been possible with counseling and medication alone, it cannot restore functioning of structurally damaged areas of the brain. However, if a spark of neuronal activity remains, neurofeedback can be effective in increasing its positive or decreasing its negative effects on clients' emotional, behavioral, or cognitive functioning.

REFERENCES

Adrian, E. D., & Matthews, B. H. (1934). The Berger rhythm: Potential changes from the occipital lobe of man. *Brain, 57*, 355–385.

Berger, H. (1929). On the electroencephalogram of man. *Journal fur Psychologie und Neurologie, 40*, 160–179.

Berners-Lee, T., & Fischetti, M. (2000). *Weaving the web: The original design and ultimate destiny of the World Wide Web.* New York: HarperBusiness.

Crane, R. A. (2009). Infinite potential: A neurofeedback practitioner looks back and ahead. In J. R. Evans (Ed.), *Handbook of neurofeedback: Dynamics and clinical applications* (pp. 3–21). New York: Informa Healthcare.

Demos, J. N. (2005). *Getting started with neurofeedback.* New York: Norton.

DiCara, L. V., & Miller, N. E. (1969). Heart-rate learning in the noncurarized state, transfer to the curarized state, and subsequent retraining in the noncurarized state. *Physiology and Behavior, 4*, 621–624.

Hoffman, D. A., Stockdale, S., & Hicks, L. L. (1995). Diagnosis and treatment of head injury. *Journal of Neurotherapy, 1*, 14–21.

Hughes, J. R., & John, E. R. (1999). Conventional and quantitative electroencephalography in psychiatry. *Journal of Neuropsychiatry and Clinical Neuroscience, 11*, 190–208.

Jasper, H. H. (1958). The ten-twenty electrode system of the International Federation. *Electroencephalography and Clinical Neurophysiology, 10*, 370–375.

Kaiser, D. A. (2005). Basic principles of quantitative EEG. *Journal of Adult Development, 12*(2–3), 99–104.

Kamiya, J. (1969). Operant control of the EEG alpha rhythm in Altered States of Consciousness. In C. Tart (Ed.), *Altered States of Consciousness* (pp. 507–517). New York: Wiley.

Kershaw, C. J., & Wade, J. W. (2011). *Brain change therapy.* New York: Norton.

LeDoux, J. (2002). *Synaptic self: How our brains become who we are.* New York: Viking.

Lubar, J. F., Swartwood, M. O., Swartwood, J. N., & O'Donnell, P. H. (1995). Evaluation of the effectiveness of EEG neurofeedback training for ADHD in a clinical setting as measured by changes in TOVA, scores, behavioral ratings, and WISC-R performance. *Biofeedback and Self-Regulation, 21*(1), 83–99.

Lutz, A., Greischar, L., Rawlings, N., Ricard, M., & Davidson, R. (2004). Long-term meditators self-induce high amplitude gamma synchrony during mental practice. *Proceedings of the National Academy of Sciences, 101*, 16369–16373.

Millett, D. (2001). Hans Berger: From psychic energy to the EEG. *Perspectives in Biology and Medicine, 44*, 522–542.

Montgomery, D. D., Robb, J., Dwyer, V., & Gontkovsky, S. T. (1998). Single channel amplitudes in a bright, normal, young adult sample. *Journal of Neurotherapy, 4*(1), 29–42.

Pfurtscheller, G. (1986). Event related desynchronization mapping: Visualization of cortical activation patterns. In F. H. Duffy (Ed.), *Topographic mapping of brain electrical activity* (pp. 99–111). Boston: Butterworth.

Quirk, D. A. (1995). Composite biofeedback training and dangerous offenders: III. *Journal of Neurotherapy, 1,* 44–54.

Schwartz, M., & Andrasik, F. (2003). *Biofeedback: A practitioner's guide.* New York: Guilford.

Skinner, B. F. (1938). *The behavior of organisms: An experimental analysis.* New York: Appleton-Century.

Sterman, M. B. (2000). Basic concepts and clinical findings in the treatment of seizure disorders with EEG operant conditioning. *Clinical Electroencephalography, 31,* 45–54.

Swingle, P. G. (1998). Neurofeedback treatment for pseudoseizure disorder. *Biological Psychiatry, 44,* 1196–1199.

Swingle, P. G. (2008a). *Biofeedback for the brain.* New Brunswick, NJ: Rutgers University.

Swingle, P. G. (2008b). *Basic neurotherapy: The clinician's guide.* Vancouver, British Columbia, Canada: Author.

Thatcher, R. W., Walker, R. A., Biver, C. J., North, D. M., & Curtin, R. (2003). Sensitivity and specificity of the neuroguide EEG normative database: Validation and clinical correlation. *Journal of Neurotherapy, 7*(3–4), 87–121.

Thatcher, R. W., Walker, R. A., Gerson, I., & Geisler. F. (1989). EEG discriminant analysis of mild head trauma. *Electroencephalography and Clinical Neurophysiology, 73,* 93–106.

Thompson, M., & Thompson, L. (2003). *The neurofeedback book: An introduction to basic concepts in applied psychophysiology.* Wheat Ridge, CO: The Association of Applied Psychophysiology and Biofeedback.

Thorton, K., & Carmody, D. (2005). Electroencephalogram biofeedback for reading disability and traumatic brain injury. *Child and Adolescent Psychiatric Clinics of North America, 14,* 137–162.

Walker, J. E., Norman, C. A., & Weber, R. K. (2002). Impact of QEEG-guided coherence training for patients with a mild closed head injury. *Journal of Neurotherapy 6,* 31–45.

Watson, J. B. (1913). Psychology as the behaviorist views it. *Psychological Review, 20,* 158–177.

Wyrwicka, W., & Sterman, M. B. (1968). Instrumental conditioning of sensorimotor cortex EEG spindles in the waking cat. *Physiology and Behavior, 3,* 703–707.

Yucha, C., & Montgomery, D. (2008). *Evidence-based practice in biofeedback and neurofeedback.* Wheat Ridge, CO: Association of Applied Psychophysiology and Biofeedback.

7

ASSESSMENT, TREATMENT PLANNING, AND OUTCOME EVALUATION

The brain is a monstrous, beautiful mess. Its billions of nerve cells lie in a tangled web that display cognitive powers far exceeding any of the silicon machines we have built to mimic it.

—William Allman

Effective neurotherapy is guided by an in-depth assessment process that allows the clinician to understand the possible origins, complexity, and impact of specific types of brain dysregulation on the client's presenting problem. This information is essential in designing an individualized treatment plan intended to help clients achieve the general goal of restoring more effective self-regulation and optimal functioning and the more specific objectives identified through their individual assessment results. Also important is a concrete plan for outcome evaluation. This establishes realistic expectations, guides the neurotherapist in assessing the effectiveness of treatment, and provides important feedback to the client regarding progress toward his or her desired goals.

This chapter will present the basic components of a thorough neurotherapy assessment. It will then outline key considerations in the development of an effective treatment plan. Finally, it will discuss realistic therapeutic expectations and several methods of outcome evaluation.

ASSESSMENT

The neurotherapy assessment process can take several hours. It involves exploration of the presenting problem, collection of a detailed psychosocial medical history, completion of psychological and behavioral checklists, a computerized test of variable attention and a quantitative electroencephalogram, and a summary of results. In clinical assessment, it is important to have multiple sources of both subjective and objective information. A subjective understanding of the nature, emotion, and impact of a client's problem on his or her life can strengthen therapeutic rapport and clinical understanding. Objective assessment of the client's behavior can offer a normative comparison of the problem's presence, intensity, or predominance. This is especially useful in more complex situations where there may be more than one presenting problem or multiple underlying sources of dysregulation. Objective assessment can be helpful with prioritization of treatment goals. Multiple sources of both subjective and objective information provide the neurotherapist with an opportunity for making more confident assessment conclusions. If both subjective and objective sources yield similar results, then a stronger conclusion may be made regarding that aspect of the client's assessment and this can be taken into account in the development and focus of their treatment plan.

Exploration of the Presenting Problem

Every step in the assessment process presents an opportunity for increasing therapeutic rapport, especially discussion of the client's presenting problem. Empathy, reflective listening, and exploration of the details of the presenting problem let the client know you care and want to understand his or her experience. Much important information needs to be gathered. Discover the nature of the problem, its physical and emotional symptoms, when it occurs, how often it occurs, how the client responds to it, the impact of the problem on his or her life, who else may be involved in the problem, when the problem started, possible stressors that lead to the problem, current triggers that intensify the problem, previous stress or trauma, substance use or abuse to cope with the problem, and use of counseling or medication. Finally the client and the clinician must clarify the expectations for neurotherapy.

Some of this information may be obtained over the phone during the client's initial call for services. The balance can be obtained in the first face-to-face interview. When collecting this information, it is important to express warmth and to be nonjudgmental. The client is looking for an ally, someone whom he or she can trust and with whom he or she can feel safe. The client is also looking for someone who is interested in his or her unique experience and who seems willing and able to help him or her. Sometimes clients can be very desperate and may be coming to you as a neurotherapist after having been down a long road of failed treatment experiences. It may be tempting to present neurotherapy as an answer to their prayers, but it is best to present neurotherapy within the limits of the research evidence, noting that individual results may vary.

Psychosocial Medical History

Usually conducted in an interview format, a typical psychosocial medical history will include inquires about family history, school history, psychological history, and medical history (Demos, 2005). The interview format allows the neurotherapist the opportunity to gather more detail in areas of significant history and less detail when significant history is not indicated. It is typical that discussion of the presenting problem and the psychosocial medical history be done in the same session. It is also important this interview be conducted with a person who is a good historian. Parents will often report on behalf of children and spouses may be present to augment what their partner may not recall. During the psychosocial medical history, the neurotherapist is especially interested in significant history that may suggest potential risk of brain dysregulation.

The first part of the psychosocial history asks about family history of bipolar disorder, ADHD, addiction, chronic depression, anxiety disorders, or other genetic disorders. These may reflect genetically acquired or environmental instability. Given the potential for epigenetic influences, it may be useful to not only inquire about family of origin (paternal, maternal, and sibling) history but also grandparent history. As previously noted in this book, research has noted a higher incidence of these disorders in families with a preexisting family history.

School history is particularly important when assessing ADHD and learning problems. Such inquiries as low report card subjects, low achievement scores, behavioral problems, learning problems, ADHD, and developmental disorders are noteworthy. It is often useful to ask whether the child has ever had an Individual Educational Plan (IEP). If yes, previous assessment and interventions have likely been attempted to help remediate these problems.

Psychological history of dissociative disorder, post-traumatic stress disorder, personality disorder, and severe psychiatric disorder (bipolar, schizophrenia, psychosis, and borderline personality disorder) suggest a higher degree of instability and brain dysregulation, as well as trauma. In addition, a history of suicidal or homicidal ideation/behavior can indicate a higher risk of harm and emotional brittleness.

Medical history begins with notation of any problems in pregnancy or birth with a special focus on exposure to alcohol or drugs, brain injury, or oxygen deprivation. Early childhood medical problems, high fever, delay in developmental milestones, and operations or hospitalizations may also be significant. These may not only cause specific dysregulation but may also be a source of emotional trauma and attachment injury. Head injuries from falls, sport mishaps, and car accidents are also important to note. Many people will minimize or dismiss what seem to them to be "minor" head injuries that didn't require medical intervention. However, these too may cause brain dysregulation. Seizure disorders, neurological disorders including stroke, cognitive problems, and sensory impairment (vision or hearing) are also notable. Substance use and abuse, including alcohol, nicotine, caffeine, illegal drugs, and extended prescription medication can also cause brain dysregulation.

In addition, lifestyle issues may also be relevant. A diet high in processed food, lack of exercise, and exposure to toxic substances, heavy metals, and petrochemicals common in agriculture and cleaning supplies also contribute to brain dysregulation. Finally, the process of aging and a lifetime with numerous surgeries and cumulative exposure to anesthesia also contribute to brain dysregulation.

While the psychosocial history is primarily an assessment tool, when tactfully conducted, it can also become an educational exercise. It can inform clients about the causes and effects of brain dysregulation and stimulate discussion about the many ways dysregulation can be prevented.

Psychological and Behavioral Checklists

Several psychological and behavioral checklists are helpful in conducting a thorough neurotherapy assessment. These include the Beck Depression Inventory, Burns Anxiety Inventory, Amen Clinic ADD Type Questionnaire, ADHD Checklist, Insomnia Severity Index, Report of Post Traumatic Stress (Child and Parent), Post Traumatic Stress Disorder Checklist, and the Problem Checklist. All of these tools involve either self-report or parent-report of observed behavior. They are not measures of actual behavior as are the computerized and EEG tests to be discussed later in this section; however, many are normed, quickly administered, easily interpreted, and very useful for differentiating the presence and magnitude of single or multiple presenting problems.

The Beck Depression Inventory (Beck et al., 1961) is a 21-item inventory that takes about 10 to 15 minutes to complete. It asks clients to rate which of four responses best describes their current thoughts and feelings. For example, "I do not feel sad. I feel sad. I am sad all the time and can't snap out of it. I am so sad or unhappy that I can't stand it." The total score is easily calculated by adding all 21 responses. A score of 1 to 10 indicates normal mood; 11 to 16, mild depression; 17 to 20, borderline depression; 21 to 30, moderate depression; 31 to 40, severe depression; and scores over 40 indicate extreme depression.

The Burns Anxiety Inventory (Burns, 1993) is a 33-item inventory that can be completed in 10 to 15 minutes. It asks clients to rate each statement by indicating how much this type of feeling has bothered them in the past several days. For example, "Anxiety, nervousness, worry or fear: Not at all, Somewhat, Moderately, or A Lot." The total score is calculated by adding up all 33 items' responses. A score of 0 to 4 indicates minimal or no anxiety; 5 to 10, borderline; 11 to 20, mild; 21 to 30, moderate; 31 to 50, severe; and 51 to 99 indicates extreme anxiety.

The Amen Clinic ADD Type Questionnaire (Amen, 2001) is a 71-item questionnaire that assesses six subtypes of ADHD including inattentive, hyperactive, overfocused, temporal lobe, limbic, and ring of fire. It takes about 20 minutes to complete. Each type relates to a specific pattern of brain dysregulation and offers ready interpretation for neurotherapy assessment.

Clients and a significant other (parent, spouse, or lover) can rate each statement by indicating how much the behavior is a problem for them. For example, "Is easily distracted: Never, Rarely, Occasionally, Frequently, Very Frequently, or Not Applicable." A scoring key is provided. Any subscale score of 4 may indicate the presence of a problem. A score of 6 is diagnostically significant. The results can help differentiate between ADHD subtypes. In addition, Amen (2001) provides recommendations for medication, food supplements, diet, exercise, and neurotherapy protocols.

The ADHD Checklist offers a more detailed assessment of common ADHD behavioral problems (Hill & Castro, 2009). It has four subscales including attention deficit, hyperactivity, impulsivity, and other symptoms that are proportionately measured. It takes about 10 to 15 minutes to complete. Clients indicate how much they have observed the behavior in the last week. For example, "Does not seem to listen when spoken to: Not Present, Very Mild, Mild, Moderate, Severe, and Very Severe." Subtotal scores are calculated for each subscale, and a percent of the total amount is determined to indicate which set of subscale behaviors is more predominant. This questionnaire is particularly helpful in identifying specific behaviors that may be targeted and tracked in neurotherapy treatment.

The Insomnia Severity Index (Morin et al., 2011) is a very brief assessment of clinical insomnia that often accompanies many types of brain dysregulation. It consists of only seven items and takes about 5 to 10 minutes to complete. Clients are asked to rate the current severity (during the last 2 weeks) of their insomnia problem. For example, "Difficulty falling asleep: None, Mild, Moderate, Severe, or Very Severe." Total scores are calculated. A score of 0 to 7 is not significant; 8 to 14, low; 15 to 21, moderate; and 22 to 28 indicates severe insomnia.

The Report of Post Traumatic Stress (Greenwald & Rubin, 1999) is designed to be completed by a child age 6 to 18 or their parent. The CROPS Student Form has 20 items. It takes 5 to 10 minutes to complete. Clients are to rate how true each statement feels for them in the past week. For example, "I daydream: None, Some, or Lots." The total score is calculated by adding up all 20 items' responses. A score of 19 or greater indicates significant symptoms of trauma. The PROPS Parent Form has 30 items. It takes about 10 minutes to complete. Parents are asked to rate how well each item describes their child in the past week. For example, "Difficulty concentrating: Not True or Rarely True, Somewhat or Sometimes True, or Very True or Often True." The total score is calculated by adding up the 30 items. A score of 16 or greater indicates significant symptoms of trauma.

The Post Traumatic Disorder Checklist (Blanchard et al., 1996) is an adult assessment of trauma. It can be completed in 10 to 15 minutes and consists of 17 items. Clients are asked to indicate how much they have been bothered by the behavior indicated in each item as these pertain to problems and complaints people sometimes have in response to stressful life experiences. For example, "Repeated disturbing memories, thoughts, or images of a stressful life experience: Not at all, A little bit, Moderately, Quite a bit, or Extremely." The total score is calculated by adding up the 17 responses. Scores from 0 to 21 indicate mild trauma; 22 to 24, moderate; and 45 or greater, severe symptoms of trauma.

The Problem Checklist (Anderson, 2010) is used to identify current problems that can become the focus of neurotherapy. The checklist consists of 60 common problems. Clients are asked to check all the current problems they are experiencing. It takes them about 5 minutes to complete. The checklist is also useful to track progress during neurotherapy. When it is used for this purpose, clients respond to selected items by indicating the degree of improvement. For example, "Impulsiveness: Better, Worse, or No Change." The checklist can also be quantified by simply calculating the total number of improved symptoms from session to session or every 10 sessions, depending upon the neurotherapist's outcome evaluation strategy. More will be presented later in this chapter on outcome evaluation.

Computerized Tests of Cognitive Ability and Variable Attention

With even stronger face and construct validity, computerized tests of cognitive ability and variable attention offer measurement of actual cognitive and attending behavior. Some of the tests commonly used in neurotherapy include the MicroCog, the Integrated Visual and Auditory Performance Test (IVA), and the Test of Variable Attention (TOVA).

The MicroCog (Powell et al., 1993) is a culturally unbiased, user friendly, computerized test of cognitive functioning for persons age 18 to 89 years old. It is available in a short and standard form and can be completed quickly, within 30 to 90 minutes. Unlike other tests of intelligence or cognitive ability, it requires only minimal assistance with a brief orientation from a testing assistant. It is used to measure problems with learning, memory, or other cognitive impairment. It consists of 18 subtests that yield summary scores in nine areas including attention/control, memory, spatial processing, reasoning/calculation, reaction time, information-processing accuracy, information-processing speed, cognitive functioning, and cognitive proficiency. The last two scores are overall scores similar to total IQ and can be used to measure improvements in IQ due to neurotherapy.

The Integrated Visual and Auditory Performance Test (IVA) is a computerized test of variable attention used to assess attention problems in children and adults (Tinius, 2003). It measures a client's response to visual and auditory stimuli. More specifically, the characters "1" and "2" are presented half visually, on the computer screen and half auditorily, through the computer's sound system. The client responds by pressing the mouse button. The test takes 13 minutes to complete and yields measures of both visual and auditory attention. Several types of brain dysregulation can result in significant attention problems. The IVA allows the clinician to determine the presence, degree, and type of attention problem, as well as allowing the tracking of changes over the course of neurotherapy.

The Test of Variable Attention (TOVA) is another computerized test to assess attention problems in children and adults (Greenberg & Waldman, 1993). It differs from the IVA in its use of non-language-based visual targets (a large rectangle with a square either at the top or the bottom) and auditory tones that the client must discriminate by pushing an attached microswitch. The microswitch allows more accurate measurement of response time. The TOVA also takes longer to complete, about 22 minutes for both the visual and auditory tests. Like the IVA, the TOVA can also be used to assess the presence, degree, and type of attention problem, as well as to track changes in attention due to neurotherapy.

Quantitative Electroencephalogram

The quantitative electroencephalogram (QEEG) offers even more direct assessment of underlying brain dysregulation by measuring the subcortical electrical activity of various brain locations found to be related to common behavioral and emotional problems. Budzynski et al. (2009) wrote that the relevance of the QEEG to the diagnosis and prognosis of brain dysfunction stems from its ability to reliably and objectively assess the distribution and amount of brain electrical energy and to compare it to a normative EEG data base. Through the use of T-tests and Z-scores, individual results can be compared to a normative database of means and standard deviations. These can then be interpreted through neuropsychological correlations, or to empirically established conditions such as ADHD, schizophrenia, OCD, anxiety, depression, epilepsy, and traumatic brain injury, with their corresponding EEG signatures.

QEEG evaluation, or brain mapping, can be conducted with different degrees of detail, complexity, and thoroughness. The most complex type of QEEG involves a full, 19-channel assessment of the standard 19 brain locations as indicated by the International 10–20 System (Homan, Herman, & Purdy, 1987). This full QEEG, requiring the purchase of specialized equipment, is most typically done when there is a known history of traumatic brain injury or complicated symptomology; however, some clinicians use them as a thorough assessment of every client they treat. A full QEEG usually takes 1 to 2 hours to complete. It involves the use of a skullcap, preparation of each sensor site, application of conductive paste, administration of the QEEG protocol for collection of brainwave data, and interpretation of the results. While most clinicians can readily learn how to collect the QEEG data, specialized training and experience is required to analyze the results and generate a normative-based treatment plan. Most clinicians use the services of QEEG experts to generate these reports (see Figure 7.1).

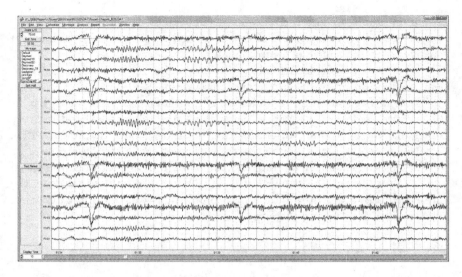

FIGURE 7.1 QEEG screen illustrating 19 channel brain locations

Permission granted from Douglas Dailey

A second, less extensive QEEG option is the MiniQ developed by Soutar & Longo (2011). It utilizes 10 key brain sites and, while not a normative database system itself, it was developed from years of Soutar's clinical experience using established QEEG databases, allowing the generation of a very useful four-part clinical report. The first part of the report looks at the technical dimensions of the EEG including a summary of brainwave magnitude, coherence, dominant frequency, and asymmetry. The second part provides a multivariate analysis of relevant cognitive and emotional information about the client. The third part presents neurofeedback protocol recommendations, and the fourth provides suggestions for dietary supplements found to help ameliorate the noted conditions. Like the 19-channel QEEG, the MiniQ also requires the purchase of special equipment and report services.

The third QEEG option is the QuickQ developed by Paul Swingle (2008). It is the least extensive of the QEEG options, providing information on only five brain sites, but its ease of use, broad clinical applicability, and low cost make it the most cost-effective option for the typical neurotherapist. The QuickQ assesses brainwave activity in the occipital lobe, the parietal lobe, the frontal lobe, and the anterior cingulate gyrus. It yields useful information about trauma, ADHD, anxiety, depression, and OCD, along with other cognitive and behavioral information. The QuickQ is available at no cost to clinicians who have completed the basic neurotherapy certification training course. Data collection involves eyes open, eyes closed, and a cognitive task condition, and can be completed in less than 20 minutes. A narrative report detailing brainwave problems and treatment recommendations can be generated in 15 minutes. The QuickQ is a very useful tool in guiding treatment planning.

Summary of Results

Once all the assessment information is collected, it must be organized and presented to the client in a way that helps him or her to more fully understand the problem, its likely underlying cause, neurological impact, and need for treatment. The first step is to review the nature of the presenting problem. This includes its typical symptoms, onset history, frequency of occurrence, triggering events (if any), and impact on the client's life. Next, the summary offers insight into possible sources of brain dysregulation from the client's psychosocial medical history. It is not unusual for more than one area of the client's history to be suggestive of dysregulation. If evident from the client's report, it may be useful to communicate some sense of a given factor's greater or lesser likelihood of impact on dysregulation so a client can better differentiate the factor's influence.

After the psychosocial medical history or context has been laid out, the results of the psychological and behavioral checklists can be presented. Both areas of significance and nonsignificance are noted because they help identify, rule out, and confirm the nature of the presenting problem and its relative need for treatment. On occasion, clients' results will tend to be all high or all low. This suggests a response bias caused by overreporting or underreporting, often related to a client's anxiety or exasperation with their problem or minimization or denial of its impact on his or her life. Should this occur, a discussion of these hypotheses would be in order and with the client's improved insight and cooperation, retesting should be done to provide more valid and clinically useful results.

The next step is to review the QEEG results. This is often of most interest to clients because it is new information about how their brain is working. In presenting the QEEG results, it is first helpful to provide a brief description of the brain areas that were evaluated and their general functions as well as the major brainwaves: delta, theta, alpha, SMR, and beta (low and high). This gives the client a framework from which to understand the QEEG summary statements that describe over- or underfunctioning of specific brain activity at specific brain sites and the resulting psychological, behavioral, or cognitive consequences associated with them. Clients are usually very grateful for this information and surprised with how consistent it is with the presenting concern, psychosocial medical history, and psychological and behavioral checklists. The concurrent evidence presented in the summary of results makes a strong case for the need for treatment, builds client confidence in the neurotherapist, and increases client hope and expectation that neurotherapy can help them resolve their problem.

The last part of the summary of results offers validation of the client's presenting problem and the need for treatment. It is not unusual for clients initially presenting with only one concern to learn that they have one or two other problems that may benefit from treatment. This can be a difficult issue because of the implication for additional length and cost of treatment. To ease this concern, it may be helpful, based upon the evaluation results, to prioritize the client's problems so that he or she can exercise some decision-making control about the treatment. Not all work has to be done in a single treatment episode, and a client may prefer treatment to first focus on the most upsetting problem. Also of concern during this last part of the summary of results is the client's expectation about treatment outcome. The client's excitement, hope, and newly established confidence from the neurotherapy assessment process may lead him or her to believe his or her problem can be completely resolved. Outcome research in neurotherapy is very impressive especially compared to traditional treatments of counseling and medication, but complete resolution of clients' problems is not realistic. It is important to check clients' expectations and temper them with research-based information and the neurotherapist's own clinical experience.

TREATMENT PLANNING

A sound treatment plan flows readily from the presenting concern, the psychosocial medical history, the psychological and behavioral checklists, and the EEG. Based upon the results of the assessment, the treatment plan addresses several areas of concern and intervention. These include an exploration of indications, contraindications and possible side effects of neurofeedback treatment; client expectations; suggestions for exercise, diet, food supplements, and other preventive measures; preparation for neurofeedback training; the role of self-regulation skills in facilitating neurofeedback; selection of neurofeedback protocols; client instruction; use of audio-visual entrainment to enhance neurofeedback; the role of medication and counseling; evaluation of progress; and completion of treatment. The treatment plan can be presented to clients in a verbal or brief written summary, but be sure to allow ample time for questions and more detailed discussion.

Indications, Contraindications, and Possible Side Effects

Neurofeedback has been found to be very helpful for many clients, but it is not for all clients. Demos (2005) wrote about indications and contraindications for neurotherapy. These are reviewed below. Overall, neurotherapy has been found to be most effective in the treatment of discreet problems known to be related to specific areas of the brain; however, it has also been used to help improve communication problems between brain regions. Some examples include ADHD (frontal and parietal lobes), anxiety (right frontal lobe), depression (left frontal lobe), trauma and substance abuse (occipital lobe and cingulate gyrus), OCD (anterior cingulate), and insomnia (parietal lobe). It is best if the clients' home or marital environment is loving, supportive, and encouraging, and their work and interpersonal stress is minimal. Clients who have the ability to pay, who are available twice a week for treatment sessions, and who are compliant with the treatment plan are most likely to complete treatment and gain its fullest benefit. Clients with minimal emotional and interpersonal problems also train well. They tend to take responsibility for their own lives and have a positive view of others in authority at school or work. This suggests they may also work well with the neurotherapist. Clients on medication may also benefit from neurotherapy, but the goal of treatment remains improving behavioral performance that may lead to reduction in the amount or need for medication.

Contraindications for neurofeedback include clients who do not have the time, availability, or money to complete treatment. Those with severe psychological or interpersonal problems such as borderline personality disorder, bipolar disorder, or dissociative disorder may have a greater need for counseling or psychotherapy than neurofeedback. Clients who are suicidal, self-injuring, or those with severe explosive behavior problems may require other stabilizing treatment before neurotherapy can be implemented. Persons in highly dysfunctional families or those immediately exposed to severe environmental stress may also struggle in optimizing their neurotherapy results. Children with conduct disorders and highly resistant teenagers with poor self-management skills may also be poor candidates for neurotherapy because treatment requires a high degree of cooperation and patience. Persons who are actively abusing alcohol, drugs, or medications are also poor candidates because their substance abuse will undermine any gains made in neurotherapy. Clients who plan to continue to experience head trauma such as boxers and football players may only temporarily benefit from neurotherapy because any recurring injury will cause further brain dysregulation and further need for additional neurotherapy.

Neurofeedback has been found to have very few side effects (Hammond & Kirk, 2008). Clients are never exposed to any direct electrical current. The equipment utilizes only two AA batteries. The neurofeedback sensors are used only to read the electrical activity of the brain, not transmit it. Some clients report quickly resolved, minor disorientation following periods of concentration or deeper relaxation involved in neurofeedback. Others report some minor skin irritation caused by the alcohol pad used to cleanse the skin before attaching a senor. Nonalcohol cleansing wipes are available for those clients with especially sensitive skin. Finally, some clients who are working to resolve trauma issues may experience abreaction as a result of some types of neurotherapy and may become allergic to their substance of choice. An abreaction can take the form of unexpected emotional material or memory flashes coming to awareness; reactivation of dreams with emotional content; or heightened emotionality, tearfulness, or unsettled physical feelings related to the processing of traumatic material. While sometimes upsetting to clients, these are signs of positive neurological change and may require some brief counseling to process. Although becoming allergic to one's substance of choice may sound like a wanted side effect, the ethical principle of informed consent dictates that clients be told of this potential side effect.

Since neurotherapy can have a significant impact on one's behavior, clients should also be informed that such changes may cause consequences for marriage and family relationships. Systems theory generally dictates that a change in one part of a system will inevitably affect other parts of that system. For example, resolution of a child's ADHD symptoms may allow greater focus on long-standing marital or family problems. No longer is parental attention focused on the child's behavior. It now refocuses on marital discord. If informed in advance, clients can be encouraged to expect these other noted side effects and reactions and view them as an indication of progress or an opportunity for further marital or family improvement.

Client Expectations

Some clients seek neurofeedback after extensive, sometimes disappointing, experience with more conventional treatments of counseling and medication. Others may have had no previous treatment for their presenting problem but are curious about what neurofeedback could do for them. Still others have done their own research on neurofeedback and are very excited about its potential benefit. This makes it very important to gauge each client's degree of skepticism, discouragement, optimism, hope, motivation, and expectations in seeking neurofeedback treatment. In addition, since most insurance companies do not reimburse for neurofeedback work, clients' required investment of time and cost are often foremost in their decision to begin treatment.

Most typical neurofeedback treatment plans involve 30 to 40 total sessions scheduled twice a week. More complicated problems such as bipolar disorder, learning problems, attachment, and autistic spectrum disorders may require 60 to 100 or more sessions. Scheduling sessions once a week seems to delay the targeted changes. Scheduling sessions more than twice a week may not allow enough recovery time from inflammation due to training new neural pathways. The typical cost of neurotherapy can run from $150 to $195 a session or $4,500 to $7,000 for a complete treatment episode. Many neurotherapists will ask clients to commit to an initial set of 20 sessions because it takes about that much time for symptomatic changes to be observed. The next 10 to 20 sessions promote neurological consolidation of the initial changes and strengthening of new neural pathways.

While the research for many emotional and behavioral problems is very impressive, as reviewed in Chapter 9, on the effectiveness of neurofeedback, neurofeedback is not a cure-all. Some clients, because of the variety of contraindicated factors noted above, do not get the full results of treatment. Others may end treatment early feeling satisfied with the initial results, limiting the changes they could have experienced had they continued. Still others choose to discontinue treatment due to limitations of time or money, impatience, or a lack of recognition of meaningful change. Managing clients' expectations is a very important part of the treatment plan. The best client mindset is one of optimism, commitment, compliance with treatment recommendations, and perseverance.

Exercise, Diet, Food Supplements, and Other Preventive Measures

As previously noted in this book, exercise, a healthy diet, targeted food supplements, and other preventive strategies are useful for optimal brain functioning. If clients decide to invest their time, money, and effort in neurofeedback training, they will likely appreciate other ways of enhancing treatment effects and strengthening their neurological health.

The general recommendation for exercise is 40 minutes of interval exercise, five times a week. This will stimulate the production of brain-derived neurotropic factor, the brain's own brand of "Miracle Gro." It will also increase cerebral blood flow found to enhance overall neurological functioning. Exercise done with others that involves a variety of enjoyable activities and that can be done at both a fast and slow pace are best. When exercise is done with others, boredom is less likely and compliance more likely. While everyone usually understands the benefits of exercise, many are unable to keep up the routine. Encourage children and adults of all ages to incorporate a moderate exercise program into their lifestyle.

Along with exercise comes a healthy diet. The brain prefers a high protein and low carbohydrate diet. This will be a challenge for children who love sugar and adults addicted to the convenience of processed and fast food. An easy way to structure a healthy diet is to limit or eliminate all white food including sugar, flour, bread, pasta, potatoes, and white rice. Be sure meals have a balance of protein, fruit, and vegetables. Nuts, seeds, and small amounts of dark chocolate make great snacks. Although more expensive, food that is free of hormones and pesticides is preferred.

The two most commonly suggested food supplements for neurotherapy clients are omega 3s or fish oil and N-acetylcysteine or NAC. Sixty percent of the brain and nerves are composed of fat. Fatty acids aid in brain cell growth and function, and omega 3s help promote overall brain health. NAC promotes improved neuronal functioning. It is especially useful when there is a personal or family history of significant neurological instability such as OCD, bipolar disorder, substance abuse, trauma, or schizophrenia. Together, omega 3s and NAC counteract inflammation, support the restoration of brain functioning, and help strengthen neurological communication. Some clients may prefer to consult their doctor or a homeopathic specialist before taking any food supplements. See Chapter 5, "Strategies for Self-Regulation," for a comprehensive list of other food supplements that may be helpful for other specific problems.

Other preventive strategies that support neurofeedback include limiting daily screen time and use of safety equipment to prevent head injury. The general recommendation is for no more than 1 to 2 hours a day of total screen time on television, computers, and video games. This limits passive brainwave entrainment to higher levels of theta waves and exposure and desensitization to traumatic, aggressive, or violent material. Carefully monitored screen time can be used as a reward for completion of homework or chores, but age-appropriate access is essential. While it may not be realistically possible to protect ourselves from all head injuries, such as those from an unexpected fall or car accident, it is possible to limit our exposure by wearing appropriate safety gear when riding bikes, skateboarding, or playing contact sports. The gains of neurofeedback can be quickly lost with even one seemingly mild head injury.

Preparation for Neurofeedback Training

Clients arriving for neurofeedback treatment should be physically and emotionally stable (Demos, 2005). That is, they should be well rested, hydrated, and satiated. It is best for them to refrain from pretraining ingestion of sugar, caffeine, alcohol, or drugs. A small protein snack is acceptable, and prescribed medication will generally not affect neurofeedback training. Clients should be free of any intense personal crisis, as this may distract their attention and present rogue high brainwave interference with training. Gum chewing and cell phones also interfere with training. Gum chewing creates muscle tension artifact that interferes with accurate EEG recording, and active cell phones interfere with the wireless communication between the EEG equipment and the computer. Overall, it is best for children to train without their parents in the room; however, very young children may be initially calmer if their parents are present during training.

Role of Self-Regulation Skills in Facilitating Neurofeedback Training

Many neurotherapists begin treatment by first teaching clients how to control their peripheral skin temperature and how to breathe diaphragmatically. These self-regulation skills can be learned in one session. They give clients experience and confidence in their own ability to control their autonomic physiological functions. They also facilitate neurotherapy training by providing skills the client can use to alter higher brainwave incursions (anxiety spikes) in their EEG. When these occur, the neurotherapist can simply suggest the client use their deep breathing and relaxation skills to make the anxiety go away. Clients are usually very successful in doing this. Since neurotherapy in its basic sense is about brainwave self-regulation, skin temperature training and diaphragmatic breathing act as early lessons in self-regulation.

Selection of Neurofeedback Training Protocols

There are many different types of neurofeedback training protocols to choose from in designing a treatment plan to resolve client's emotional and behavioral problems. Chapter 8, "Neurofeedback Training, Protocols, and Case Studies," will review these in much more detail. The selection of a specific protocol is determined by the client's assessment results, the research literature on effective protocols for specific problems, and the client's priorities for treatment. In general, neurofeedback training begins from the center of the brain at the sensory motor strip or the parietal lobe, then proceeds to the front of the brain or the frontal lobes, and concludes at the midline or the cingulate gyrus (Soutar & Longo, 2011).

Work at the sensory motor strip has been found to promote physiological and perceptual calming and begins to correct underlying brain communication networks. This is helpful for such problems as ADHD, seizures, and insomnia, and involves training SMR brainwaves to correct theta and beta wave problems. Training at the frontal lobes most typically focuses on alpha wave imbalance related to problems with anxiety and depression. High alpha at the left frontal lobe is related to depression, and low alpha at the right frontal lobe is related to anxiety. Beta wave training for depression and alpha and SMR wave training for anxiety are indicated. Training at the midline or the cingulate gyrus helps resolve problems with OCD, trauma, and substance abuse. This training focuses on synchronizing alpha and theta waves and is often used for assessed problems at the occipital lobe. It is important to note that more than one protocol may be necessary to resolve several presenting problems.

Neurofeedback training sessions usually take about an hour to complete. The first few minutes involve checking in with the client about how they are doing since their last visit. Then time is needed to prepare the client's scalp and attach the EEG sensors. Actual training may take 20 to 30 minutes of the hour and can be broken into 10-minute segments, giving the client a few minutes to relax between segments. This can be especially helpful for younger children who may become bored or restless, or any client who needs a short break from the concentration and focus required during treatment. Sometimes more than one protocol will be used in a particular session, so a natural break occurs while the neurotherapist is relocating the sensors. Sessions end with another brief check-in with the client to discuss their experience during treatment, removal of the sensors, cleaning of the scalp, and completion of billing paperwork and rescheduling. As previously noted, training twice a week seems to provide sufficient time for recovery and optimal treatment effects.

Client Instruction

In neurofeedback training, clients use their brains to influence or control audio-visual playback. More specifically, they learn to increase desired brainwaves to play a music or video reward. They also learn how to decrease undesirable brainwaves associated with annoying sounds or alerts. It is this method of operant conditioning that trains the brain and helps resolve neurologically based emotional and behavioral problems. As a practical matter, some clients will not know what to do. They may try too hard and become frustrated in being unable to affect the audio-video playback. It is best to explain to clients that neurofeedback involves a more passive/unconscious attention. That is, their brain will be naturally motivated to want to see the video or hear the audio and will search for a way to become successful. When it discovers what to do, the video and audio will play. When it wanders away, the video and audio will stop.

It's also important to tell clients they will not be successful all the time. This minimizes frustration they might feel when they are unable to maintain the reward. In fact, the software is intentionally set up for them to be successful only about 75% of the time. This keeps the brain working at the task. In addition, the neurotherapist will periodically increase the difficulty of success as the client gets better at achieving it. Over the course of neurofeedback treatment, this is what strengthens the brain's ability to access the desired brainwave states and limit the undesired brainwave states.

Use of Audio-Visual Entrainment to Enhance Neurofeedback

Soutar and Longo (2011) recommend the use of audio-visual entrainment at the beginning of neurofeedback training to enhance neurofeedback's effectiveness. These researchers have found that visual entrainment alone is adequate for this purpose, and they prefer to use sinusoidal white light impulses. Their research has indicated that clients do better on the third trial of entrainment. They caution that prospective clients be screened for a personal or family history of seizures because visual entrainment can trigger a seizure response. Their procedure is to entrain the brainwave frequency targeted for up-training or reward. They noted that down-training a brainwave frequency is more complicated. They also use visual entrainment for client management. If clients come in sleep deprived, they will give them 20 minutes of 10 Hertz visual entrainment. For ADHD kids, they will give them 10 minutes of 14 Hertz entrainment along with their favorite music.

Other neurotherapists including Swingle (2008) and Thompson (2007) have used audio entrainment and therapeutic harmonic CDs to facilitate neurofeedback and extend its benefits long after treatment has concluded. These tools are ideal for home use. They are easy to use and have been found to help strengthen and maintain the gains achieved in neurofeedback treatment.

Role of Medication and Counseling During Neurofeedback

Clients who are taking medication during neurofeedback should continue taking their medication until their prescribing physician determines they can reduce or altogether cease its use. Neurotherapy often results in significant reduction in presenting symptoms. The brain is functioning differently and may no longer require medication assistance. If not adjusted, agitation, sedation, or increased side effects may result. Clients are best advised to coordinate their neurotherapy treatment with their physicians and communicate any needed medication adjustments as they become necessary. Also note, continued medication use after neurotherapy can sabotage neurotherapy's beneficial effects. It is important that clients be prepared to take an active role in their medical treatment and to assert their needs with their doctors.

Clients who need therapy due to personal, marital, or family conflict; environmental stress; or chronic personality disorders may choose to continue therapy during neurofeedback treatment. This can become expensive and time consuming but can be necessary because neurofeedback as a more technological intervention will not sufficiently address clients' more immediate emotional and interpersonal needs. When therapy clients become relatively stable, a break from counseling could be done to allow for a period of neurotherapy treatment. It has been our clinical experience that clients who have been in counseling for months or years have made substantial strides after completing neurofeedback, becoming able to implement changes not possible or evident during counseling. Some clients who have chosen to stop counseling to begin neurofeedback find that their counseling needs resurface during neurofeedback. Demos's (2005) rule of thumb is that if a client requires 25 minutes of counseling in a neurofeedback session, neurofeedback may need to take a back seat to the client's more pressing counseling needs. Another alternative is to take a brief break from neurofeedback for a session or two of counseling and then return to neurofeedback when the counseling needs have been addressed.

Evaluation of Progress

Client progress during neurofeedback training can be monitored in three ways. These include the client's self report, completion of a Symptom Checklist, and observation of the client's training performance. The most important goal of neurofeedback is the reduction of the symptoms related to the client's presenting concern. The brief check-in conversation at the beginning of each treatment session can be very informative. It can tell the neurotherapist whether the client is feeling better, worse, or experiencing no change. The client's response can stimulate a discussion about current life stressors, training expectations, counseling needs, medication issues, positive signs of treatment affects, lack of treatment effects, or the need for a different training protocol.

Completion of the Symptom Checklist, presented earlier in this chapter, is another source of valuable information on client progress. Some neurotherapists will administer a checklist every session. Others have found that a Symptom Checklist completed every 10 sessions is very effective in noting client progress. The checklist often makes obvious to the client symptom changes he or she has not consciously recognized, as well as identifying areas for continued treatment. This is usually a very encouraging experience for the client and the neurotherapist. The feedback is very useful for ongoing treatment planning. In general, we have observed that half of clients' symptoms improve after 10 sessions of neurotherapy, another 25% after 20 sessions, and most improve after 30 to 40 sessions. When a stubborn symptom is identified, it may suggest more work is needed with the same treatment protocol or another altogether different protocol should be considered.

The third method of gauging session progress is evaluating the client's training performance. This is an observational and neurotherapy software–driven approach and involves monitoring and noting session-to-session changes in threshold levels, summary statistics, and client performance. As a client develops the skill to meet the threshold for increasing or decreasing a specifically targeted brainwave, this threshold can be noted and tracked over the course of training. In general, the reward threshold level should increase and the inhibit threshold decrease. When individual session summary statistics are calculated, the average brainwave scores may also reflect this change, but more importantly, the variability of the brainwave will change. This suggests that the client has learned how to access and change (increase or decrease) the range of amplitude of the desired brainwave. Observationally, the neurotherapist can also test the client's performance by challenging him or her to increase or decrease a specific brainwave associated with a specific video or audio reward or inhibit. The better the client is able to produce or stop the video or audio, the stronger his or her ability to identify and change the associated brainwave. This enhanced self-regulation of the brainwaves is the primary goal of neurotherapy.

Completion of Treatment

Neurofeedback treatment is completed when the client's presenting concerns and symptomatic behavior is meaningfully reduced. As previously noted, this usually takes about 30 to 40 sessions, with the first 10 to 20 sessions focused on symptom reduction and the last 10 to 20 sessions focused on consolidation or strengthening of the changes. Some clients feel inclined to stop treatment after 20 sessions, but the value of consolidation or overtraining has been well documented (Demos, 2005). Some neurotherapists will advise once a month relapse prevention training, to keep the newly established self-regulation skills strong. However, most brainwave changes will persist well after training has been completed. The exception is alpha wave training, or brain brightening, for seniors, which involves four sessions of ongoing neurofeedback, four times a year, to maintain the change. In summary, the changes made in neurotherapy are best compared to learning how to ride a bicycle. Barring reoccurrence of brain dysregulation, once your brain learns how to do it, it never seems to forget.

OUTCOME EVALUATION

Evaluating the overall outcome of neurofeedback treatment can be complicated because neurological change may be less obvious with some indicators and more obvious with others, and it can occur well beyond the completion of the training episode. For example, while dramatic changes in specific brainwave amplitudes suggest change has occurred, sometimes the average amplitude doesn't change that much, but the client's ability to activate underlying neural networks does change. In addition, change begun in neurotherapy treatment has been found to expand or generalize months to even a couple of years after treatment (Demos, 2005). This is due to the slowly evolving generative benefits of the client's healthier neurological engagement in their personal, interpersonal, academic, and/or work life. There are three general approaches to treatment outcome evaluation. These include client self-report, objective assessment, and observational information. All three of these methods are important to consider because they each have their associated strengths and limitations but together provide a fuller picture of neurofeedback's impact on a client's life.

Client Self-Report

As previously noted, the most powerful and meaningful indicator of neurofeedback outcome is the client's verbal or written problem checklist report of symptom reduction and resolution of his or her presenting concern. Who better than the client to judge differences between pretreatment and posttreatment emotional and behavioral problems? In psychotherapy, counselors rely very heavily on clients' subjective report of change and often weigh it even more heavily than objective sources of information. However, a significant limitation of self-report information and a criticism of neurofeedback in particular is the placebo effect. Clients have invested a great deal of time and money in the neurotherapy process and have developed rapport with the neurotherapist whom they may not want to disappoint. The positive bias that can develop from such factors should not be minimized when weighing the value of the client's self-report. Therefore, self-report alone is not a sufficient treatment outcome measure.

Objective Assessment

There are many sources of objective information available to the neurotherapist to assess the outcome of neurotherapy treatment. These can involve posttreatment administration of psychological tests and behavioral checklists, a Test of Variable Attention, a QEEG, and a trend analysis of brainwave changes across the treatment episode. The value of valid and reliable psychological tests and behavioral checklists of anxiety, depression, trauma, ADHD, insomnia, and cognitive functioning is that they provide a quantifiable measure of change. Their primary limitation is that a pretreatment–posttreatment administration schedule without a control group doesn't account for other factors of change such as maturation or learning from the first administration. However, having a number that reflects significant change does strengthen self-report information.

Readministration of the Test of Variable Attention (TOVA) is especially useful for clients with ADHD and is often reported in the research literature documenting neurotherapy effectiveness. Positive change can be indicated by normalization of visual and auditory performance or by improvement in the desired directions. Since other emotional and behavioral problems can also cause problems with attention, the TOVA can also be used to quantify improvements in non-ADHD clients. Not all neurotherapy clients have problems with attention, so the TOVA may not be of use for all clients.

Some neurotherapists rely very heavily on the QEEG for initial assessment, treatment progress, and outcome measurement. Other neurotherapists use it only for treatment planning. The benefit of the QEEG is that it generates a quantifiable measure of brainwave activity and neuronal communication networks as compared to a normative sample. Neurofeedback training is then done to move the client's EEG more toward the norm. Critics of the use of the QEEG for this purpose have two concerns. The first is that clients are unique, and while pretreatment assessment can help with general treatment planning, client individuality suggests that what is the norm for one person may not be the norm for another. The second critique is that the tasks required in a QEEG assessment (eyes open, eyes closed, and reading or math task) do not measure the client's ability to access and use the changed brainwaves or neural network in their fuller personal, interpersonal, school, or work life and are thus less meaningful indicators of change.

A neurotherapy software–driven trend analysis of brainwave changes across treatment can yield some potentially interesting information; however, as previously noted, it too has significant limitations. Most neurofeedback software platforms allow the neurotherapist to track, statistically analyze, and generate a graphic trend report of changes in average brainwave amplitude or variability across the treatment episode. Caution must be exercised in expecting changes in average amplitude. Some clients' treatment may indeed evidence such changes, but it is more likely that changes in brainwave variability will be observed, since this reflects improved access and self-regulation of the particular brainwave. A further limitation of statistical trend reports is that they cannot illustrate changes in underlying neural networks that are evident only when the client is calling upon them to perform a real-life task, such as attending in the classroom or remaining calm in a previously upsetting situation.

Observational Information

As in basic science, the best researchers and the most experienced neurotherapists rely on well-developed observational skills. Often, it is the unsolicited report of third parties in the client's life that provide the most compelling evidence of positive treatment outcomes. These may be comments from parents, teachers, coaches, friends, and doctors. Some examples include a psychiatrist who worked with a child with ADHD all her life and has never observed such dramatic change, a teacher who notices marked improvement in reading ability, a parent who notes his or her child is sleeping much better and no longer has violent nightmares, an orthodontist who notices their client is no longer grinding his or her teeth, a coach who comments on marked improvement in an athlete's performance, a family who is grateful that an adult son is now able to face family conflicts avoided for 5 years, and a mother whose previously traumatized and avoidant son is described as a new person.

Also observable are changes in medication needs have been observed as a result of neurofeedback. As the brain changes its ability to self-regulate, it no longer requires the assistance of medication to do so. In fact, medication may create too much stimulation, agitation, or sedation, as well as other unwanted side effects. Another indicator of successful neurofeedback is the reduction or cessation of previously needed medication. This of course must be done in collaboration with the client's doctor but is often a very welcome outcome in a client's life.

Finally, many clients are slow to observe changes in their own lives. The effects of neurofeedback are often subtle and unfold over time. Steinburg and Othmer (2004) described the transformation as, "The problem is running our lives" to "What problem?" Families with children who have ADHD are very familiar with the daily stress of disorganization, hyperactivity, impulsive control, emotional reactivity, struggles to complete tasks, and sleep cycle problems. After neurofeedback, many families observe that life is calmer, relationships less tense, and their child much happier and more successful.

CONCLUSIONS

This chapter explored the value of an in-depth assessment of brainwave dysregulation for individualized treatment planning, the many components of a comprehensive treatment plan, and three general methods to evaluate the outcome of neurofeedback training. A thorough assessment procedure involves several types of information including a psychosocial medical history, psychological and behavioral checklists, a test of variable attention, and a quantitative EEG. Once completed, the assessment guides the neurotherapist in the development of an individualized treatment plan designed to educate clients about the neurofeedback treatment process and other strategies they can employ to improve their neurological self-regulation.

Comprehensive treatment plans review indications, contraindications, and possible side effects of neurotherapy treatment. They assess client expectations, explain the commitment they must make, and offer realistic research-based information on potential outcomes. They include recommendations for exercise, diet, food supplements, and other preventive strategies. They prepare clients for neurofeedback by letting them know what they can do to get the most out of each neurofeedback session. Treatment plans explain the benefit of skin temperature and heart rate variability training in enhancing self-regulation skills found to facilitate neurofeedback work. They explain the reasons for recommended treatment protocols, provide understandable instructions so clients know what to do during a training session, and present the benefits of audio-visual entrainment in enhancing neurofeedback treatment. In addition, treatment plans inform clients about the role of medication and counseling during neurofeedback, help them understand how to evaluate progress along the way, and explain when it's time to complete neurofeedback training.

Finally, this chapter reviewed three methods for evaluating treatment outcomes that included the value and limits of client self-report, objective assessment, and observational information. Alone, any one method may not be sufficient in assessing meaningful change, but together, all three provide a multifaceted and convincing basis for evaluating the outcome of neurofeedback treatment.

REFERENCES

Allman, W. F. (1989). *Apprentices of wonder: Inside the neural network revolution.* New York: Bantam Books, Random House.

Amen, D. (2001). *Healing ADD: The breakthrough program that allows you to see and heal the six types of ADD.* New York: Putnam.

Anderson, J. S. (2010). *Professional EEG biofeedback certification training.* St. Louis Park, MN: Minnesota Neurotherapy Institute.

Beck, A. T., Ward, C. H., Mendelson, M., Mock, J. J., & Erbaugh, N. (1961). An inventory for measuring depression. *Archives of General Psychiatry, 4,* 561–571.

Blanchard, E. B., Jones-Alexander, J., Buckley, T. C., & Fornevis, C. A. (1996). Psychometric properties of the PTSD Checklist (PCL). *Behavior Research and Therapy, 34*(8), 669–673.

Budzynski, T. H., Kosan Budzynski, H., Evans, J. R., & Abarbanel, A. (Eds.). (2009). *Introduction to quantitative EEG and neurofeedback: Advanced theory and application.* New York: Academic.

Burns, D. D. (1993). *Ten days to self-esteem.* New York: Quill.

Demos, J. N. (2005). *Getting started with neurofeedback.* New York: Norton.

Greenberg, L. M., & Waldman, I. D. (1993). Developmental normative data on the test of variables of attention (T.O.V.A.). *Journal of Child Psychology and Psychiatry, 34*(6), 1019–1030.

Greenwald, R., & Rubin, A. (1999). Assessment of posttraumatic symptoms in children: Development and preliminary validation of parent and child scales. *Research on Social Work Practice, 9*(1), 61–75.

Hammond, D. C., & Kirk, K. (2008). First, do no harm: Adverse effects and the need for practice standards in neurofeedback. *Journal of Neurotherapy, 12*(1), 79–88.

Hill, R. W., & Castro, E. (2009). *Healing young brains: The neurofeedback solution.* Charlottesville, VA: Hampton Roads.

Homan, R. W., Herman, J., & Purdy, P. (1987). Cerebral location of international 10–2-system electrode placement. *Electroencephalography and Clinical Neurophysiology, 66*(4), 376–382.

Morin, C. M., Belleville, G., Belanger, L., & Ives, H. (2011). The insomnia severity index: Psychometric indicators to detect insomnia cases and evaluate treatment response. *Sleep, 34*(5), 601–608.

Powell, D. H., Kaplan, E. F., Whitla, D., Catlin, R., & Funkenstein, H. H. (1993). *MicroCog: Assessment of cognitive functioning version 2.1.* San Antonio, TX: Psychological Corporation.

Soutar, R., & Longo, R. (2011). *Doing neurofeedback: An introduction.* San Rafael, CA: ISNR Research Foundation.

Steinberg, M., & Othmer, S. (2004). *ADD: The 20-hour solution.* Bandon, OR: Robert D. Reed.

Swingle, P. G. (2008). *Brain neurotherapy: The clinician's guide.* Vancouver, British Columbia, Canada: Author.

Thompson, J. (2007). *The brainwave suite.* Retrieved from www.TheRelaxationCompany.com

Tinius, T. P. (2003). The integrated visual and auditory continuous performance test as a neuropsychological measure. *Archives of Clinical Neuropsychology, 18*(5), 439–454.

8

NEUROFEEDBACK TRAINING, PROTOCOLS, AND CASE STUDIES

Whatever happens in the mind of man is represented in the actions and interactions of brain cells.

—C. E. Boklage

This chapter will present the nuts and bolts of conducting neurofeedback training. It will discuss neurofeedback lab design; necessary furniture, equipment and supplies; the importance of the client–neurotherapist relationship; client preparation for training; different general approaches to neurofeedback training; specific training protocols; and case examples. It will also explore several procedural considerations necessary to facilitate effective neurotherapy. These include sensor preparation and placement, managing distorted EEG and artifact interference, setting training thresholds for rewards and inhibits, length of training, evaluation of change during training, and the resolution of training problems.

The process of neurofeedback training requires a delicate balance between a knowledge and comfort with computer and EEG technology and therapeutic skill essential in observing, empathizing, communicating, and connecting with the client. Some therapists may feel intimidated by the technical aspects of the work; however, like any new skill and knowledge base, this can be learned through a commitment to study, supervision, and practice. In time, confidence will emerge, questions not even yet imagined will be answered, and beneficial results for clients will motivate even further skill development and expertise in neurofeedback.

This "how to" chapter, although meant to cover a wide range of practitioner questions, is not meant to replace the standard 45-hour EEG neurofeedback certification training course. This course is invaluable in its depth and experiential design in preparing prospective neurotherapists to begin their acquisition of neurotherapy knowledge and skills.

NEUROFEEDBACK TRAINING AND NEUROFEEDBACK LAB DESIGN

Basic neurofeedback equipment includes a computer, an EEG amplifier, and a comfortable chair. These can be readily assimilated into most clinicians' current offices; however, some neurotherapists choose to set up a special room or lab that is specifically designed for neurofeedback training. The lab is usually situated in a quiet location. Overhead florescent lighting is replaced with indirect incandescent lighting because florescent lighting can interfere with accurate EEG readings. The lab is also best located away from any heavy electronic equipment, electrical power sources such as air conditioners, copiers, or high power lines and radio frequency disturbance. This also minimizes 60 Hertz interference that can distort EEG readings. Some labs are further equipped with special mats that reduce the risk of static electricity that can also alter accurate EEG readings.

The neurotherapy lab is also designed to be comfortable and functional. Many are set up with a dual computer monitor capacity that allows the neurotherapist to view and operate an administrative neurofeedback training screen and the client to view a second stimulus screen. The administrative screen typically includes a graphic representation of the client's full EEG, specific brainwave graphs extracted from the full EEG, an indication of DC Offset or the strength of electrical connection between the sensors, a muscle or EMG artifact indicator that warns about muscle tension that can interfere with accurate EEG readings, and several brainwave bar graphs with adjustable threshold settings that allow the administrator to increase or decrease the reward or inhibit requirement of the training task. In most treatment protocols, one or two brainwaves are being increased or rewarded, and one, two, or three other brainwaves are being decreased or inhibited.

The client stimulus screen presents a visual and/or auditory task that the client must perform by using his or her brain. More specifically, the client uses a passive awareness of different brainwave states to alter a visual and/or auditory stimulus. For example, a client with ADHD may learn to identify and increase his or her sensory motor rhythm (SMR) brainwave by making a video play and certain annoying background noises (bird chirping or bleep sound), associated with high theta and high beta waves, stop. Learning how to focus on and increase or decrease the targeted brainwaves occurs through operant conditioning. In other words, the client's new skill, improved brainwave self-regulation, is reinforced by the video playing and the annoying background noises becoming silent. Over numerous training sessions, this new skill becomes strengthened and the client becomes better able to access it when needed outside the neurotherapy lab. For children with ADHD, that means less distraction, daydreaming, or anxiety in the classroom and improved behavior, attention, and learning in school.

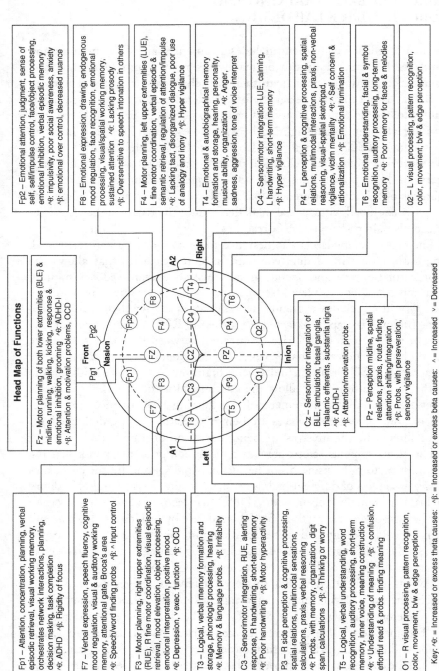

FIGURE 8.1 Head Map of Functions showing the 10-20 system of brain site locations and functions

Permission granted by © John S. Anderson

The client's brainwave activity is acquired through sensors, attached with conductive paste, that are designed to pick up the small amounts of electrical activity produced by the brain. The sensors are attached to a cable that relays the information to a battery-operated EEG amplifier. The amplifier is battery operated so there is no risk of shock to the client. At no time is electrical current ever being sent to the client. Once amplified, the EEG signal is then sent via Bluetooth wireless technology to the computer software. It is the software that controls, displays, and operates the administrative and stimulus screens described above, facilitating neurofeedback training.

A well-equipped neurotherapy lab has many necessary supplies. These include reference diagrams of the International 10–20 System of brain site locations, reference charts of the functions of different brain locations, different types of sensors for head and ear placement, conductive paste and wooden application sticks, alcohol pads and abrasive gel for cleaning application sites, clips or gauze medical tape to stabilize cable wires, and tissue to help clean sensors and clients' hair of conductive paste after each session.

Other lab equipment can include good quality speakers and DVD player, a blanket should a client become cold while training, head bands to help stabilize sensors, entrainment CDs for clients' home use, audio-visual entrainment equipment, handheld thermometers for skin temperature training, other computer software for heart rate variability training and various testing materials, take-home handouts, symptom checklists, and training protocol reference information. Finally, some neurotherapists stock their labs with a treasure chest filled with small giveaways to help reward and motivate younger clients. After 30 or 40 neurotherapy sessions, many children will accrue an extensive home collection.

THE CLIENT–NEUROTHERAPIST RELATIONSHIP

As in all therapeutic relationships, rapport in the client–neurotherapist relationship is very important. This involves maintenance of an understanding, empathetic, and reassuring connection. Many clients enter neurofeedback training with some apprehension; after all, it proposes to alter their brain functioning. What if something should go wrong? What if they are not able to succeed at the task? What if the time and money they have spent turn out to be a poor investment? These doubts can be best addressed when the neurotherapist responds with openness, creates an environment of trust, closely observes and attends to the client's emotional needs, and is prepared to alter training as indicated by the client's response.

Not all clients are emotionally ready for neurofeedback training even though they have agreed to it. Some are reluctant participants being urged to participate by their parents or spouses. Others are experiencing such overwhelming life distress that they can't sufficiently focus on neurofeedback.

Still others have not stopped their substance abuse, are not eating or sleeping well enough for effective training to be done, or are in such a resistant or rebellious state that neurofeedback training is not indicated for them at this time in their lives. The best clients are those who are optimistic about neurofeedback, who are voluntary participants, and who have a relatively stable lifestyle.

One way to reduce client apprehension is to provide a brief orientation to the neurofeedback training process. This can begin with a clear written description of the process, its benefits, procedures, research base, indications and contraindications, and potential side effects. This information can be concisely included in the client service or informed consent agreement. Similar information can also be placed in a client-friendly brochure or added to the neurotherapist's website with links to national and international neurotherapy association websites.

Perhaps the best way to reduce client apprehension is to gradually expose clients to the process, demonstrate the equipment, and provide a full description of everything you are doing so that the "mystery" of neurofeedback is replaced with "calm understanding." This can be accomplished with a tour of the neurotherapy lab, a demonstration of the software, an explanation of both the administrative and stimulus training screens, and a full description of the equipment and procedures that are used in a typical training session.

Also important is to provide clients with some sense of what is expected of them during a neurofeedback training session. They need to know what to do. Many will presume they must exert some sort of intentional effort to affect the stimulus screen to make the video or music play. Some may become frustrated because they feel they are failing at the task, seeing the screen grow dark, the music go silent, and the annoying background sounds persist. The best client mindset is one of passive awareness. The brain will naturally want to seek stimulation if given the opportunity. When a client relaxes and permits his or her mind to explore what is in front of him or her, the brain will learn what to do and become aware of itself, or more specifically, of the particular brainwave activity required to keep the stimulation going or to decrease the annoying background sounds. This usually occurs within the first few minutes of training.

After the client has become comfortable with using his or her brain to successfully affect the stimulus screen, the neurotherapist must adjust the challenge thresholds to make the task a little more difficult to accomplish. This is what over time and over numerous training sessions, strengthens the client's ability to increase the desired brainwave and to decrease the undesired brainwaves. However, the continued effort to succeed at the task can be discouraging to clients. It is very important to explain this process to clients so they understand why the video and/or music still stops and the annoying sounds still occur. After a while, the client will recognize when you have adjusted a threshold and will look forward to meeting the next challenge.

Shaping client expectations and nurturing this attitude of continuous challenge is critical for neurofeedback to be effective.

A strong and trusting client–neurotherapist relationship is also needed to effectively monitor client progress across sessions. At the beginning and end of each session, a skillful neurotherapist will check in with his or her client to assess both the client's positive and negative experiences since the last session or during the current session. A client who is too worried about "failing" or "disappointing" the neurotherapist will not give honest and specific feedback about their experience. To counter these influences, the neurotherapist must create an atmosphere of nonjudgmental acceptance. This is done by inviting, acknowledging, and accepting the client's experience, both positive and negative, so he or she feels fully free in letting the neurotherapist know what is going on with the training experience. This information can help the neurotherapist encourage the client's positive changes, be aware of problems that could be resolved by adjusting or changing the training protocol, and address any environmental issues (stress, lifestyle, or emotional needs) that need attention with a referral for counseling. Demos (2005) noted that if 25% of a neurotherapy session is used to talk about a client's personal matters, then the client may need more counseling than neurotherapy and perhaps neurotherapy should be suspended until the emotional matters are better addressed.

CLIENT PREPARATION FOR TRAINING

There are several strategies clients can employ to prepare themselves for neurofeedback training. If done conscientiously, these can optimize the impact of neurotherapy, decrease the long-term impact of stress, and promote overall neurological health. These include taking certain dietary supplements, learning how to increase peripheral skin temperature, developing the skill of diaphragmatic breathing, and being physically and mentally ready to perform during the neurofeedback session.

As noted in Chapter 5, *Strategies for Self-Regulation*, there are many types of dietary supplements that enhance brain functioning. Some of the most beneficial are omega 3s found in fish oil, N-acetylcysteine, turmeric, and Vitamin D. Since brain tissue is composed of a significant amount of fat, the fatty acids found in fish oil have a positive effect in promoting overall brain functioning. Many clients will come to neurotherapy already taking fish oil. Those who do not but who are investing in neurotherapy may appreciate knowing that a daily course of fish oil is an easy way to ensure healthier brain functioning. N-acetylcysteine improves neuronal glutamatergic functioning. It too reduces neuronal inflammation likely already present in clients presenting with significant mental health problems. Turmeric also works to assist the body in generating a healthier inflammatory response.

Finally, Vitamin D has been found to support the immune system and is useful in reducing a variety of mental health problems. It is important to note that neurofeedback training can increase brain inflammation via the formation of new neural pathways. This makes dietary supplements a very useful adjunct to neurotherapy.

During neurofeedback clients are asked to create a state of passive awareness. They are also commonly called upon to reduce anxiety (high beta waves) or reduce drowsiness (high theta waves) when they hear annoying background noises (bird chirping or bleep sound). It is much easier for clients to do this if they have learned two simple methods of behavioral self-regulation. These are peripheral skin temperature training and diaphragmatic breathing.

Peripheral skin temperature training is very easy to learn. A small hand-held thermometer or an inexpensive digital thermometer with a skin temperature sensor can be attached to a client's big finger on the nondominant hand with gauze medical tape. The client's baseline skin temperature can then be noted. Next, simply instruct the client to increase their skin temperature any way they can. Some will be able to do this and others will require some assistance. If assistance is required, ask them to close their eyes, take a few deep breaths, and suggest they imagine their skin warming, muscles relaxing, and blood flowing ever more easily through their veins. Sometimes it can be helpful to use a few metaphors such as soaking in a warm bath, lying on a beautiful beach, or floating like a gentle cloud. Most clients will be able to increase their peripheral skin temperature by 5 to 10 degrees. Increases in the 92- to 96-degree range indicate a strong relaxation response.

The second self-regulation skill is diaphragmatic breathing. Demos (2005) offered a very detailed description of this technique. He suggested clients place one hand on their stomach and the other on their chest. When they inhale, the hand on their stomach should move outward. When they exhale, the hand on their stomach should move inward. The hand on their chest should stay still. This will not feel familiar to "chest breathers" who take many short breaths from their chest but with practice, they can learn to take fewer and deeper breaths from their diaphragm, improving the oxygenation of their lungs and heart and sending relaxation and recovery messages to their brain and body. Another way to learn diaphragmatic breathing is to use the Emwave computer software program from HeartMath Corporation. It is more expensive to purchase but gives the client several types of biofeedback signals (sound, color, graphic, numeric) to enhance their ability to learn diaphragmatic breathing. Most clients can learn skin temperature training and diaphragmatic breathing in one session. Once learned, the neurotherapist can simply remind clients to use their self-regulation skills when they need to decrease high beta or high theta, or to enhance passive awareness during neurofeedback training.

General guidelines for clients to be physically and mentally prepared to do neurofeedback training involve sleep, hydration, food, substance use, and relative freedom from illness or upsetting distraction. If clients are too tired when they arrive for a session, their focus may be affected and they may fall asleep during training. The same applies to hunger and thirst. Clients should feel satiated with healthy food and drink and maintain good hydration during training. Sugar-based foods or caffeinated beverages are not recommended. Clients should also refrain from substance abuse, feel generally healthy, and not be overly distracted by home or work stress. All of these can interfere with focus and neuronal functioning, decreasing the benefits of neurofeedback training. Clients who are taking prescription medication may continue doing so; however, in some cases, it too may affect performance in neurofeedback. For example, in later stages of training, children on stimulant medication may become more agitated and with their doctor's approval, may reduce their medication. Also note that psychotropic and other medications can cause brainwave disregulation and may undermine progress in neurofeedback. Feedback from the client and consultation with their prescribing physician is recommended.

Other necessary guidelines include no gum chewing, poor posture, or cell phones. Gum chewing along with other mouth, jaw, facial, neck, and head movements can cause muscle tension and EMG artifact interference with the EEG. Slouching, leg crossing, and foot bouncing can also cause EMG artifact and must be limited. If a client has difficulty controlling these behaviors, several small breaks can be taken during the training session to allow the client an opportunity to relax and release their pent-up energy. For young children, it may be best to have them use the rest room before training begins, otherwise sensors and equipment will have to be removed and reapplied. Some very young children may train better if their parents are in the room; however, it is usually less distracting if parents are not present. Finally, clients cannot bring active cell phones or other electronic devices into the neurotherapy lab because the cell phone signals can interfere with the wireless Bluetooth communication between the EEG amplifier and the computer. In addition, other heavy metal objects such as pocketknives, belt buckles, and jewelry must be removed because they can attract 60 Hertz interference and distort EEG readings.

PROTOCOL SELECTION: GENERAL APPROACHES TO NEUROFEEDBACK TRAINING

There are two general approaches to neurofeedback training. These are single-channel and two-channel training. Demos (2005) presented a detailed description of each approach. Single-channel training allows targeted intervention on one specific neurological region of the brain. Its goal is to increase or decrease the amplitude of the brainwaves at a given location known by research to be related to a certain neurological function. Two-channel training allows intervention on and between two selected areas of the brain. Its goal extends beyond the improvement of single brainwave amplitude by also improving the communication between two separate regions of the brain.

Single-channel training records the raw EEG signal and separates it, through electronic filters, into the respective brainwave bandwidths of delta, theta, alpha, beta, and gamma. There are two types of single-channel montages or patterns of sensor placement. Both require the use of three cable leads connecting the sensors to the EEG amplifier. One lead, called the ground, is attached to the ear lobe or the mastoid bone behind the ear. These areas have little electrical activity and serve well to ground the circuit between the primary leads. A second lead is called the referent. It is attached to the other ear lobe or mastoid bone behind the ear. The referent is attached to the same side of the head as the active lead or in the case of a midline placement, either ear. The third lead, called the active lead, is attached to the brain location targeted for neurofeedback intervention.

The most common type of single-channel training involves a referential or monopolar montage. It yields an absolute value of amplitude because the referent (at the ear) has an amplitude value of zero. This permits full measure of the total amplitude at the given site. For example, single-channel training for ADHD usually involves training the sensory motor rhythm at Cz with a ground at one ear and a referent at the other. A limitation of single-channel training is that it can be prone to muscle tension (EMG) artifact from facial movement or jaw tension and heartbeat contamination from the ear lobe. Use of the mastoid bone can minimize these artifacts.

The other type of single-channel training involves a sequential or bipolar montage. In this sensor pattern, both the referent and active sensors are attached to the scalp and the ground to either ear lobe. This montage does not yield an absolute value. Its value is incremental or the mathematical difference between the referent and scalp sensor positions. This montage is more resistant to artifact interference and allows two areas of the brain to be simultaneously trained. The two sites can be aware of and communicate more effectively with each other. For example, clients struggling with cognitive inefficiency may benefit from midline alpha training. The active sensor could be attached to Cz, a referent to Fz, and the ground to an ear.

Two-channel training offers the neurotherapist access to the brain's underlying communication patterns. Regions of the brain, while identified with specialized functions, do not operate independently of each other. They communicate front to back, side to side, across and within the hemispheres in complex neurological networks. Two-channel training utilizes two independent EEG signals, each with its own set of electronic filters, that breakdown the raw EEG into its frequency bandwidths (delta, theta, alpha, beta, and gamma). This allows the neurotherapist an opportunity to compare and simultaneously train two brain regions. Typical goals of two-channel training include coherence training to improve communication between two regions;

asymmetry training to promote bilateral differences; and alpha theta synchrony training for peak performance, trauma, and addiction.

In coherence training, the neurotherapist is concerned about increasing the similarity of the brainwave frequency between two sites on the scalp. In other words, it involves a comparison of the waveforms or patterns rather than their amplitudes. The client is reinforced when the amplitude of the brainwaves at both sites increases. Coherence training can be applied to problems of hypercoherence, hypocoherence, and phase. In hypercoherence, two brain areas share too much of the same waveform. This occurs in problems of head injury and mental retardation. In hypocoherence, two brain areas share too little of the same waveform. This occurs in problems related to learning disabilities and trauma. In phase problems, the timing of the waveforms has been disrupted. This occurs in traumatic brain injury.

Asymmetry training is used when contralateral brain regions have been found to have normatively deviant asymmetry. That is, their waveforms are more dissimilar than they are supposed to be. An example is the presence of mood disorders when F3 and F4 alpha are too asymmetrical. Demos (2005) presented the BAT triad model to illustrate this concept. He noted three normative patterns involved in comparing left hemisphere (LH) and right hemisphere (RH) beta, alpha, and theta (BAT). More specifically, LH beta should be greater than or equal to RH beta, RH alpha should be greater or equal to LH alpha, and RH theta should be roughly equal to LH theta. If RH beta exceeds LH beta, suspect anxiety or anxiety mixed with depression. If LH alpha exceeds RH alpha, suspect depression. If RH and LH theta are not equal, expect other mood problems. Rosenfeld (2000) and Baehr et al. (1999), using specially designed cables, developed an alpha asymmetry two-channel protocol for the treatment of mood disorders using an active lead on F3, an active lead on F4, both referents at Cz, and a ground to the ear.

Alpha theta synchrony (ATS) training, also called deep state training, involves increasing the activity of two brainwaves, in two regions of the brain, at the same time. This enhances their synchronicity or the degree to which their amplitudes rise and fall together. It also facilitates alpha theta crossover and improves the phase of alpha and theta. Alpha states are associated with calm focus and theta states with meditation, healing, and recovery. They disarm the limbic system (Demos, 2005) and permit a bridge from the internal to the external world (White, 1999). When theta amplitude surpasses alpha, it permits awareness and insight of suppressed material. When both alpha and theta simultaneously increase, two to three times their normal amplitude, a phase reset has occurred. This promotes insight, cognitive understanding (often nonverbal), processing, and integration of previously unavailable and sometimes traumatic material. Alpha theta synchrony training has been used to treat personality disorders (White, 1999), trauma and addiction (Peniston & Kulkosky, 1999), and peak performance (Gruzelier, 2009). Alpha theta synchrony utilizes two active leads, two referent leads to each ear, and a ground to the bony part of the upper chest. An example is two-channel alpha theta synchrony neurofeedback training at Pz and Fz for trauma. Dailey (2009) enhanced this protocol by adding 5 minutes of gamma training to help consolidate cognitive integration of processed material. His protocol is called theta alpha gamma (TAG) synchrony training.

SINGLE-CHANNEL PROTOCOLS

There are many commonly used single-channel neurofeedback training protocols. They are chosen because a specific type of problem has been identified by the psychosocial medical history, psychological assessment, computerized testing, or EEG evaluation, and because research and/or clinical practice has demonstrated efficacy in reduction of that presenting problem. Below are listed several typical mental and behavioral health problems, their associated neurofeedback protocols, a brief description of their use, and references for further information.

ADHD

The most widely used protocol for ADHD is rewarding the sensory motor rhythm (SMR) at 12–15 Hz training at Cz with inhibits on theta at 4–7 Hz and beta at 15–18 Hz. It involves placing an active sensor at Cz, a referent at one ear, and a ground at the other. This training has been referenced by many practitioners including Tansey (1993), Lubar (1995), Sterman (2000b), Amen (2001), Thompson and Thompson (1998, 2003), Othmer (2008), and Hill and Castro (2009). It usually takes 30 to 40 sessions to complete. Changes can be seen within the first 10 to 20 sessions, but 30 to 40 sessions are recommended to consolidate the changes. Recent research (Russell-Chapin et al., 2013) has found this protocol also reactivates the underactivated default mode network in children with ADHD. An active default mode network is necessary for internal reflection, memory consolidation, integration, and application of external experience.

Depression

The customary protocol for depression requires placement of the active sensor at F3, the referent at the left ear, and the ground at the right ear. Treatment involves rewarding low beta at 14–18 Hz and inhibiting alpha at 8–12 Hz and theta at 5–7 Hz. If clients report becoming too activated, the upper range of beta may be lowered 1 Hz at a time. Neurofeedback training for depression usually takes about 10 sessions to complete. This protocol has been cited by Amen (2001), Thompson and Thompson (2003), and Hammond (2005).

Anxiety

There are two protocols for the reduction of anxiety. The first is a quick relief method developed by Fisher (2004). It is known as the Sebern Fisher Bliss Protocol. It involves placement of the active sensor at FPO2, between the right eyebrow and nose on the line where the eyelids meet. The referent sensor is attached to the right ear and the ground to the left. To attach the active sensor, you must remove the blue plastic sensor pad and attach only the metal sensor with conductive paste to the eyebrow with medical gauze tape. The training should be done lying down in order to activate slow wave activity. This protocol rewards theta and mediates the emotional reactivity of the amygdale. Initially, start the training at the 6–9 Hz range and proceed to the 5–8 or 4–7 Hz range if needed. Inhibit the upper range of delta to the lower range of theta from 2–4 or 2–5 Hz. Train up to 9 minutes at a time. Also note, this protocol can increase smell sensitivity and reduce appetite.

The second protocol for anxiety reduction involves rewarding high alpha at Cz from 11–13 Hz and/or SMR from 13–15 Hz while inhibiting high beta from 20–23 Hz or 24–32 Hz. This training usually requires 10 to 20 sessions of neurofeedback. Increases of alpha have also been known to increase immune system functioning and improve general physical health. This protocol has been documented by Moore (2000), Hammond (2005), and Thompson and Thompson (2003).

Cognitive Inefficiency

Cognitive efficiency is very important in learning, emotional health, and overall physiological functioning. It is related to peak alpha efficiency at Cz. Alpha waves have been described as the brain's reset or idle position. Healthy alpha waves allow calm focus; access to creative states; increased problem solving; centered emotions; optimal athletic performance; decrease in fear, tension, and anxiety; internal awareness; enhanced learning; improved immune functioning; and increased serotonin production. Persons with high peak alpha efficiency have been found to be very good meditators, socially extroverted, and have superior memory. Those with low alpha peak efficiency display dementia, fibro fog associated with fibromyalgia, or cognitive inefficiency.

The neurofeedback protocol for improved cognitive efficiency involves increasing low alpha. The active sensor is attached at Cz, and the referent and ground are attached at either ear. Alpha is rewarded at 8–12 or 10–12 Hz. High beta at 20–30 Hz and low theta at 4–7 Hz are inhibited. Training can extend from 10 to 20 sessions. Budzynski, Budzynski, and Tansey (1999) developed a procedure called brain brightening to increase the peak alpha efficiency of seniors. Alpha tends to decline as we age, and the brain brightening procedure, four alpha sessions four times a year, can help keep it strong. Demos (2005), Swingle (2008), and Soutar and Longo (2011) discussed the value of peak alpha efficiency training.

Insomnia, Pain Control, Migraine Headaches, Tics, Dystonia, and Seizures

In some cases, one neurofeedback protocol can have many applications. This is true of the single-channel SMR protocol for insomnia, pain control, migraine headaches, tics, dystonia (a movement disorder related to Parkinson's disease), and seizures. The active sensor is attached to Cz, and SMR at 12–15 Hz is rewarded, while theta at 4–7 Hz and high beta at 20–30 Hz are inhibited. The referent and ground sensor can be attached to either ear. The number of sessions necessary to treat these conditions varies. For example, insomnia can be generally treated in 10 sessions; migraine headaches and tic disorders in 10 to 20 sessions; and pain control, dystonia, and seizure disorders may require an initial 30 to 40 sessions with ongoing maintenance training. This training protocol calms down the body's sensory motor functions and has been supported by the work of Ayers, (1995a), Sterman, (2000a), Thompson and Thompson, (2002), Hammer et al. (2011), and Soutar and Longo (2011).

TWO-CHANNEL PROTOCOLS

There are several two-channel neurofeedback protocols used when an underlying neuronal network is presumed to be the source of brainwave dysregulation. As previously noted, this may involve problems with front-to-back, side-to-side, and across- or within-hemisphere communication. After a thorough psychosocial medical history, psychological assessment, computerized testing, and an EEG evaluation have determined a problem with a mood disorder, trauma, addiction, obsessive-compulsive disorder, personality disorder, or peak performance, a two-channel protocol may be appropriate for neurofeedback training.

An important clarification before reviewing the following protocols is to understand that the earliest neurofeedback training approaches that utilized one or two brainwave frequencies at a single or two site location, typically did so by employing standard amplitude training. These included among others, Budzynski (1979), Peniston et al. (1993), Demos (2005), Othmer (2007), and Anderson (2010). A major shift occurred when Dailey (2009) developed a two-channel "synchrony" protocol that allowed fine tuning of two brainwaves and observation of phase resets. Phase resets allow emotional material to be processed and integrated into conscious understanding and have been observed in the clinical setting to result in significant behavioral changes in the client. He later extended that work to include cross-frequency coupling between multiple brainwave frequencies (Dailey, 2013). This was important because it allowed even greater benefit from neurofeedback training by coupling or synchronizing specific brainwaves over the entire cortex, which has been found to consolidate underlying infra-slow neuronal networks such as the default mode network (Jirsa & Muller, 2013; Kahn, 2013).

Mood Disorders

Alpha asymmetry between F3 and F4 is related to mood disorders. When right frontal alpha at F4 is less than left frontal alpha at F3, depression is indicated. The two-channel neurofeedback treatment for alpha asymmetry involves placement of active sensor one at F3, active sensor two at F4, the two referents at Cz, and the ground at either ear. Alpha at 8–12 Hz is rewarded at F4 and inhibited at F3. Rosenfeld (2000) and Baehr et al. (1999) found this training can take from 30 to 60 sessions.

Dailey (2013) also utilized a two-channel protocol, Theta Alpha Gamma synchrony (TAG Sync), at F3 and F4 to regulate frontal symmetry. Since F3 has been found to be related to positive emotions and reaching out behavior and F4 to negative emotions and withdrawing behavior, frontal symmetry allows improved access to both behavioral options. After employing a midline TAG Synch protocol from Fz to Pz, the F3/F4 protocol helps self-regulate frontal alpha synchrony. This has been found to be associated with fluid intelligence and strong leadership skills.

Trauma

Low alpha at Cz and O1 have been found to be related to emotional trauma (Swingle, 2008). Early work in trauma and addiction was described as slow wave training because it focused on increasing alpha and theta waves. The original work in this area was done by training the posterior at O1 and Cz but also involved training P3 and P4 (Othmer, 2007) and Pz (Anderson, 2010). It is important to note that this work was done in an eyes closed condition that reduced activation of the vigilance network and created a hypnogogic state of drowsiness observed by the appearance of theta-alpha crossover. This permitted integration of previously practiced self-improvement scripts and allowed new insights into otherwise suppressed emotional material. The standard alpha theta amplitude (ATA) protocols that trained the posterior did not consider phase resets and did not train the long-distance networks known to be disturbed in post-traumatic stress disorders (Daniels et al., 2011).

Dailey (2009) advanced neurofeedback treatment of trauma by training the midline from the posterior to the anterior of the brain, thus connecting the posterior and anterior hubs of the default mode network in what was called Alpha Theta Synchrony (ATS) training. This allowed fine tuning of the alpha and theta reward frequencies, observation of phase resets and significant behavioral change in clients. The treatment protocol for ATS involves attaching the active 1 sensor to Fz, the active 2 sensor to Pz, the 1 reference to the left ear, the 2 reference to the right ear, and the ground where convenient. In ATS training both alpha at 9–12 Hz and theta at 4–7 Hz are rewarded and any high beta inhibited. Training is usually done with eyes open and alpha-theta crossover is limited. Progress is noted by the occurrence of phase resets. ATS typically requires 5 to 10 sessions although some applications may require 20 to 40 sessions. The goal of traditional ATA protocol is to reduce the effects of trauma by achieving a profound deep reflective state, allowing previously blocked material to emerge and become nonverbally processed and integrated. During alpha theta crossover, when alpha states decrease and theta states increase, images of meaningful material spring forth. Sometimes clients present with elevated theta and decreased alpha and do not generate alpha theta crossovers. Up-training of alpha can help these clients generate this material and have spontaneous visualizations. Some clients may experience therapeutic abreactions or emotional release. It is not necessary to have clients verbalize these events; however, some may moan, become tearful, or express an "aha" feeling. Others will show no obvious reaction. Still others will report renewed dreaming and want to discuss their feelings and insights. Counseling can be helpful if more thorough verbal processing is necessary.

Of more significance in ATS training is a phase reset. This occurs when timing of theta and alpha simultaneously increase or resets, two to three times their normal amplitudes. This suggests emotional material has become processed and integrated into more conscious understanding. It is often interesting to question clients about their reactions at such moments. Their comments often confirm something meaningful has shifted in their insight, understanding, and acceptance.

A later extension of the ATS protocol called TAG Sync training involves cross-frequency coupling between multiple brainwave frequencies to reestablish resting state integration of the default mode network, necessary for effective internal reflection and creative problem solving (Dailey, 2013). During TAG Sync training, clients first work on theta and alpha synchrony. Later they work on the synchrony of theta and gamma, alpha and gamma, and cross-frequency coupling. Gamma waves are implicated in high levels of cognitive performance, synaptic potentiation, and learning. They act to consolidate the benefits of ATS by generating a sense of insight, pleasure and satisfaction. The protocol procedure involves changing the alpha reward to gamma at 32–48 Hz and then continuing theta gamma synchrony training for at least five more minutes. More information about ATS two-channel training can be found in the work of Budzynski (1979), Peniston et al. (1993), Demos (2005), and Dailey (2009).

Addiction

Another application of traditional ATA training is in the area of addictions. Peniston and Kulkosy (1989, 1990) reported impressive reduction in the relapse rates of alcoholics who participated in traditional substance abuse treatment but also completed ATA neurofeedback training with seven pre-neurofeedback treatment sessions of peripheral skin temperature biofeedback training. They noted up to a 60% improvement in relapse rates after 4 years of treatment. Their early work also found that a third of the subjects developed an aversion to their previously abused substance. Later research extended ATA neurofeedback's application in addiction work. Scott and Kaiser (1998) and Scott et al. (2005) found adding beta training at 12–18 Hz to the ATA protocol helped mixed substance abusing subjects reduce relapse rates 33% more than a nontreated control group. The length of ATA training for the treatment of substance abuse can range from 20 to 40 sessions. Given the financial cost, lifestyle impact, and emotional duress of substance abuse treatment, neurofeedback offers a significant advantage in greatly improving the effectiveness of traditional substance abuse treatment and reducing the likelihood of a second treatment episode.

Obsessive-Compulsive and Personality Disorders

Negative internal chatter or self-defeating internal dialogue is a frequent symptom of clients struggling with obsessive-compulsive and other self-defeating personality disorders. White (1999), using traditional ATA training, reported a case study of a trauma client who scored in the clinically significant range on several scales of the Minnesota Multiphasic Personality Inventory and the Millon Clinical Multiaxial Inventory. After ATA training, remarkably, this client scored in the average range on these inventories and maintained these changes after one- and seven-year follow-ups.

Dailey (2013) offered a modification of the TAG Sync protocol to more directly promote the reduction of internal negative chatter. After completing midline, Pz/Fz TAG Sync training, this protocol involves attaching the active 1 sensor to F3, the active 2 sensor to P4, the 1 referent to the left ear, the 2 referent to the right ear, and the ground to the chest or where convenient. This protocol has been found to calm internal dialogue, giving clients an increased ability to feel more settled in interpersonal interaction and to recover more quickly should they become upset. This allows clients the ability to more effectively manage their irrational thoughts and feelings and to better control the physiological reactions that fuel obsessive-compulsive and personality disordered behavior.

Additional Protocols

The research literature is filled with a variety of neurofeedback protocols for many other mental health, learning, and behavioral health problems. Soutar and Longo (2011) cataloged dozens of protocols used by many established neurofeedback practitioners. Of particular interest is Joel Lubar's a list of the protocols supported by peer-reviewed journal articles and other early Othmer protocols (J. Lubar, personal communication, August 2001). The Othmers continue to refine their protocols and are now training in what they call the infra-low frequency range of 0.01 Hz within the reward bandwidth (Othmer, 2008). The efficacy of neurofeedback protocols varies based upon the quality of controlled research studies conducted to evaluate their effectiveness. The additional protocols described below have been applied to learning problems, autism, traumatic brain injury, tinnitus, and peak performance.

Learning Problems

Specific learning problems can be treated by generally activating the brain location associated with the specific problem. For example, dyslexia, an information-processing problem, can be trained by rewarding beta at 16–18 Hz at T3 and/or P5, while inhibiting theta and high beta as needed (Walker & Norman, 2006). This training usually requires 5 to 10 sessions.

Autism

Autism and Asperger's disorder describe a spectrum of pervasive developmental disorders characterized by significant impairment in social interaction and communication and restricted, repetitive, and stereotyped patterns of behavioral interests or activities that limit learning, interpersonal, and occupational functioning. Since many areas of neurological dysregulation are implicated, the length of neurofeedback treatment is long, sometimes 60 to over 100 sessions. Jarusiewicz (2002) presented a good review of neurofeedback for the treatment of autism. A specific protocol for Asperger's disorder was offered by Thompson and Thompson (2003). It involved beta training at 13–16 Hz at T6 with inhibits set to decrease any dominant slow wave activity.

Traumatic Brain Injury

Traumatic brain injury causes functional injury to the brain, often in multiple locations, by slowing normal brain activity and impacting the functions related to that area of the brain. Ayers (1987, 1995a, 1995b) worked with traumatic brain injury, coma patients, and clients with absence seizures (minimally detectable seizures that cause persons to appear to be daydreaming, aloof, or momentarily detached). Her primary protocol for brain injury was to reward beta at 15–18 Hz and inhibit theta at 4–7 Hz at the location of the injury. Common treatment sites are T3/C3, T4/C4, F4/T4, F3/T3, F7/T5, and O1/O2. A full 19-channel QEEG can be helpful in identifying areas for treatment, but assessed functional problems can also guide active sensor location. Treatment may require up to 24 sessions.

Tinnitus

Tinnitus is a chronic condition that causes perception of sound in the absence of an objective physical source. The sound is usually a high frequency or ringing in the ears. There is no generally accepted view how this phantom sound comes about and no cure. It is thought that it may be caused by changes in the central nervous system. Chronic tinnitus can limit quality of life, impair normal functioning, and contribute to depression. Two protocols for tinnitus have been noted in the literature. The single-channel protocol involves rewarding alpha at 8–12 Hz and inhibiting delta at the temporal lobes, T3, and T4 (Dohrmann et al., 2007). The two-channel protocol involves alpha theta synchrony training at T3/C4 and T4/C3 (Shulman & Goldstein, 2002). Research has indicated that a 50% reduction in tinnitus symptoms can be expected.

Peak Performance

Using many different single- and two-channel neurofeedback protocols to enhance SMR, alpha and alpha theta synchrony, low beta, and gamma, neurotherapists have helped athletes, golfers, musicians, actors, physicians, opera singers, and businesspersons improve their peak performance. This has allowed clients more controlled access to sensory perceptual control; calm focus; better reaction time; and deeper states of creativity, recovery, and satisfaction. Swingle (2008) wrote that optimal performance training focuses on increasing the brain's efficiency when processing information and on rapid change to the restorative quiet state when sharp focus is no longer required. In other words, efficiency and peak performance can be achieved when using the right brainwave, at the right time, for the right task.

Some neurotherapists have specialized in doing peak performance training and have developed and marketed their own proprietary protocols and equipment. One example of this is Jon Cowan's Peak Achievement Trainer (Cowan, 2007, 2009). Sokhadze (2011) reported that 12 sessions of prefrontal EEG feedback, using "Focus, Alertness, and 40 Hz Neureka" protocols resulted in improved selective attention and other cognitive functions in both clinical and nonclinical populations. More information on the use of neurofeedback for peak performance can be found in Gruzelier and Egner (2003), Gruzelier (2009), and Strack, Linden, and Wilson (2011).

CASE STUDIES

Swallowed Up by Failure

A 29-year-old male college graduate experienced a series of career failures involving being passed over by a college professor for a government service program, having to leave an international service project after becoming ill while abroad, and not being able to get another international project successfully off the ground. Feeling defeated, embarrassed, and humiliated, he cut off all ties with his last project planning team, played far too many hours of daily video and online games in the basement of his father's home, and was unable or unwilling to initiate any sort of job search.

His psychosocial medical history noted early birth trauma and oxygen deprivation. As a child, he was diagnosed with ADHD and as a young adult, treated for depression. His parents were divorced when he was 2 years old. He lived as a young child with his mother who had significant psychopathology. He described her as "very irrational." As a teen, he lived with his father who was an attorney, but he felt overshadowed by a brother who was much more athletic and aggressive than he. He described himself as more creative and intellectual and felt detached and isolated from peers. He enjoyed theater in college but had few significant relationships. When arriving for help, he said he felt like a child who can't move into adult life and complained about significant body tension and sleep problems. At the time, he was taking both stimulant and antidepressant medication and had completed 34 sessions of counseling with little notable progress.

His neurotherapy assessment indicated moderate trauma, inattentive ADHD, mild anxiety, and moderate depression. His computerized Test of Variable Attention (TOVA) found significant problems with both visual and auditory attention, suggesting ADHD. His quantitative electroencephalogram found problems with his occipital lobe, suggesting trauma and sleep problems. His initial problem checklist indicated 19 problems. This client completed 30 total sessions of neurofeedback (NFD) training including 10 sessions of sensory motor rhythm (SMR) work at Cz, 10 sessions of theta alpha gamma (TAG) synchrony work at Fz and Pz, and 10 sessions of TAG at F3 and P4.

The results of his NFB included improved sleep and cessation of night terrors. He also began to sort through and discard some of his old project papers. Then he decided to call several of his most recent project team members who wondered what had happened to him, validated his analysis that the project had to stop, and encouraged him to begin a job search. This was a huge hurdle for him to overcome in confronting his sense of failure, shame, and discouragement. Then in a matter of weeks, he put together a resume, interviewed for a job, and landed a position using many of his specialized skills and talents. His final problem checklist noted 29 improved problems including 12 of his original complaints: anxiety, anger, obsessive thinking, negative thoughts, happiness, being organized, having your act together, motivation, morning routine, feeling a dull memory, and empathy for others. After 2 years of counseling, it was the NFB that seemed to catapult him further down the road in activating many of the goals and action plans he could previously only contemplate but never dare enact.

Homebound and Searching for Confidence

A 22-year-old female college graduate was struggling with her decision to stay near home and attend a local graduate school or enroll in a large urban university several hours away from home. Her appearance was very shy, quiet, and anxious. She wore her long black hair over her face and said only a few words when directly questioned. She reported two significant dating relationships that lasted only a few months before she broke them off. She described her mother as very involved in her life and her father much less so.

Her psychosocial medical history noted a childhood hospitalization for breathing problems and a head injury from an ice skating accident. She also reported a school age incident of attacking another child with a pair of scissors and being diagnosed with ADHD. In addition, she said her father had a history of depression. She has been under the care of a psychologist and psychiatrist since childhood and was currently taking stimulant and antidepressant medication.

Her neurotherapy assessment indicated inattentive ADHD with near clinically significant anxiety problems. Her depression and trauma scores were in the average range. Her TOVA found average visual but significant auditory attention problems. Her QEEG found problems with her occipital and frontal lobes, suggesting trauma, sleep problems, and frontal ADHD. Her initial problem checklist indicated 12 problems. This client completed 30 sessions of sensory motor rhythm (SMR) neurofeedback (NFB) at Cz.

The results of her NFB included much improved interpersonal interaction, sleep, and personal confidence. She began to wear her hair off of her face, her mood greatly lightened, and she initiated extended casual conversation both before and after sessions. Her psychiatrist was reportedly astounded at her change of personality and behavior, never having seen such interpersonal comfort and confidence in her. Her medication was reduced, and after 30 sessions of NFB she reported improvement on eight of her initial 12 problems and 15 other problems not previously recognized. These included impulsiveness, aggression, overfocus, agitation, anxiety, compulsiveness, body tension, hyperactivity, feeling jumpy, can't slow down, being organized, attention and concentration, reading, spaciness or fogginess, motivation, energy, depression, ability to complete tasks requiring several steps, irritability, eye contact with others, talkative, voice calmer or lower, and work preparation. Perhaps most profoundly, she also developed the confidence to leave home and attend graduate school out of town at a large urban university.

Addicted to Avoiding Family Conflict

A 37-year-old male with a college education had a history of disappointment, shame, and guilt surrounding his family relationships; sense of inferiority; and lack of sustained personal achievement. He grew up as the youngest child in an alcoholic family of origin with reportedly successful siblings. He struggled with enuresis into his teenage years and recalled physical conflict with his alcoholic father. Despite several attempts at establishing a meaningful career path, he seemed to become unsettled whenever conflict emerged and soon found a way to escape. Then after mounting frustration with his sister and falling short yet one more time, he cut off all ties with his family and moved across the country. His lengthy detachment from his family ended after his mother, checking upon his whereabouts, made her continued concern for him known. He said something within him woke up and he began to make his way back toward his family. He also noted he had used marijuana and/or alcohol on a daily basis but felt it was not a significant problem for him.

His psychosocial medical history noted paternal alcoholism and maternal codependency. He recalled the occurrence of a significant head injury in the fourth grade, and in high school, several likely concussions from playing football. As an adult, he also had a DUI car accident involving air bag deployment. He reported some counseling in his teenage years and 14 more recent sessions both before and after neurofeedback (NFB). His diagnosis was dysthymia and alcohol and cannabis dependence.

His neurotherapy assessment indicated moderate trauma, a tendency toward inattentive ADHD, and significant problems with visual attention (TOVA). His anxiety and depression scores were in the average range. His QEEG found problems at the occipital and frontal lobes and suggested trauma, sleep problems, frontal ADHD, depression, anxiety, and cognitive inefficiency. Many of these are typical of long-term substance abuse. His initial problem checklist indicated 17 problems. He completed 20 sessions of theta alpha gamma synchrony (TAG) NFB at both Fz and Pz and at F3 and P4.

The results of his NFB included improved sleep, less agitation, decreased negative internal chatter, and a generally calmer disposition, allowing him to become less upset when facing conflict and better able to emotionally rebound when emotions became strong. His problem checklist noted improvement in impulsiveness, anxiety, anger, obsessive thoughts, racing thoughts, awareness of dreams, clear thinking, loss of emotional control, and voice calmer and lower. Near the end of NFB, he began to have meaningful conversations with his father and felt ready to face the unresolved and previously daunting issues with his sister. During their first conversation in years, he was able to remain calm, express his thoughts and feelings, empathize with her, and discuss how he might reconnect with his brother-in-law and nieces. He also sought and found meaningful employment, investigated further educational options, and has maintained his sobriety begun 9 months earlier.

Too Stressed to Clean the Silverware

A 71-year-old female entered counseling when her son was sent to jail and her husband was suffering from health complications due to a stroke. She was struggling with many difficult life transitions. She was anxious and drinking alcohol on a daily basis. The initial 10 sessions of counseling focused on assertiveness training to help her "express her voice," on a fairly regular basis. During a particularly difficult counseling session, she exhibited a regular throat-clearing behavior. This tic seemed to occur when she was talking about a highly stressful topic. It was at this time the potential benefits of neuro-therapy were discussed. She decided to begin the assessment process and start a course of neurofeedback training.

Her psychosocial medical history indicated some school age struggle with mathematics. It was also found she had fallen three times in the past 4 years. Two of these falls caused injury to the back of her head, resulting in tender-ness for some time. Finally, her history noted current use of four medications: two for cholesterol, an antidepressant, and a medication for high blood pressure.

Her neurotherapy assessment indicated problems with insomnia and mild anxiety. Her depression score was in the average range. Her Quick QEEG assessment noted problems with low alpha at the midsection resulting in problems with short-term memory and problems at the occipital lobe, suggesting traumatic emotional stress, sleep problems, and self-medicating behavior. Her initial problem checklist indicated seven problems. After initial skin temperature and heart rate variability training, she completed 20 sessions of neurofeedback. As she learned to breathe more deeply and increase her peripheral skin temperature, her tic behavior decreased. Eight sessions of neurofeedback focused on increasing her alpha brainwave at Cz and O1. The remaining sessions worked on her trauma response with theta alpha gamma (TAG) training. She was able to significantly change her peripheral skin temperature after three sessions from 75 to a consistent 90 degrees. She also reported improved sleep. She said, "I am sleeping so well, and even a good friend said I seem so relaxed." Later in training she said, "For some reason, I am handling all my difficult decisions so easily." Her most surprised comment came after week 8, when she said, "All of a sudden, I felt like polishing my sterling silver! I haven't accomplished that in 3 years." Her final problem checklist noted changes in six problems.

When My Body Turned on Me

A 58-year-old, highly educated female inquired about neurofeedback, as it seemed all other medical interventions had not helped her immune deficiency problems. She was depressed and in the past had conquered obsessive-compulsive disorder with medications and counseling. Overeating and consuming too much alcohol were prevalent coping mechanisms currently. During her psychosocial evaluation, a childhood fall with injury to the right side of the head and a traumatic sexual event were discussed. Her adult trauma inventory score was in the moderate category. The results of the Swingle Quick Q, five-channel EEG assessment, showed decreased short-term memory and retention of information with low alpha at the midsection. Traumatic emotional stress and the trauma signature were prevalent throughout her report, with low alpha at the left occipital lobe. There were reported sleep problems, and this, too, was uncovered in the evaluation, with a need for increased theta/beta ratio at the occipital lobe. At the beginning neurofeedback session, five symptoms were marked on the symptom problem checklist. Fifteen neurofeedback sessions of SMR at the midsection were completed. The second round of 15 sessions was theta alpha gamma synchrony. During these sessions, the patient began exclaiming that she felt "positive, calm, tingly, and alive!" She changed her antidepressant and began having vivid dreams about a new house where she was getting rid of old baggage. A few weeks later, another dream was discussed about her new house where an older, bad lady had to move out. At this session of TAG, she declared that her brain was warm and clear. At the end of our TAG protocols, she exclaimed that she was feeling safe. Her neurotherapist asked when she had last felt safe. Her reply came slowly: "Since before my rape." The remaining 10 sessions were completed at the midsection and the left occipital lobe to increase alpha. At session 39, she told of a lemon tree that she planted after her father's death. It was blooming for the first time. At her final session, she marked no symptoms and declared she felt organized, clear, and motivated.

PROCEDURES FOR EFFECTIVE NEUROFEEDBACK TRAINING

Conducting effective neurofeedback training requires much more than attending to the clinical issues noted above. Details with regard to sensor application, artifact management, working with thresholds, length of training, evaluating session progress, and the resolution of training problems are very important in assuring training success. Without attention to these details, the most skillful assessment, protocol selection, and neurofeedback training may become ineffective.

Sensor Preparation and Placement

Sensors come in a variety of forms. The most typically used sensor has a round metal body that snaps into a blue plastic ring. Other types of sensors clip to the client's ears or are attached to the back of the ear, on the mastoid bone, with a self-adhesive backing. The purpose of all sensors is to conduct or read the electrical activity of the brain. Some neurotherapists refer to sensors as electrodes; however, this may unintentionally alarm a client who may think they transmit electricity to the brain. This, of course, is not the case.

The first step in attaching a sensor is identifying where you want to place it. Sensor placement is guided by the International 10–20 System and the specific neurofeedback protocol being used for training. Sensor location charts, a three-dimensional Styrofoam head map, or an EEG skullcap can guide precise sensor placement. Another method is to manually locate Cz by finding the midpoint between the nasion (point between the eyes at the bridge of the nose) and the inion (point just below the back of the skull bone and the top of the neck vertebrae). This is done by spreading your hands, touching your thumbs, and placing one middle finger on the nasion and the other on the inion. The place where your thumbs fall on the head, centered between the ears, is the Cz location. All other locations can be found by measuring from Cz. Some neurotherapists mark this spot with a grease pencil so they can retain this reference point.

The second step is cleaning the scalp and hair of naturally occurring body oils. This is not a personal hygiene issue but rather a means to abrade the skin surface and secure a good connection to the neurofeedback equipment. Two products are useful in scalp preparation. These are alcohol pads with pumice and abrasive skin preparation gel. Gently pull back the client's hair and rub the identified area with the alcohol pad or abrasive gel. The gel is especially effective for areas of the scalp that have been exposed to the sun. It is important to note that the best electrical connection occurs when the scalp has been mildly abraded. Some clients may be sensitive to alcohol pads. For these clients, abrasive gel and a nonalcohol wipe may sufficiently remove the body oils.

The third step is attaching the sensors. Begin by attaching the sensor to the EXG cable lead. Blue-ringed sensors are attached with 10–20 conductive paste. Squeeze out about a pea- to a marble-sized amount of paste and spread it on the sensor. A wooden craft stick is a useful tool for this purpose. Next pull back the client's hair and gently press and hold the sensor in place. Heat from the client's scalp will cause the paste to soften and spread between the hair to the scalp. To attach ear clip sensors, spread a small amount of conductive paste on the sensor and clip to the ear lobe, gently pressing the clip so it attaches. To attach a self-adhesive sensor, begin by first attaching an EXG cable lead to the sensor. Then slowly pull the cloth backing from the sensor sheet. These are available in sheets of six sensors. Next, without touching the adhesive backing, carefully secure it to the mastoid bone, rubbing the edges of the sensor cloth and pressing on the lead to be sure it is in place.

Once the sensors are in place, it is important to test the strength of your connections. This can be done by turning on the EEG amplifier, opening up the neurotherapy software program, and checking the DC (direct current) offset reading. If the DC offset reading is above 60 Hz, it is possible the connections are weak and one or more sensor must be reattached. This can also be observed by noticing an unusually high, variable, or absent EEG reading. Sometimes sensors are inadvertently placed over a vein. This can cause a heart rate artifact and is observed by a persistent pulse in the EEG. It can be corrected by moving the sensor slightly from the original location.

Managing Distorted EEG and Artifact Interference

Factors other than poor sensor connections can also interfere with an accurate EEG reading. These include 60 Hz electrical interference, client posture and muscle tension, clients' physical and emotional status, and sensor movement or equipment failure. As previously noted, 60 Hz interference can be caused by florescent lighting, electrical power lines, motorized equipment, and radio waves. Client jewelry and cell phones can also cause interference. Jewelry can act like an antenna, drawing in electrical interference, and cell phones can disrupt Bluetooth communication from the EEG amplifier to the computer software. The primary way to manage 60 Hz interference is to avoid it by keeping the EEG equipment away from its influence. Turn off florescent lights, set up the neurotherapy lab away from heavy electrical interference, and ask clients to remove heavy metal jewelry and turn off cell phones before they begin neurofeedback.

Clients' posture and muscle tension can also significantly distort the EEG reading, causing EMG (electomylograph) interference. Clients are best advised to sit up and not cross their legs. Slouching or having their heads pushed forward or too far back can cause muscle tension that will be picked up in the EEG and observed as unusually high EEG readings. Other EMG interference can be caused by teeth clenching, gum chewing, neck and shoulder tension, and eye blinking. These can be managed in a variety of ways. Some-times bringing the problem to the client's attention and offering a simple instruction can be sufficient. For example, say, "Relax your jaw." Other times, a biofeedback instrument, such as an EMG sensor, can be used to provide the client ongoing feedback in reducing the problem. Another way to reduce the problem is to set a neurofeedback inhibit to sound an alarm when the client's high wave (beta) electrical activity is too excessive. An opposite problem involves clients who become too sleepy during training. This can be managed by setting a low inhibit to sound as alarm when the client's slow wave (theta) activity is too high. In time, the client will become able to reduce or increase the interfering artifact.

Another more subtle, but nonetheless very important, type of artifact interference is caused by clients' physical and emotional status. Clients who are thirsty, hungry, tired, or mood altered by drugs or alcohol, and clients who are too cold, too hot, or too distracted by emotional or immediate life issues will not train well. Their EEG readings will be distorted and will not provide an accurate source of feedback. These issues can be managed by providing clients a set of instructions in preparation for neurotherapy. Should they be unable to comply, neurotherapy may be rescheduled and other supportive interventions such as counseling or drug and alcohol treatment recommended. Young children and children with ADHD may also be unable to initially sit for a full neurofeedback training session. Several breaks may be taken during a session to allow them to move around, get a sip of water, or talk before resuming the session. It may also be helpful to alter the training stimulus. For example, children often attend best to audio and video feedback from their favorite DVD. A parent's presence in the room may be useful for the first session until a younger child has developed some comfort in working alone with the neurotherapist. Resistant teenagers who are opposed to training and are only participating at a parent's insistence will also have distorted EEG readings. Personal and family therapy may be advisable before the teen is ready to resume neurofeedback with greater personal motivation.

The last type of artifact interference involves sensor movement and equipment failure. Sometimes during neurofeedback training, the sensor may move due to a client shifting in the chair, heat from the client's head loosening the conductive paste, or thick client hair pushing the sensor out of position. These problems can be managed by using a head band to restrict sensor movement or removing the plastic blue ring and attaching only the metal sensor to the scalp. This reduces the natural tendency of thick hair to move back in place, pushing the sensor off the scalp. Most frustrating to neurotherapists is a problem with equipment failure. This can occur when the batteries are running low, a lead has become corroded, or a lead wire has become damaged. Most EEG amplifiers will signal when the battery power is running low; however, sometimes the battery power will be low and the signal will not be tripped. Some neurotherapists address this problem by routinely replacing the batteries whether or not the low battery signal has tripped. Corroded leads can be cleaned by carefully using a cotton swab to remove greenish corrosion. A broken lead wire must be replaced. Most neurotherapists keep an extra set of lead and ground wires on hand should they fail. An inexpensive ohmmeter can be used to determine if a lead is not functioning properly.

Even after doing all that is possible to reduce the impact of artifacts on the EEG, some artifact interference will still occur. This can be removed from the record with software artifact procedures so accurate assessment and data analysis can be conducted.

Setting Thresholds for Rewards and Inhibits

The clinical art of neurotherapy is knowing where to set and how to adjust the reward and inhibit thresholds within a given neurofeedback protocol. Rewards are set to the brainwave or brainwaves that are targeted for increase, and the inhibits are set for the brainwave or brainwaves targeted for reduction.

In general, both high and low brainwaves (theta and high beta), are inhibited and moderate brainwaves (low beta, SMR, and alpha) are rewarded.

Thresholds can be understood as criteria references. When a client meets an established criterion, the client's brainwave behavior is either rewarded or inhibited. For example, if a client increases his or her alpha brainwave, he or she is presented a video and/or auditory reward that plays his or her favorite music or movie. On the other hand, if a client becomes too sleepy or too anxious, his or her behavior is inhibited by being presented with an auditory alert or warning that repeats until the client reduces the brainwave associated with the alert, causing the annoying sound to stop. For example, a chirping bird alert sounds until the client becomes more alert or a bleep alert sounds until he or she becomes more relaxed.

Thresholds are initially set at the client's current level of performance and then slowly increased for rewards and decreased for inhibits. Most neurotherapists set thresholds so that the client will succeed at the given task 70–90% of the time. The purpose of this is to encourage the client and maintain high motivation for optimal learning. As the client gets better at the task, the threshold is reset, to make the task a little more challenging. Over time, clients strengthen their ability to increase the desired and decrease the undesired brainwave.

It is important to note that threshold levels are not consistent from session to session. Many factors can affect client performance during a given session including the time of day it is conducted, clients' physical and mental status, the effort they are willing to extend that day, and the time between training sessions. Brainwaves change over the course of a day. In general, they are higher earlier in the day and lower as the day progresses. As previously noted, a client's physical and emotional status can also affect training. Some days may be more stressful than others; a client may have had a rough night's sleep or may be coming down with a cold. Also, too short a time between training can impede neuronal recovery, disallowing the resolution of inflammation caused by neurofeedback training. Just as muscles become inflamed after exercise, exercised neuronal pathways also become inflamed. As previously noted, dietary supplements can decrease this problem, but sufficient time between training sessions is indicated to reduce training-induced inflammation. Finally, to make matters even more complicated, while in general we expect brainwaves to increase or decrease over the course of training, sometimes they do not. Instead, a client's ability to access a needed state improves, as does activation of their underlying neural networks.

Length of Training

As presented in the single-channel and two-channel protocol section of this chapter, neurofeedback training can take anywhere from a few sessions to 100 sessions, depending upon the selected protocol, to be effective. Most typical one-channel training takes about 30 to 40 sessions to complete. This includes treatment for ADHD, insomnia, chronic pain, migraine headaches, tics, dystonia, and seizures. Typical two-channel training takes about 10 to 20 sessions to complete, although when used for addiction and mood disorders it may take 20 to 40 to 60 sessions. Other types of training may take 10 to 20 sessions. This includes training for depression, anxiety, and cognitive efficiency. Finally, training for autism spectrum disorders, requiring the use of several treatment protocols, can take from 60 to 100 neurofeedback sessions.

The number of training sessions needed to complete treatment depends upon the needs of the individual client and his or her trainability, adherence to training preparation instructions, and reported symptom reduction. Many clients will report observable change after as few as 5 to 10 sessions; however, they should be encouraged to continue training to consolidate and strengthen the gains they've made in early treatment.

Most training sessions last about 1 hour. The first few minutes involve checking in with the client and setting up the neurofeedback sensors, equipment, and software. Checking in is very important because it will provide feedback about progress, problems associated with training, or the need for other assistance such as counseling. The usual time needed to train one site is about 20 to 30 minutes. If two sites are being trained in a single session, then 10 to 15 minutes are spent on each site. Two-channel training takes about 25 minutes, with 20 minutes focused on the main protocol, such as alpha theta synchrony, and 5 minutes on the secondary protocol, gamma training. The last few minutes of a session are used to remove the sensors; clean the client's hair of any residue conductive paste; discuss any reactions to the training session; and handle administrative details such as billing, rescheduling, and session notes.

Evaluating Change During Training

Clinical observation skills, client feedback, problem checklists, and changes in brainwave amplitude are the main methods used to evaluate change during neurofeedback training. Clients' nonverbal reactions to training can be very informative. Do they appear to be emotional, dizzy, bored, fatigued, excited, relaxed, unsettled, or disoriented? Are their overall reactions positive or negative? A simple way to confirm clinical observation is to seek verbal feedback from the client. This can be done by asking an open-ended question such as, "How do you feel?" or "What are you thinking?" If a client has difficulty verbalizing his or her feelings, the neurotherapist can ask a scaling question such as, "On a scale of one to 10, where one equals calm and 10 equals anxious, how would you rate your current feelings?"

Clients who have initial negative reactions to training may be adjusting to the strain of focus required to do neurotherapy, may be experiencing new, unfamiliar feelings they are trying to process, or may be having a negative reaction to some aspect of the training protocol. Be sure to explore the specific nature of their reaction and do not rush to judgment. What appears to be a negative reaction may be a normal response to deeper states of relaxation or a reasonable emotional reaction to a release of pent-up emotional trauma.

If clients become fatigued during training, consider taking several small breaks. If clients become bored, consider changing the training reward from visual to audio (eyes open to eyes closed task) or from one type of stimulus task screen to another (video game to puzzle pictures). If a client reports dizziness or disorientation, have him or her sit quietly until he or she feels better, then slowly walk around, get a drink of water, and readjust to his or her surroundings before driving home in a car. Also ask disoriented clients to monitor their reaction through the rest of the day and follow up with them at the beginning of the next session. If a client's performance during a session increases and then decreases, this may be a sign of fatigue. Consider finishing the session, taking a break, or training another scalp location. If a client becomes tearful after alpha theta synchrony training, do not be alarmed. He or she is likely having an abreaction and processing some previously unavailable emotional material. Let the client take a few moments to work through it, verbally reflect his or her comments and feelings, reassure him or her of its therapeutic value, or refer the client for counseling should he or she need more help in processing the new insight. Finally, if a client's negative reaction is related to the training protocol, consider changing the threshold setting, the protocol, or the sensor scalp location. Demos (2005) discussed such reactions and suggested switching from training on the right hemisphere to the left or from the anterior (front of the brain) to the posterior (back).

Many clients will have very positive reactions to training. They will feel more relaxed, experience a release of tension, gain a new sense of clarity or insight, and feel in a better mood. Some will report relief from a headache, less brain fog, an invigorated tingliness, or new-felt body warmth. Others will report improved sleep, restored dreaming, and better interactions with others. It is important to acknowledge these experiences, as they are signs of meaningful progress but not necessarily indications of completed treatment. Completed treatment is also associated with presenting symptom reduction. Be aware that some clients may become so excited about their initial symptom relief that they may consider discontinuing treatment. Overtraining or training beyond initial symptom relief has been found to consolidate and strengthen overall neurofeedback training results.

The use of a symptom checklist is a very effective way of tracking within and across session progress. It offers an operational bridge from brainwave activity to real-life behavioral changes. As part of the initial neurotherapy assessment, clients usually complete a symptom checklist. It is not uncommon for them to indicate problems with 15 or more of some 60 possible symptoms. After 10 sessions, clients typically report half of their symptoms have improved. A symptom checklist is also helpful for clients who lack self-awareness. The items bring to mind areas of improvement not previously noticed. In fact, many clients will report improvement over the course of neurotherapy in several areas not indicated in their initial checklist. Checklists can be administered after each session or after every 10 sessions.

A final method of evaluating change during training is to monitor the baseline amplitude of targeted brainwaves. Within-session change in brainwave variability and changes in amplitude (increases or decreases) are meaningful. They suggest the client has strengthened his or her ability to access and change the targeted brainwave. Across-session changes of 15–20% in baseline brainwave amplitude also indicates significant change. For example, consider a child with ADHD who has too much slow wave (theta) brainwave activity. A decrease in the theta wave from 32 Hz to 26 Hz is significant and will likely result in a meaningful decrease in that child's inattentive behavior. If a child can access and change a targeted brainwave during a neurofeedback session, this new ability will generalize to real-world settings at home and school.

Resolving Training Problems

Even after attending to the issues noted above that can influence effective neurofeedback training, some clients still may not train well. These are clients who are highly anxious, experiencing other immediate psychosocial stressors, overly medicated, poorly motivated, possessing unrealistic expectations, or unable to learn from neurofeedback training. While some interventions may assist these clients in benefiting from neurotherapy, other clinical interventions may be necessary before they can resume neurofeedback training.

Highly anxious clients may be too preoccupied with their physiological distress and cognitive ruminations to sufficiently focus on the task required for effective neurofeedback. They may benefit from skin temperature training and diaphragmatic breathing skills; hypnosis or mental imagery work; or psychotherapy intended to help them recognize, challenge, and decrease their internal negative dialogue. In addition, the neurotherapist can keep watch for rogue beta spikes, indicative of high anxiety, in the client's EEG and set inhibits to alert the client and help them down-train their distracting anxiety.

Clients who are distracted by immediate psychosocial stressors such as overwhelming family conflict, divorce, job loss, death of a loved one, legal problems, or serious physical illness may also be unable to attend to the task of neurofeedback. Despite the potential benefit of neurotherapy to help them resolve the impact of personal distress, their attention may be better focused on their needs for personal adjustment, counseling, legal guidance, and medical treatment. When ready, initial neurotherapy may best focus on deep state training to resolve any emotional trauma related to the distress before attending to other specific problem areas.

Clients sometimes begin neurofeedback training on some type of medication prescribed by their physician or psychiatrist for medical, psychological, or behavioral problems. This is usually not a problem. As neurotherapy proceeds, their need for medication may decrease. As long as there is open communication between the neurotherapist and the prescribing professional, these adjustments can be coordinated. However, in some cases with poor communication and lack of coordination, continued medication use can sabotage neurofeedback training, distort the EEG, and inhibit training progress. A direct discussion with the client about this problem is advisable so that he or she can make an informed decision about continuing or discontinuing neurofeedback.

Although most clients are highly motivated to begin neurotherapy, some are not. A notable example includes resistant teenagers from highly dysfunctional families. They may have been forced into treatment as a consequence of longstanding misbehavior. Their rebellious attitude and defiant position will make their cooperation in neurofeedback difficult, if not impossible, to gain. Another example are clients who refuse to change an unhealthy lifestyle such as clients in an abusive relationship, clients with poor diet or sleep hygiene, or clients with ongoing substance abuse problems. Neurotherapy at this time of their lives may not be helpful because these issues will interfere with its effectiveness. After they become willing to address these problems and grow more stabilized with their lifestyle, neurotherapy may be more effective.

Clients with unrealistic expectations may also be disappointed in neurofeedback's benefit in their lives. The neurofeedback research, while impressive, does not suggest clients will have 100% resolution of their problems, and some problems are more complicated, requiring additional types of intervention to remedy. For example, consider the problems of weight loss and school performance. While neurofeedback may help resolve anxiety, depression, and the influence of trauma and personality disorders involved in weight gain, weight loss also requires a change of diet and exercise. The same is true with school performance. Neurofeedback can help resolve ADHD and specific learning disorders, but it cannot teach study skills or make students do their homework. These behaviors require another set of skills and organizational abilities that, when combined with neurofeedback, can achieve a satisfying outcome. Neurofeedback can provide a sound neurological platform but cannot fully resolve all clients' presenting concerns.

Finally, other clients may not benefit from neurofeedback training because they may be unable to learn from the methods neurofeedback employs, utilizing visual and auditory operant conditioning of brain electrical activity. Visually and hearing-impaired persons, clients with severe structural brain damage or mental retardation, and clients in prolonged unconscious states or comas may have great difficulty benefiting from neurofeedback training. Some work has been done in using tactile forms of stimulation and in working with clients who are in mild coma states (Ayers, 1999); however, this work has not found its way into the repertoire of most trained neurotherapists.

CONCLUSIONS

Effective neurofeedback training requires a delicate balance between knowledge of neuroscience and neurotherapy; confidence with computer software and EEG technology; and therapeutic skill in observation, empathy, and communication. This chapter presented the nuts and bolts of neurofeedback training. It detailed the basic design of the neurotherapy lab. It stressed the importance of the client–neurotherapist relationship, and it reviewed several considerations in preparing the client for training.

The chapter also highlighted the general approaches of single-channel and two-channel neurofeedback training. It provided an overview of the most common neurofeedback training protocols, described their use, sensor placement, and the brainwaves they target for change. Several case examples were presented. They illustrated some of the more common protocols and offered a brief summary of their impact in reducing both the client's presenting concern and other concerns only recognized by the client after neurofeedback training was completed.

Finally the chapter outlined several procedural concerns necessary to ensure neurotherapy's effectiveness. These included sensor preparation and placement, managing EEG and artifact interference, setting reward and inhibit thresholds, length of training, evaluation of change during training, and resolution of training problems.

Learning to become an effective neurotherapist is a challenging task. The required knowledge base and technical skill set is very unfamiliar to most therapists. However, when brought together, the technical knowledge and clinical expertise of a trained therapist provides a powerful synergy for client change.

REFERENCES

Amen, D. G. (2001). *Healing ADD*. New York: Putnam.

Anderson, J. (2010). *Professional EEG Biofeedback Certification Training*. San Rafael, CA: Stens Corporation.

Ayers, M. E. (1987). *Electroencephalographic neurofeedback and closed head injury of 250 individuals*. Paper presented at the National Head Injury Conference, Beverly Hills, CA.

Ayers, M. E. (1995a). Long-term follow-up of EEG neurofeedback with absence seizures. *Biofeedback and Self-Regulation, 20*(3), 309–310.

Ayers, M. E. (1995b). EEG neurofeedback to bring individuals out of level two coma (Abstract). *Proceedings of the 26th Annual Meeting of the Association for Applied Psychophysiology and Biofeedback,* 9–10.

Ayers, M. E. (1999). Assessing and treating open head injury, coma, and stroke using real-time digital EEG neurofeedback. In J. R. Evans & A. Abarbanel (Eds.), *Introduction to quantitative EEG and neurofeedback* (pp. 203–222). New York: Academic.

Baehr, E., Rosenfeld, J. P., Baeher, R., & Ernest, C. (1999). Clinical use of an alpha asymmetry neurofeedback protocol in the treatment of mood disorders. In J. R. Evans & A. Abarbanel (Eds.), *Introduction to quantitative EEG and neurofeedback* (pp. 181–201). New York: Academic.

Boklage, C. E. (1977). Discussion paper: Embryonic determination of brain programming asymmetry—a caution concerning the use of data on twins in genetic inferences about mental development. *Evolution and Lateralization of the Brain, 299,* 306–308.

Budzynski, T. H. (1979). Biofeedback and the twilight states of consciousness. In D. Goleman & R. J. Davidson (Eds.), *Consciousness: Brain, states of awareness, and mysticism* (pp. 142-144). New York: Harper & Row.

Budzynski, T., Budzynski, H. K., & Tansey, H. Y. (1999). Brain brightening: Restoring the aging mind. In J. R. Evans (Ed.), *Handbook of neurofeedback: Dynamics and clinical applications* (pp. 231–258). New York: Informa Healthcare.

Cowan, J. (2007). *Peak Achievement Trainer manual and workbook.* Goshen, KY: Neurotek LLC.

Cowan, J. (2009). *Peak Brain Happiness Trainer manual.* Goshen, KY: Neurotek LLC.

Dailey, D. (2009). *Alpha-theta synchrony user's guide.* Santa Clara, CA: Mind Growing.

Dailey, D. (2013). Theta-Alpha-Gamma Synchrony: Operations-Introduction. A Matter of Mind. Santa Clara, CA. www.tagsynchrony.com.

Daniels, J. K., Frewen, P., McKinnon, M. C., & Lanius, R. D. (2011). Default mode alterations in posttraumatic stress disorder related to early life trauma: A developmental perspective. *Journal of Psychiatry and Neuroscience, 36*(1) 56–59.

Demos, J. N. (2005). *Getting started with neurofeedback.* New York: Norton.

Dohrmann, K., Weisz, N., Schlee, W., Hartmann, T., & Elbert, T. (2007). Neurofeedback for treating tinnitus. *Progress in Brain Research, 166,* 473–485.

Fisher, S. (2004). *FPO2 Protocol Outline.* Glendale, CA: EEG Spectrum International.

Gruzelier, J. (2009). A theory of alpha/theta neurofeedback, creative performance enhancement, long distance functional connectivity and psychological integration. *Cognitive Process, 10,* 101–109.

Gruzelier, J. H., & Egner, T. (2003). Ecological validity of neurofeedback modulation of slow wave EEG enhances musical performance. *Neuroreport, 14*(9), 1221–1224.

Hammer, B. U., Colbert, A. P., Brown, K. A., & Ilioni, E. C. (2011). Neurofeedback for insomnia: A pilot study of z-score SMR and individualized protocols. *Applied Psychophysiology and Biofeedback, 36*, 251–264.

Hammond, D. C. (2005). Neurofeedback treatment of depression and anxiety. *Journal of Adult Development, 12*(2–3), 131–137.

Hill, R. W., & Castro, E. (2009). *Healing young brains.* Charlottesville, VA: Hampton Roads.

Jarusiewicz, B. (2002). Efficacy of neurofeedback for children in the autism spectrum: A pilot study. *Journal of Neurotherapy, 6*(4), 39–49.

Jirsa, V., & Muller, V. (2013). Cross-frequency coupling in real and virtual brain networks. *Frontiers in Computational Neuroscience, 7*(78). doi: 10.3389/fncom.2013.00078

Kahn, S. (2013). Local and long-range functional connectivity is reduced in concert in autism spectrum disorders. *Proceedings of the National Academy of Sciences, 110*(8), 3107–3112.

Lubar, J. F. (1995). Neurofeedback for the management of attention-deficit hyperactivity disorders. In M. S. Schwartz and Associates (Eds.), *Biofeedback: A practitioner's guide* (2nd ed., pp. 493–522). New York: Guilford.

Moore, N. C. (2000). A review of EEG biofeedback treatment for anxiety disorders. *Clinical Electroencephalography, 31*(1), 1–6.

Othmer, S. (2007). *EEG info presents protocol guide: Case study with Sue Othmer, BCIAC.* Woodland Hills, CA: EEG Institute.

Othmer, S. (2008). *Protocol guide for neurofeedback clinicians.* Woodland Hills, CA: EEG Info.

Peniston, E., Marrinan, D., Deming, W., & Kulkosky, P. (1993). EEG alpha-theta brainwave synchronization in Vietnam theatre veterans with combat-related post-traumatic stress disorder and alcohol abuse. *Advances in Medical Psychotherapy, 6*, 37–50.

Peniston, E. G., & Kulkosky, P. J. (1989). Alpha-theta brainwave training and beta-endorphin levels in alcoholics. *Alcoholism: Clinical and Experimental Research, 13*(2), 271–279.

Peniston, E. G., & Kulkosky, P. J. (1990). Alcoholic personality and alpha-theta brainwave training. *Medical Psychotherapy, 3*, 37–55.

Peniston, E. G., & Kulkosky, P. J. (1999). Neurofeedback in the treatment of addictive disorders. In J. R. Evans & A. Abarbanel (Eds.), *Introduction to quantitative EEG and neurofeedback* (pp. 103–143). San Diego, CA: Academic.

Rosenfeld, J. P. (2000). An EEG biofeedback protocol for affective disorders. *Clinical Electroencephalography, 31*(1), 7–12.

Scott, W., & Kaiser, D. (1998). Augmenting chemical dependency treatment with neurofeedback training. *Journal of Neurotherapy, 3*(1), 66.

Scott, W., Kaiser, D., Othmer, S., & Sideroff, S. (2005). Effects of an EEG biofeedback protocol on a mixed substance abuse population. *American Journal of Drug and Alcohol Abuse, 31*(3), 455–469.

Shulman, A., & Goldstein, B. (2002). Quantitative electroencephalography: Preliminary report—tinnitus. *International Tinnitus Journal, 8*(2), 77–86.

Sokhadze, E. T. (2011). Peak performance training using prefrontal EEG biofeedback. *Biofeedback, 40,* (1) 7–15.

Soutar, R., & Longo, R. (2011). *Doing neurofeedback: An introduction.* San Rafael, CA: ISNR Research Foundation.

Sterman, M. B. (2000a). Basic concepts and clinical findings in the treatment of seizure disorders with EEG operant conditioning. *Clinical Electroencephalography, 30*(1), 45–55.

Sterman, M. B. (2000b). EEG markers for attention deficit disorder: Pharmacological and neurofeedback applications. *Child Study Journal, 30*(1), 1–22.

Strack, B. W., Linden, M. K., & Wilson, V. S. (2011). *Biofeedback and neurofeedback applications in sports psychology.* Wheat Ridge, CO: Association for Applied Psychophysiology and Biofeedback.

Swingle, P. G. (2008). *Biofeedback for the brain: How neurotherapy effectively treats depression, ADHD, autism, and more.* Piscataway, NJ: Rutgers University Press.

Tansey, M. A. (1993). Ten year stability of EEG biofeedback results for a hyperactive boy who failed fourth grade perpetually impaired class. *Biofeedback and Self-Regulation, 18,* 33–44.

Thompson, L., & Thompson, M. (1998). Neurofeedback combined with training in metacognitive strategies: Effectiveness in students with ADD. *Applied Psychophysiology and Biofeedback, 23*(4), 243–263.

Thompson, M., & Thompson, L. (2002). Biofeedback for movement disorders (dystonia with Parkinson's disease): Theory and preliminary results. *Journal of Neurotherapy, 6*(4), 51–70.

Thompson, M., & Thompson, L. (2003). *The neurofeedback book: An introduction to basic concepts in applied psychophysiology.* Wheat Ridge, CO: Association for Applied Psychophysiology and Biofeedback.

Walker, J. E., & Norman, C. A. (2006). The neurophysiology of dyslexia: A selective review with implications for neurofeedback remediation and results of treatment in twelve consecutive patients. *Journal of Neurotherapy, 10*(1), 45–55.

White, N. E. (1999). Theories of the effectiveness of alpha-theta training for multiple disorders. In J. R. Evans & A. Abarbanel (Eds.), *Introduction to quantitative EEG and neurofeedback* (pp. 341–364). San Diego, CA: Academic.

9

NEUROFEEDBACK EFFICACY RESEARCH

The brain is designed to grab what input it can and then boil it up into a froth of understanding.

—John McCrone

The role of research is important in the development of any therapeutic intervention. This is especially true of any new, relatively unknown intervention that potentially challenges conventional treatment methods and assumptions. Although neurofeedback laboratory research began many decades ago, with the advent of advanced electroencephalography (EEG) and computer technology, it has today experienced a resurgent clinical interest. It is now practical for individual practitioners to become trained and supervised, purchase the equipment, and provide neurofeedback training as another clinical strategy in the treatment of many psychological and behavioral disorders. As a third clinical option, alongside counseling and medication (Russell-Chapin & Chapin, 2011), neurofeedback research has exploded with over 250 studies in the past 7 years (Myers & Young, 2012). However, many important questions remain to be answered in fully evaluating its efficacy. This is no simple matter. While many outcome studies have reported impressive results, their designs have been criticized, casting doubt on neurofeedback's benefit to clients. More recent work with extensive reviews, meta-analyses, improved research design, and brain imaging studies have improved neurofeedback's efficacy ratings, with many respected mental health and medical professionals calling for its use in clinical practice.

The purpose of this chapter is to review neurofeedback's outcome and efficacy research. This will be done by first discussing several research issues. These will include the differences between outcome and efficacy research, the primary criticisms of neurofeedback research as these relate to issues of research design, demand characteristics and the placebo effect, different types of research and their value in demonstrating efficacy, and the Association for Applied Psychophysiology and Biofeedback and American Psychological

Association's efficacy rating criteria. Next, the chapter will review the current efficacy rating and relevant outcome research of the major applications of neurofeedback to include attention deficit hyperactivity disorder, anxiety, depression, substance abuse, and post-traumatic stress disorder. It will then present a brief summary of the research and current efficacy of several other treatment applications including chronic pain, epilepsy, headaches, insomnia, traumatic brain injury, autism spectrum disorders, cognitive efficiency, and personality disorders. The chapter will conclude by presenting several valuable resources for further review of current neurofeedback research and endorsements from several respected mental health and medical experts.

RESEARCH ISSUES

Clinical research is a complicated but essential endeavor. Without it, practitioners cannot be certain whether the impact they are observing is caused by the intervention or a host of other factors that can also influence treatment results. Although encouraging, it is not enough to observe positive outcomes. Confidence in any single intervention is most fully experienced when its efficacy has been demonstrated. What is the difference between outcome and efficacy research? What are the major criticisms of neurofeedback research? How do different types of research affect conclusions about efficacy, and what does the American Psychological Association have to say about the matter of efficacy research? These are a few of the questions whose answers will provide the foundation to help evaluate the existing neurofeedback research and its clinical value to clients and practitioners.

DIFFERENCES BETWEEN OUTCOME
AND EFFICACY RESEARCH

In health care, the terms "outcome research" and "efficacy research" are often used interchangeably. While they are both interested in evaluating the effect of clinical interventions, they do so from very different perspectives (Mulley, 1990). In general, outcome research is interested in looking at the benefits to a client or patient, and efficacy research is interested in clarifying the impact of a specific intervention on the outcome.

The outcome of a clinical research study is most often focused on the resolution or reduction of a targeted problem or complaint such as improved attention, reduced feelings of depression, or fewer panic attacks. Many factors come into play to achieve this end. Some of these might include type of counseling, type and amount of medication, biofeedback, or group therapy, not to mention other factors such as length of treatment, therapist's expertise, and client motivation. In outcome research, the focus is on the ends more than the means, although it can be very useful to know which means produce the best outcomes.

In efficacy research, the focus is on evaluating the effectiveness of a specific intervention apart from all the other influences, so that a conclusion about its relative benefit can be confidently made. In efficacy research, as many factors as possible must be accounted for and controlled, so they do not influence the actual effect of the specific intervention. This allows any conclusion about the value of the intervention to be attributed primarily to the intervention and not to the other factors. This is a very challenging task and requires a specialized knowledge of rigorous research design.

Clinical efficacy research is especially challenging because it involves human subjects in a nonlaboratory, less controlled setting, struggling with serious problems, often conducted by clinicians, not researchers, with limited funding and assistance, and a bias toward client care, not rigorous research design. In general, clinicians care more about outcomes than efficacy. They tend to be less concerned about control groups, double-blind interventions, and the placebo effect. This bias is what influenced much, but not all, of the early neurofeedback research and led to many often legitimate criticisms by more tough-minded researchers (Robbins, 2008). Although politics and professional turf issues were also implicated, the gauntlet was thrown down and the research issues could not be ignored. Even with very impressive outcomes, the efficacy of neurofeedback as the primary intervention was yet to be demonstrated. This motivated neurofeedback researchers to develop a template or set of guidelines to evaluate the clinical efficacy of its interventions (La Vaque et al., 2002) and stimulated a quality improvement effort that continues today, to rate the clinical efficacy of neurofeedback interventions based upon a periodic and critical review of the current research.

CRITICISMS OF NEUROFEEDBACK RESEARCH

Robbins (2008) documented several criticisms of neurofeedback research made by prominent experts in ADHD including Russell Barkley and Sam Goldstein and a national expert in addiction treatment, Norman Hoffman. These included limitations of the case study method, lack of control for the placebo effect, insufficient data, nonrandomized assignment to treatment conditions, little follow-up to assess duration of change, too few subjects, and failure to use trained research assistants to deliver the interventions. He also noted criticisms from fellow neurotherapists, Edward Taub and Lester Fehmi, and a failed replication attempt by Ken Graap, a Ph.D. candidate, and David Freides, a psychologist at Emory University in Atlanta. Their criticisms included the use of a treatment package confounding the specific impact of the neurofeedback intervention, the lack of a sham or convincing fake control condition, huge demand characteristics of a charismatic clinician likely increasing the placebo effect, failure to replicate, inconsistent controls on subjects' use of medication during intervention, reported use of Omni Prep (an abrasive cleanser) as a conductance paste, and too much hype about impressive results that got ahead of the science.

Although Robbins (2008) exposed many of the flaws and biases behind some of the criticisms noted above, the damage to the reputation of neurofeedback research was significant. It did not matter that Barkley clearly lacked information about neurofeedback and had a clear bias toward medication treatment for ADHD, or that Goldstein had a blind spot in failing to recognize neurofeedback as a nonmedication method to improve the IQ and performance of children with ADHD. It also did not matter that Hoffman, despite 20 years of reviewing addiction research, had never reviewed a neurofeedback study, or that Graap's and Freides's inexperience with neurofeedback may have contributed to their failure to replicate previous research. Despite the exciting and positive outcomes in neurofeedback research, what mattered were the obvious flaws in research design and the resulting limitation in evaluation of its efficacy.

RESEARCH-BASED CRITERIA FOR LEVELS OF CLINICAL EFFICACY

According to La Vaque et al. (2002), there are 10 levels of clinical trial design that form an accepted hierarchy of "scientific power" to determine whether a particular intervention is empirically supported or validated. These can be further grouped into five levels of efficacy, from "not empirically supported" to "efficacious and specific," and parallel the research efficacy rating system of the American Psychological Association.

The first five of the 10 levels of clinical trial design, from the weakest to the strongest, is anecdotal evidence. It is a narrative report of an observation that a certain treatment seems to have worked. It is considered to be without scientific value but may motivate further examination. The second level of design is an uncontrolled case study. It is also scientifically weak but may have defined independent and dependent variables and can lead to a more controlled study. The third level of design is historical control. It assumes that the nature of the disorder is so well known that controls are unnecessary in demonstrating that the intervention has been effective. This rarely occurs, but an example would be an intervention that prolongs the life of an Alzheimer's patient. The fourth level of design is observational study. It involves retrospective or prospective studies that are case controlled but not randomized or blind. The validity of observational studies has been found to be near those of randomized and blind studies. The fifth level of design is a wait list or intention-to-treat control group. This is commonly used in clinical settings and typically involves random assignment to the wait list or treatment condition. This design controls for maturational factors but does not control for experimenter bias and other nonspecific factors. It does carry with it ethical concerns regarding failure to treat the waiting list subjects and does risk influence from lack of a sham treatment in a repeated measures design.

The sixth of the 10 levels of clinical trial designs is the within-subject and intrasubject replication design or the "A-B-A" design. It involves giving the intervention, reversing it, and giving it again. This is a powerful design but may be less so unless the experimenter is blind to the reversal condition. It also has ethical issues in intentionally reversing the subjects' symptoms. The seventh design is single-blind, random assignment control with a sham or active treatment condition. In this design, the subject is blind to the treatment but the experimenter is not. It controls for nonspecific subject influences but not for experimenter bias. It too involves ethical problems in not treating some subjects. The eighth design is the double-blind control study with sham or active treatment and random assignment. This blinds both the subject and the experimenter and is a very strong design. The ninth design level involves a treatment equivalence or treatment superiority design. An example would be comparing a known drug treatment to an unknown, nondrug treatment. All subjects are being treated, thus avoiding that ethical issue, but known placebo effects must be considered in comparing the outcomes. The 10th level of design involves more sophisticated designs such as a Solomon Four Square design that involves repeated measures and controls for priming or learning effects from pretest administration or meta-analyses, reviewing multiple research studies and concluding significant effect sizes across these studies.

In addition there are five specific levels of efficacy in determining a particular intervention's demonstrated effectiveness. From weakest to strongest is Level 1: not empirically supported. This involves anecdotal reports or case studies. The second is Level 2: possibly efficacious. This involves at least one study with sufficient statistical power and outcome measures but lacks random assignment to a control condition. The third is Level 3: probably efficacious. This involves multiple observational studies, clinical studies, wait list controls, and within-subject and intrasubject replication of efficacy. The fourth is Level 4: efficacious. This involves a no-treatment, alternate treatment, or sham control using random assignment, with sufficient statistical power, appropriate statistical analysis, and valid and reliable outcome measures. It must be conducted with a sample that meets inclusion criteria indicative of the treated problem, and all procedures must be clearly defined to allow replication. In addition, the research results must have been found in two independent research settings. The fifth is Level 5: efficacious and specific. The intervention must be shown to have been superior to a sham therapy, medication, or alternative bona fide treatment in at least two independent settings.

The American Psychological Association also developed a set of guidelines and criteria for evaluating the efficacy of clinical interventions. Its guidelines focused on mental disorders and the psychological aspects of physical disorders (APA, 1995, 2002). Its intent was to design a method to review existing clinical research toward the establishment of evidence-based clinical practice. The La Vaque et al. (2002) criteria, used by the Association for Applied Psychophysiology and Biofeedback, and the APA (1995, 2002) guidelines are very similar. They both have as their highest level of efficacy empirically supported interventions that are both efficacious and specific, and as their lowest, research indicating the intervention is not empirically supported.

The reason both sets of guidelines are important is that the professionals within each organization provide treatment for many of the same psychological and physiological problems. Among these are ADHD, anxiety, depression, substance abuse, and trauma. Each organization necessarily retains oversight of its member's practices, but territorial influence can and does overlap. At times this can lead to a challenging debate, especially when differing opinions about the level of efficacy of neurofeedback for a particular problem seem to pit one group against the other. Regardless of any potential political, financial, or professional turf issues, both clients and practitioners are best served when strong efficacy research more fully demonstrates the positive outcomes noted in clinical practice.

NEUROFEEDBACK EFFICACY RATING AND OUTCOME RESEARCH

Major Applications

Any review of the efficacy rating and outcome research for neurofeedback must acknowledge several assumptions and limitations. First, a low efficacy rating does not necessarily mean the intervention is not effective. It may mean that the available research is not strong enough to confidently demonstrate efficacy. Second, many of the studies cited below present impressive intervention outcomes based upon valid and behaviorally meaningful dependent measures, but because of weaknesses in the research design, these outcomes could also be due to other factors previously noted in this chapter. Third, the most recent comprehensive review of the neurofeedback research is relatively old. Its efficacy ratings date to 2008 (Yucha & Montgomery, 2008).

The original goal of the efficacy review committee was to update its report every 3 years. This is an enormous task. Since 2008, much additional research, with stronger design, has been conducted but has not made its way into Yucha and Montgomery's (2008) comprehensive updated evidence-based review of neurofeedback. Therefore, some of the recent research studies, a few calling for improvement of the current efficacy rating, will be included in the following brief review of highlighted neurofeedback research. Finally, it is important to note that the determination of efficacy is an ongoing process that is open at any point in time to differences in interpretation, professional opinion, and sometimes heated debate. However, from a purely clinical perspective, at the end of the day, clients make the final determination of the personal value of any intervention on changing and improving their lives.

Attention Deficit Hyperactivity Disorder

The flagship application of neurofeedback has been ADHD and its outcome, and efficacy research has spawned the greatest debate of any application. As previously noted, Russell Barkley, an expert in ADHD, has been an especially vocal critic of neurofeedback for ADHD, but he has also acknowledged the utility of the electroencephalogram in studying the brain processes of children with ADHD (Loo & Barkley, 2005). More specifically, Barkley has recognized the work of Monastra et al. (1999), who found higher frontal and central theta and lower beta brainwaves in children with ADHD, leading to the use of the theta–beta ratio as a diagnostic tool in the assessment of ADHD. Barkley remains outspoken about the weaknesses of neurofeedback research and recommends better-controlled studies with larger sample sizes before it can be rated as an efficacious and specific treatment for ADHD.

The initial neurofeedback research was conducted by Lubar et al. (1995). In that study, he and his colleagues provided 40 hours of neurofeedback to 19 youth from 8 to 19 years old. Using a pretest–posttest design, 12 of the 18 subjects who showed EEG responsiveness also showed significant improvements on a computerized test of variable attention, and on parent and teacher behavioral ratings. In addition, 10 of the EEG responsive subjects showed a 12-point increase in intelligence test scores.

Better-controlled studies compared neurofeedback to medication treatment. Rossiter and La Vaque (1995) found both neurofeedback and stimulant medication were effective in improving inattention, impulsivity, and information processing. Alhambra, Fowler, and Alhambra (1995) found that 16 of 24 patients were able to reduce or discontinue their medication. Shouse and Lubar (1979), using six different medication and neurofeedback conditions, found that combining neurofeedback and medication resulted in better behavioral performance than drugs alone. Further, the behavioral changes persisted even after the medication was discontinued. Finally, in a very large study of 100 children who were receiving Ritalin, parent counseling, and academic support, Monastra, Monastra, and George (2002) found only the 50 children who had neurofeedback and medication sustained their improvement without the Ritalin.

Other studies investigated the effects of neurofeedback on neurological functioning. Kropotov et al. (2005) recorded the evoked response potentials in 86 children with ADHD, who were divided into groups of good and bad performers after 15 to 22 sessions of neurofeedback. They found that good performers had improved activation of the frontal cortical area associated with the training. A functional magnetic resonance imaging (fMRI) study conducted by Beauregard and Levesque (2006) with 20 unmedicated children with ADHD found the 15 children treated with neurofeedback had activation of several subcortical areas as compared to the control group. They concluded neurofeedback has the capacity to functionally normalize the neuronal networks that mediate attention and response inhibition. Russell-Chapin et al. (2013), in another fMRI study, investigated the default mode network (DMN) of children with ADHD. Pretest assessment found all subjects to have little activation of the DMN in the resting state. After 40 sessions of neurofeedback, the treatment group had more fully activated the DMN network. This is important because the DMN is necessary for internal processing of external experience, and it suggests that neurofeedback can activate complex neuronal networks.

In several review articles, the value of neurofeedback as a nonmedication treatment for ADHD has been well documented. Monastra et al. (2005), after reviewing the empirical evidence and applying the joint efficacy guidelines of the Association for Applied Psychophysiology and Biofeedback and the International Society for Neuronal Regulation, concluded that neurofeedback resulted in significant clinical improvement for approximately 75% of the patients in the published research and therefore warranted a rating of "probably efficacious." Hirschberg, Chui, and Frazier (2005), in a review of brain-based intervention for children and adolescents, stated that neurofeedback meets the American Academy of Child and Adolescent Psychiatry clinical guidelines for evidence-based treatment. Arns et al. (2009), in their meta-analysis of the neurofeedback treatment literature for ADHD, reported a large effect size for inattention and impulsivity and a medium effect size for hyperactivity. They concluded that the more recent research utilizing active sham control groups warranted the highest level of efficacy rating: "efficacious and specific." Sherlin et al. (2010), in a position paper on neurofeedback for the treatment of ADHD, concurred and detailed a list of conclusions and recommendations.

The conclusions were that neurofeedback for ADHD meets the criteria for "efficacious and specific." Neurofeedback has been found to have long-term effects, lasting 3 to 6 months, but more research should be done to study the effects after 3 to 5 years. Neurofeedback appears to offer similar effects to medication for inattention and impulsivity. Additional research should focus on the mechanisms of neurofeedback. Further research should also focus on effective methods to decrease the number of required sessions. Neurofeedback is efficacious for inattention and impulsivity, but hyperactivity may be better treated with medication. Neurofeedback can be effectively used with a medication regimen. Licensed health care providers who provide neurofeedback for ADHD should be appropriately trained, and they should consider neurofeedback as a potential modality for the treatment of ADHD.

Continuing research on neurofeedback and ADHD, sponsored by the National Institute of Mental Health, is currently underway. Arnold and Lofthouse of The Ohio State University completed a limited pilot study of neurofeedback for children with ADHD, in which 36 children, ages 6 to 12, were assigned to treatment and sham control conditions and provided 40 sessions of neurofeedback. Their results led them to recommend a large sample, similarly sham-controlled study be conducted by a team of both proponents and critics of neurofeedback with improved subject selection criteria and treatment procedures. Short of this research, their review of neurofeedback treatment of pediatric ADHD led them to conclude neurofeedback is "probably efficacious" for the treatment of ADHD (Lofthouse et al., 2012). The debate and the research continue. At its lowest rating by its strongest critics, neurofeedback for ADHD has been found to be "Level 3—probably efficacious," and at its highest rating by its strongest proponents, it has been found to be "Level 5—efficacious and specific."

Anxiety Disorders

There are several types of anxiety disorders that have different treatment strategies and related outcome research. These include generalized anxiety, phobic, obsessive-compulsive, post-traumatic stress, and panic disorder (Moore, 2000). Post-traumatic stress and panic disorders will be addressed in a separate part of this chapter. It is also important to note that various biofeedback and neurofeedback techniques have been found equally effective in reducing anxiety (Yucha & Montgomery, 2008). Some of the effective biofeedback techniques include electromyography (EMG), galvanic skin response (GSR), skin temperature training (thermal), and heart rate variability (HRV) feedback. In some cases, a combination of EMG and neurofeedback has been found effective. The present discussion will focus primarily on the efficacy of neurofeedback in the reduction of anxiety disorders. Given that anti-anxiety medication can only be used for a short period of time and can be accompanied by unwanted side effects and risk of dependency, biofeedback and neurofeedback treatments for anxiety disorders offer an effective and safe alternative.

Hardt and Kamiya (1978) observed that people with high anxiety have low alpha brainwaves and that increasing or enhancing alpha with five sessions of neurofeedback is useful in reducing anxiety, while decreasing alpha increases state but not trait anxiety. Rice, Blanchard, and Purcell (1993) investigated generalized anxiety, EMG, and five sessions of alpha increase and alpha decrease neurofeedback. They found that all groups had comparable decreases in anxiety and psychosomatic symptoms, but the alpha increase condition also had a significant decrease in heart rate reactivity to stress. Sittenfeld, Budzynski, and Stoyva (1976) investigated EMG and neurofeedback theta increase to reduce stress. They found high frontal EMG subjects were less successful than low frontal EMG subjects in increasing theta and suggested this technique could be helpful with anxiety reduction and problems with sleep onset insomnia. Vanathy, Sharma, and Kumar (1998) compared increased alpha with increased theta neurofeedback and found both procedures effective in reducing anxiety.

Regarding phobias, Garrett and Silver (1976) compared alpha enhancement with EMG biofeedback for students struggling with test anxiety. They found that alpha training increased alpha production from 64–78% and that both techniques were effective in reducing test anxiety. They also found that combined EMG and alpha increase neurofeedback were superior to a relaxation control and no-treatment control group, suggesting the improvement was due to the feedback and not the placebo effect.

Mills and Solyom (1974) reported the absence or decrease of ruminations of five subjects with obsessive-compulsive disorder (OCD) after 20 sessions of alpha enhancement training. However, Glueck and Stroebel (1975), working with inpatients with a variety of psychiatric disorders including OCD, found 20 hours of alpha enhancement training was less effective than transcendental meditation (TM) in improving ruminations. They noted that higher levels of psychopathology were related to decreased ability to produce spontaneous alpha, and TM has been found to produce more relaxing theta than alpha brainwaves.

In a later study that investigated the effectiveness of a third type of neurofeedback, beta or SMR (sensory motor rhythm) training, in reducing the anxiety of 38 cardiac patients, Michael, Krishnaswamy, & Mohamed (2005) found that patients with unstable angina or myocardial infarction could significantly reduce their anxiety after five sessions of beta neurofeedback. This study suggests that in addition to theta and alpha neurofeedback, beta training may also effectively reduce anxiety and have significant benefit in the rehabilitation of cardiac patients.

In a review article on neurofeedback treatment for anxiety disorders, Moore (2000) concluded that there is strong evidence that both alpha and theta enhancements are effective in treating anxiety disorders. Hammond (2005), in his review of neurofeedback treatment for anxiety, recommended 7–12 sessions of neurofeedback to treat anxiety disorders. He also highlighted a study by Passini et al. (1977), who gave 10 hours of alpha neurofeedback training to anxious alcoholics. Not only did they report a significant reduction of anxiety, but also follow-up assessment 18 months later was essentially identical, speaking to neurofeedback's enduring impact (Watson, Herder, & Passini, 1978). Hammond went on to conclude in that review that neurofeedback for the treatment of anxiety disorders warrants an efficacy rating of "Level 3— probably efficacious." Yucha and Montgomery (2008) reported the combined efficacy of biofeedback and neurofeedback interventions for anxiety as "Level 4—efficacious."

Depression

The outcome and efficacy research for neurofeedback and depression is relatively limited. Most of the studies utilized a small case study method that did not allow control group comparisons. However, some of the reported clinical outcomes are very impressive. The literature noted three different neurofeedback approaches. These included alpha asymmetry training (Baehr et al., 1999), beta training (Hammond, 2005), and a new protocol combining alpha asymmetry and beta training with an added control for anxiety or high beta (Diaz & Deusen, 2011). Similarly to the case of anxiety disorders, antidepressant medication has been found to have a limited impact. Its effectiveness is just slightly better than a placebo and is accompanied by unwanted side effects such as weight gain, decreased libido, and loss of pleasure, making neurofeedback an attractive alternative treatment for depression.

Davidson (1998a, 1998b) offered a summary of a large number of EEG studies documenting that depression is related to frontal asymmetry. That is, the left frontal area, normally associated with positive affect and memories, is underactivated, and the right frontal area, normally involved in negative emotion or anxiety, is overactivated. This corresponds to higher, calming alpha waves on the right and lower, less calm alpha waves on the left, resulting in problems with depression and anxiety. A more recent meta-analysis of 31 studies also concluded that depression and anxiety are related to prefrontal asymmetry and confirmed that excess alpha activity on the left side of the brain is related to depression (Thibodeau, Jorgensen, & Kim, 2006). Deslandes et al. (2008) found that a cohort of elderly persons with major depression had a greater activation of alpha on the left frontal lobe but had lower Beck depression scores. They suggested different manifestations of depression (reactive versus chronic) may have different EEG correlates. Finally, Bruder et al. (2008) found that alpha asymmetry could be used to predict the response of different antidepressant medications at the beginning of pharmacologic treatment. Clearly, alpha asymmetry and left frontal lobe alpha activation is related to depression, and this is a useful marker in its clinical treatment.

Baehr et al. (1999) described the clinical use of an alpha asymmetry neurofeedback protocol to treat mood disorders. It was designed to decrease left frontal alpha and increase right frontal alpha. In that study, six depressed subjects were given 18 to 34 sessions of alpha asymmetry neurofeedback. They were also administered pre- and posttest measures of depression (Beck Depression Inventory) and personality (Minnesota Multiphasic Personality Inventory-2 or MMPI-2) to assess their emotional functioning. Five of the six subjects showed significant reductions in depression, and several reduced or discontinued their antidepressant medication. One subject did not improve. She was diagnosed with bipolar disorder, and although her mood swings were substantially reduced, she continued to struggle with depression. A follow-up study of three of the six subjects 1 to 5 years after treatment found they had maintained their normal alpha asymmetry and had normal Beck Depression Inventory scores (Baehr, Rosenfeld, & Baehr, 2001). This suggested the alpha asymmetry neurofeedback had a long-term and enduring effect in reducing depression.

Hammond (2005) investigated the effectiveness of a lobeta (15–18 Hz) neurofeedback protocol with nine serious to severely depressed patients. He administered an average of twenty-one 30-minute neurofeedback sessions. One patient reportedly discontinued after five sessions due to time conflicts. Pre- to posttreatment changes on the MMPI found a mean decrease in depression t-scores of 28.75 points from near the middle 90s to the middle 60s, the normal range. Several other significant MMPI scores also fell into the normal range. He concluded that near 80% of the cases made significant improvement. He added that the treatment not only improved medication-resistant and severe depression but also reduced anxiety and rumination, decreased withdrawal and introversion, and increased ego strength.

A more recent evolution of neurofeedback treatment for depression was presented by Diaz and Deusen (2011). Combining the alpha asymmetry protocol with the beta protocol, and adding a high beta inhibit to control anxiety, they reported the results of an initial single case study. Using 10 sessions of neurofeedback on the left and right frontal lobes, they reported "moderate and consistent change" in alpha and beta performance, high beta reduction, and a notable increase in the percent of time the subject passed all three conditions, from 15% success after the first session to 26% success after the 10th. The subject also reported a significant, 43% reduction in mental suffering (anxiety, irritation, negative thoughts, obsessive thoughts, agitation, frequent crying, and difficulties falling asleep).

All of the above neurofeedback studies acknowledged the limitations of their small samples and case study methodology. They also recommended that larger, no-treatment control investigations be conducted to account for placebo and other effects unrelated to the neurofeedback treatment. However, as clinicians, they also reported the benefit of neurofeedback treatment in reducing depression, as indicated by valid dependent measures (MMPI and Beck Depression Inventory) and documented the enduring impact of the treatment from 18 months to 5 years. Despite the strength of the outcome measures, the limits of the research design caused Yucha and Montgomery (2008) to report the current efficacy of neurofeedback for the treatment of depression as "Level 2—possibly efficacious."

Substance Abuse

Like anxiety disorders, the outcome and efficacy research on substance abuse indicates that both biofeedback and neurofeedback interventions are useful in the treatment of substance abuse. More specifically, both have been found to significantly reduce relapse rates by addressing the physiological, emotional, and personality factors that underlie addiction and dependency. In addition, the research on neurofeedback and substance abuse also benefited from better-controlled studies. The type of neurofeedback employed in these studies was alpha theta and beta neurofeedback.

A meta-analysis conducted by Mathew and Wilson (1991) concluded that while alcohol and drug abuse causes an immediate increase in cerebral metabolism and blood flow, chronic abuse decreases both, and such negative changes are not corrected by abstinence alone, especially during the early stages of recovery. For example, Herning et al. (2003) found chronic marijuana abusers to have decreased brainwave power that persisted 4 weeks after cessation of use. As has been noted in this book in Chapter 3, on sources of brain dysregulation, alcohol, marijuana, and prescription medication all cause changes in brainwave electrical activity. Some examples include deficiency in slow alpha and theta in alcohol abuse, increase in frontal alpha (ADHD) in marijuana abuse, decrease in delta and alpha and increase in beta in antidepressant use, and decrease in slow wave activity in the use of benzodiazepines. It is clear that substance abuse affects neuronal EEG activity.

Early research on neurofeedback and substance abuse focused on helping chronic alcoholics strengthen their alpha and theta brainwaves (Twemlow & Bowen, 1976; Twenlow et al., 1977). The results of these uncontrolled studies found alpha and theta was reliably increased, depression decreased, other positive personality changes promoted, spirituality increased, and alcohol abuse decreased in 67–97% of the subjects. Later, better-controlled research by Peniston and Kulkosky (1989), Peniston and Kulkosky (1990), and Saxby and Peniston (1995) compared chronic, treatment-resistant alcoholics who had traditional substance abuse treatment to a control group who received traditional treatment and fifteen 30-minute sessions of alpha theta neurofeedback. The Peniston protocol involved deep relaxation training with skin temperature biofeedback and autogenic training, instruction about EEG neurofeedback, and a standard induction script that put subjects into a hypnagogic state of deep reverie. During this state, the subject reportedly accesses and resolves painful deep memories that he or she has suffered with for many years. In addition, counseling was provided after each session to help process any abreactions (upsetting thoughts, feelings, and memories) that occurred during the neurofeedback treatment.

The results of the Peniston and Kulkosky (1989) original study, the 1-year follow-up (Peniston & Kulkosky, 1990), and the Saxby and Peniston (1995) 21-month follow-up investigation found that the group who had neurofeedback and traditional substance abuse treatment strengthened their alpha and theta waves, had greater reduction on the Beck Depression Inventory, and had substantial positive personality changes as measured by the Millon Clinical Multiaxial Inventory. Specific changes were reported on the schizoid, avoidant, passive-aggressive, schizotypal, borderline, paranoid, anxiety, somatoform, dysthymia, alcohol abuse, psychotic thinking, psychotic depression, and psychotic delusional scales. Most importantly, these studies found a dramatically lower relapse rate after 1 year of discharge of 20% for the neurofeedback treatment group as compared to 80% for the traditional substance abuse control group. They further found, after a 21-month follow-up investigation, a sustained prevention relapse rate near the original 20% for the neurofeedback group.

Fahrion (1995) conducted the first large controlled study of alpha theta neurofeedback on persons who abused drugs other than alcohol. His subjects were convicted male felons in a prison-based treatment program who abused cocaine and marijuana. He compared 39 subjects who received thirty 30-minute alpha theta neurofeedback sessions to a control group and found after 6 and 12 months from the date of their release, 67% of the treatment group as compared to 53% of the control group had both clean urine drug screens and violation-free parole status. He also noted that alpha theta neurofeedback was more effective for non-stimulant-abusing felons and less effective for those who abused cocaine.

Scott and Kaiser (1998) investigated adding beta neurofeedback to the alpha theta treatment for 48 persons who abused stimulant drugs. Using a control group design, the treatment group first received 10 to 20 beta neurofeedback sessions and then 30 alpha theta sessions. They found a significant improvement in the ability to sustain attention; positive personality changes as measured by the Minnesota Multiphasic Personality Inventory on depression; decreases on hypochondriasis, hysteria, psychasthenia, social introversion, and psychopathic deviance scales; a lower substance abuse program drop-out rate; and a decreased likelihood of relapse following discharge. Scott et al. (2005) expanded the initial research using a mixed-substance-abusing sample (alcohol, heroin, crack/cocaine, and methamphetamine) of 120 volunteers undergoing inpatient substance abuse treatment. Subjects were again assigned to treatment and control conditions. The same neurofeedback beta, alpha theta treatment protocol was used. The results noted a 41% increase in substance abuse program completion; improved ability to sustain attention and inhibit impulses; decreased anxiety, depression, and psychopathic deviance; and a 23% 12-month relapse rate for the treatment group versus a 56% relapse rate for the untreated controls.

Demonstrating the benefits of biofeedback interventions in the treatment of substance abuse disorders, Taub et al. (1994) assigned 118 chronic alcoholics to one of four treatment conditions. These included routine treatment of Alcoholics Anonymous and counseling, routine treatment and transcendental meditation, routine treatment and electromylographic biofeedback (EMG), and routine treatment and neurofeedback. The results in self-reported abstinence were 25%, 65%, 55%, and 28%, respectively. The meditation and EMG treatment groups did better than counseling and neurofeedback groups, illustrating the value of meditation and EMG biofeedback in the treatment of substance abuse.

Finally, in a position paper on the applicability of neurofeedback to treat substance abuse disorders in adolescents, Trudeau (2005) noted the high co-morbidity of substance abuse and ADHD, and described ADHD as an antecedent for substance abuse, conduct disorder, and antisocial personality disorder. He further reported a high incidence of childhood ADHD in adults with chronic substance abuse, especially stimulant abuse, and suggested that neurofeedback has a special applicability to teens who may be predisposed to ADHD, conduct disorder, or substance abuse. Also in a recent review of neurofeedback treatment for substance abuse disorders, Sokhadze, Cannon, and Trudeau (2008) concluded that alpha theta training either alone for alcoholism or in combination with beta training for stimulant and mixed substance abuse, with traditional substance abuse treatment, is "probably efficacious." In addition, they echoed past recommendations including, among others, stronger research design, more detailed disclosure of treatment technical information, replication studies with diverse populations, research on the treatment of co-morbid conditions, study of involved physiological and psychological processes, and QEEG studies that evaluate EEG changes after treatment.

The outcome and efficacy research on neurofeedback and biofeedback treatment for substance abuse is relatively strong. Given the high emotional, family, legal, career, health, and financial impact involved in substance abuse and its treatment, neurofeedback offers a demonstrated means to reduce the risk of relapse and significantly enhance the effectiveness of traditional substance abuse treatment. Yucha and Montgomery (2008) concluded that biofeedback and neurofeedback interventions for substance abuse warrant a rating of "Level 3—probably efficacious."

Post-traumatic Stress Disorder

Post-traumatic stress disorder (PTSD) has been found to decrease the brain's slow wave activity, causing a suppression of traumatic experience and resulting in emotional, behavioral, and physiological consequences. Trauma does not have to be "severe" to cause such reactions, although severe trauma such as that experienced in war, rape, or natural disaster is especially likely to result in PTSD. Other emotionally overwhelming experiences such as early childhood attachment injury, emotional and physical abuse, car accidents, victimization by crime, and unexpected losses can also lead to PTSD. Alexander and McFarlane (2010) wrote of the long-term costs of PTSD and its related psychological and physiological consequences. They said PTSD was associated with a significant amount of dysregulated cortical arousal, neurohormonal abnormality, chronic pain, hypertension, hyperlipidaemia, obesity, and cardiac disease. The outcome research for treatment of PTSD suggests that both biofeedback and neurofeedback strategies may be beneficial; however, more research needs to be done to demonstrate stronger efficacy.

Early work in the treatment of PTSD with biofeedback and neurofeedback was conducted by Peniston and Kulkosky (1991) with 29 Vietnam veterans who had been diagnosed with combat-related PTSD. Subjects were divided into two groups: a traditional medical care (medication and counseling) control group and a traditional care plus neurofeedback treatment group. The treatment group was given eight 30-minute sessions of skin temperature biofeedback training and thirty 30-minute sessions of alpha theta neurofeedback. The results found significant decreases in MMPI scores on hypochondriasis, depression, hysteria, psychopathic deviance, masculinity–femininity, paranoia, psychasthenia, schizophrenia, hypomania, and social introversion, as compared to the control group, which only showed decreases on the schizophrenia scale. It was also found that all 14 subjects in the treatment group had reduced their medication, as compared to only one in the control group. In addition, a 30-month follow-up investigation found all of the traditional care subjects had relapsed, as compared to only three of the 15 neurofeedback subjects, reflecting an 80% success rate.

In an earlier study, Peniston et al. (1993) used a new neurofeedback protocol with 20 Vietnam veterans who had 13 to 15 years of history with PTSD and alcohol abuse. This study utilized an alpha theta synchrony neurofeedback treatment, designed to increase the phase and frequency of alpha and theta between two areas of the brain. All subjects received five or six 30-minute skin temperature biofeedback sessions and thirty 30-minute alpha theta synchrony neurofeedback sessions. The results found a significant increase in the percent of alpha theta synchrony and alpha and theta amplitude. In a follow-up study, 26 months after neurofeedback training, only four of the 20 experimental subjects had relapsed, resulting again in an 80% recovery rate from flashbacks, nightmares, anxiety, and panic. It was postulated that alpha theta synchrony neurofeedback provided a type of creative, anxiety-free imagery that allowed an integration of self-awareness and healing.

A later study by Pop-Jordanova and Zorcee (2005) investigated the benefits of biofeedback and neurofeedback in mitigating the effects of PTSD in children with attachment trauma. Ten children (average age of 9 years old) with PTSD were given supportive and cognitive behavioral therapy and 20 sessions of skin temperature biofeedback and SMR (12–16 Hz) neurofeedback. The results found a significant decrease in PTSD and a significant increase in skin temperature and SMR amplitude. The research concluded that the lack of secure attachment in the children contributed to their early predisposition to PTSD and nondevelopment of the right orbital frontal cortex. It further concluded biofeedback and neurofeedback are good complementary tools for assessment and treatment of children with PTSD.

The most recent work on neurofeedback and PTSD has been done by Othmer (2012, 2009) and involves what he described as low frequency and ultra low frequency neurofeedback. He said this type of neurofeedback uses signal following or waveform following feedback similar to what is used in peripheral biofeedback (for example, skin temperature training). Over 20 to 40 sessions of neurofeedback, a client follows the time course of the differentially amplified slow cortical potential. His work began at the very low bandwidth of 1.5 Hz and has since reportedly been extended to 0.0001 Hz.

He further explained that as the brain recognizes its relationship with the slow signal, it attempts to project the signal forward and bring it under its own control. He described PTSD as essentially a disorder of the resting state network, which is reregulated with this type of neurofeedback. He has reported detailed case studies and results on over 400 cases with very impressive results, noting the percentage of cases with resolved or subsided symptoms as follows: flashbacks (75%), panic attacks (80%), agitation/irritability (70%), anger (75%), and anxiety and depression (80%). He's also begun a large-scale, not-for-profit program with the United States military at Camp Pendleton called "Homecoming for Veterans."

Moore (2000), in his review of neurofeedback for anxiety disorders including PTSD, noted its association with clinical improvement. Hammond (2005) went further, suggesting that the research on PTSD was sufficiently rigorous to warrant consideration of the status of "probably efficacious." Peniston (2007), reviewing the research on the Peniston Kulkosky Protocol, presented a strong case for the benefit of alpha theta synchrony neurofeedback as a future psychotherapy for alcoholism, PTSD, and behavioral medicine. However, given the lack of sufficiently controlled investigations but acknowledging the positive clinical outcomes, Yucha and Montgomery (2008) rated biofeedback and neurofeedback's efficacy in the treatment of PTSD as, "Level 2—possibly efficacious." Perhaps the more recent, large sample work of Othmer (2009, 2012), although not involving controlled studies, might warrant a reconsideration of the efficacy rating to "Level 3—probably efficacious."

Additional Neurofeedback Efficacy and Outcome Research

The Yucha and Montgomery (2008) review of the outcome and efficacy research for biofeedback and neurofeedback interventions evaluated nearly 40 different applications. The five most common applications have been detailed above. This section of the chapter will briefly present a few more of the typical applications including chronic pain, epilepsy, headaches, insomnia, traumatic brain injury, autism spectrum disorders, cognitive inefficiency, and personality disorders. Only a brief narrative description will be provided below so the reader may gain a sense of the many applications of biofeedback and neurofeedback and their current outcome and efficacy rating. A more complete research review can be found in Yucha and Montgomery (2008).

Chronic Pain

An extensive body of research on chronic pain has found biofeedback and neurofeedback to be as effective as traditional medication treatment and generally more effective than no-treatment control groups. It has also noted the overall effectiveness of a multidisciplinary pain management program

(Singh, 2005). The many different types of interventions include relaxation training, exercise, progressive muscle relaxation, mental imagery, autogenic training, meditation, music therapy, electrical stimulation, hypnosis, cognitive therapy, counseling and support groups, acupuncture, desensitization, biofeedback, and neurofeedback. The specific types of effective biofeedback techniques used included EMG, skin temperature, and heart rate variability. The neurofeedback techniques included SMR (12–14 Hz) and beta (15–18 Hz) neurofeedback. A recent randomized, controlled, rater-blind study by Kaviran et al. (2010) found SMR neurofeedback to be effective in improving the pain, psychological symptoms, and impaired quality of life of persons with fibromyalgia. Since chronic pain can have a specific focus or be pervasive and widespread, both general and specific approaches have been found to be effective. Overall, Yucha and Montgomery (2008) rated the outcome and efficacy of biofeedback and neurofeedback for chronic pain as "Level 4—efficacious."

Epilepsy

Some of the earliest work in neurofeedback was done by Sterman and Friar (1972) on epilepsy. They initially began work on animals but then applied their findings to humans with a history of medically uncontrolled seizures. Their neurofeedback technique involved increasing SMR (12–15 Hz) and decreasing theta (4–8 Hz). In a later review of 18 studies of neurofeedback for the treatment of seizures, Sterman (2000) reported that 142 (82%) of 174 patients showed clinically significant improvement. Other biofeedback and neurofeedback techniques have also been found effective for refractory epilepsy. These included galvanic skin response and slow cortical potential (Seth, Stafstrom, and Hsu, 2005). Yucha and Montgomery (2008) rated the efficacy of neurofeedback for the treatment of epilepsy as "Level 4—efficacious."

Headaches

Much research has also been conducted on the efficacy of biofeedback and neurofeedback interventions for tension, migraine, and mixed headaches, with very positive results. The primary biofeedback techniques used forehead and trapezius muscle (EMG), skin temperature, and blood volume pulse (BVP) training. A meta-analysis of 55 studies found a medium effect size for biofeedback that was stable over 17 months and a higher effect size for BVP than skin temperature or EMG training (Nestoriuc & Martin, 2007). In a review of various meta-analyses and evidence-based reviews, Andrasik (2007) concluded behavioral treatments were superior to various control conditions and similar to medication treatment. In addition, a recent study of 40 sessions of SMR and beta neurofeedback (8–18 Hz in multiple locations) and biofeedback (skin temperature and hemoencephalography) on 37 migraine suffers found 70% experienced at least a 50% reduction in headaches, as compared to a medication-alone treatment where 50% experienced a 50% reduction (Stokes & Lappin, 2010). Yucha and Montgomery (2008) rated the efficacy of biofeedback and neurofeedback for headaches as (Level 4—efficacious).

Insomnia

Biofeedback and progressive muscle relaxation, along with other nonpharmacological strategies for the treatment of insomnia, have been recommended by the American Academy of Sleep and have been found to be effective in the treatment of both primary and secondary insomnia (Morgenthaler et al., 2006). Morin, Jarvis, and Lynch (2007), in a similar review, listed the non-pharmacological options as stimulus control, sleep hygiene education, sleep restriction, paradoxical intention, relaxation therapy, biofeedback (for example, skin temperature and heart rate variability), and cognitive behavioral therapy. More recently, Cortoos et al. (2010) demonstrated that neurofeedback was superior to relaxation biofeedback, and Hammer et al. (2011) demonstrated the utility of SMR neurofeedback for the treatment of insomnia. Using fifteen 20-minute sessions of SMR neurofeedback, they found clients significantly improved sleep and daytime functions, becoming "normal sleepers." Yucha and Montgomery (2008) rated the efficacy of biofeedback and neurofeedback for the treatment of insomnia as "Level 3—probably efficacious" but given the more recent research, consideration of increasing this rating to "efficacious" may be warranted.

Traumatic Brain Injury

Some of the early work in the use of neurofeedback to treat traumatic brain injury was done by Ayers (1987). A student of Sterman, she reported a 95% success rate with 250 patients using theta (4–7 Hz) decrease and beta (15–18 Hz) increase neurofeedback. Her work was criticized for lack of control comparisons. Head injury can be structural and functional. Even after structural damage has been ruled out, in 85% of cases, functional damage or severe postconcussive sequelae can persist due to diffuse axonal injury. TBI can be caused by a blow to the head, high fever, or oxygen deprivation caused by a stroke or heart attack. Neurofeedback can help improve memory, attention, and behavioral performance. Walker, Norman, and Weber (2002) found 88% of TBI patients showed more than 50% improvement in EEG coherence (neuronal network communication) scores and were able to return to work. In a review of the research on neurofeedback and TBI, Thorton and Carmody (2005, 2008) presented the theoretical justification for neurofeedback and demonstrated its effectiveness beyond traditional rehabilitation methods. Larson, Harrington, and Hicks (2006) reported on the effectiveness of low-energy neurofeedback in reducing 15 different symptoms with 100 TBI patients.

Based on this research Yucha and Montgomery (2008) rated the efficacy of neurofeedback for the treatment of TBI as "Level 3—probably efficacious."

Autism Spectrum Disorders

Autism is at one end of a spectrum of developmental disorders and consists of three groups of symptoms including impaired social functioning; deficits in communication; and restricted or repetitive stereotyped behavior, interests, routines, and motor patterns. What differentiates autism from Asperger's disorder, at the other end of the spectrum, is that persons with Asperger's have higher cognitive functioning, engage in literal pedantic speech, have difficulty comprehending implied meaning, struggle with fluid movement, and display inappropriate social interactions (APA, 2000). The complexity of these two disorders makes them one of the most complicated problems to treat with neurofeedback. Treatment usually requires 40 to 60 or more sessions and involves multiple brain locations and several types of neurofeedback including theta decrease, alpha decrease, SMR increase, and beta decrease neurofeedback (Coben, Linden, & Myers, 2010). Benefits have also been observed in the use of respiration, skin temperature, and heart rate variability biofeedback (Thompson et al., 2010a).

A controlled study of 37 autistic patients by Coben and Padolsky (2007) reported symptom improvement in 89% of the cases, with a 40% reduction of core autistic symptomatology (parent ratings); reduction in cerebral hyperactivity; and improvement in attention, visual perceptual functioning, executive function, and language skills. Coben, Linden and Myers (2010), in a review of the literature on neurofeedback and autism, concluded that it should receive an efficacy rating of Level 2, possibly efficacious, "with potential," as do most other current interventions for autism. Thompson et al. (2010b), in discussing the use of neurofeedback for Asperger's disorder, suggested it should focus on improving problems with reading and mirroring emotions, poor attention to the outside world, poor self-regulation skills, and anxiety. They recommended the use of heart rate variability biofeedback and theta decrease, alpha decrease, beta decrease, and SMR increase neurofeedback. In a recent review of 15 years of their clinical work with 150 clients with Asperger's and nine with autism, they described effective use of metacognitive strategies (education in social understanding, spatial reasoning, reading comprehension, and math provided while clients are relaxed and focused), biofeedback, and 40 to 60 sessions of neurofeedback (Thompson et al., 2010b). Their results included decrease in core symptoms; decrease in problems with attention, anxiety, aprosodias, and social functioning; and improved academic and intellectual functioning (average gain of 9 full-scale IQ points). Yucha and Montgomery (2008) rated the efficacy of biofeedback and neurofeedback for autism as "Level 2—possibly efficacious." No rating was provided for Asperger's disorder, but the outcome research suggests these clients make stronger improvements. Better-controlled research is needed for both.

Cognitive Inefficiency

The efficacy of neurofeedback for cognitive efficiency has not been reviewed by Yucha and Montgomery (2008), but it has been demonstrated in several outcome research studies focusing primarily on alpha increase neurofeedback. Early research on the relationship of alpha to cognitive efficiency was done by Obrist (1979) and Duffy et al. (1984), who respectively noted the decline of alpha with physical aging and longevity, and suggested high alpha (10–12 Hz) was the hallmark of good memory. Budzynski (1996, 2007), building on this work, developed a program called "brain brightening," intended to increase the cognitive efficiency of seniors with five sessions of alpha increase neurofeedback. Later research on seniors, with control group design, found that alpha increase did not improve memory but did improve other important cognitive functions including processing speed and executive functions (attention, planning, organization, problem solving, and performance) (Angelakis et al., 2007). Swingle (2008) noted that slow peak alpha, under 9.5 Hz, was related to mental sluggishness, eventual Alzheimer's disease, and other types of dementia. The question this research presented was "Could alpha increase neurofeedback be beneficial to a normal population?"

Suldo, Olson, and Evans (2001) found that the alpha peak efficiency of children who were precocious readers, as compared to their peers, was 5.2% higher than grade level. Hanslmayr et al. (2005), in a pretest–posttest design, found that alpha increase neurofeedback increased cognitive performance as measured by a mental rotation test. More recently, in a control group design, Zoefel, Huster, and Herrmann (2011) also found that five sessions of alpha increase neurofeedback enhanced cognitive performance. In additional studies, alpha increase along with other types of neurofeedback, including SMR training, have been found to improve semantic processing and working memory and increase reading scores, time reading, reading comprehension, and verbal and full-scale IQ in 6th, 7th, and 8th graders with learning problems (Vernon et al., 2003; Orlando & Rivera, 2004). Despite its lack of review by Yucha and Montgomery (2008), the above outcome research does suggest that alpha increase neurofeedback is effective in improving the cognitive functioning of children and adults.

Personality Disorders

Like cognitive efficiency, the efficacy of neurofeedback for personality disorders was not reviewed by Yucha and Montgomery (2008); however, the outcome research has demonstrated some compelling results. As noted above in the substance abuse section, Peniston and Kulkosky (1989, 1990, 1991) studied the efficacy of alpha theta neurofeedback on the treatment of alcoholism and trauma. In addition to significant increases in abstinence and reductions in symptoms of trauma, they found that abnormal scores on the Beck Depression Inventory, Millon Clinical Multiaxial Inventory, 16 Personality Factor, and Minnesota

Multiphasic Personality Inventory had become "normalized." This was an astounding result. While symptoms of depression and anxiety may have been expected to decrease, personality disorders, thought to be more deeply rooted, would likely remain stable. White (1995, 1999, 2008) also employed the Peniston alpha theta protocol. She added 5–10 sessions of SMR neurofeedback to help first settle clients down before alpha theta synchrony training. She also used the MMPI and the MCMI as dependent measures and found normalization of symptoms and personality disorders. She concluded that neurofeedback was effective, "despite the severity or multiplicity of diagnoses" (p. 264).

Later research began to focus on the underlying causes of change. Gruzelier (2009) reported that alpha theta synchrony neurofeedback seemed to stimulate a process of "psychological integration." White (2008) said it caused a "non-linear clearing of trauma and dropping in of a new program of behavior that caused a dramatic personality transformation" (p. 261). More recent applications of neurofeedback on personality disorders have focused on the use of individual QEEG assessment and multiple neurofeedback protocols to successfully treat such previously considered intractable problems of antisocial personality disorder and schizophrenia (Surmeli & Ertem, 2009; Surmeli et al., 2012). Results again found normalization of personality measures along with significant improvements in recidivism, attention, and noted reduction in positive and negative symptoms of schizophrenia and psychopathic deviance, as well as 68% 2-year compliance with medication as compared to only 26% typically reported in the literature. Swingle (2008) noted that neurofeedback was emerging as a "first choice treatment" for many severe disorders including personality disorders because it works without adverse effects, the changes are permanent, and clients are not harmed by dependency on medication. Despite its lack of review by Yucha and Montgomery (2008), alpha theta synchrony neurofeedback appears to be an effective treatment for the normalization of personality disorders.

RESOURCES AND ENDORSEMENTS

This chapter has presented much of the current key outcome and efficacy research that supports the use of neurofeedback for many emotional and behavioral problems. It has highlighted the ongoing professional debate regarding the quality of that research and the demonstrated utility of neurofeedback, particularly in treating ADHD. It has also traced the challenges and advancements made in improving that research while pointing out the need for further work in investigating the efficacy of neurofeedback. Provided below is a list of resources for further review of the neurofeedback literature. Also presented is a brief summary of key endorsements to offer some perspective on the acceptance of neurofeedback among mental health practitioners, researchers, and their respective professional organizations.

Resources

The primary resource repeatedly referenced in this chapter is the work of Yucha and Montgomery (2008), who reviewed the outcome and efficacy research of biofeedback and neurofeedback in treating 45 different disorders. In their *Evidence-Based Practice in Biofeedback and Neurofeedback*, they presented a summary of the research literature and offered an efficacy rating based on La Vaque et al. (2002). It is important to note that their effort represents a work in progress. Their latest update was done in 2008. Much research has continued since the last update of their review, and the current efficacy rating does not necessarily indicate that an application is not helpful. It may reflect a lack of controlled research, replication studies, or large sample investigations. It may also reflect the limitation of the group research approach in evaluating and effectively treating the unique constellation of individual clinical variability. Any individual client may or may not respond to even a demonstrated effective neurofeedback intervention because of characteristics germane only to that individual.

Another set of resources includes those provided by the biofeedback and neurofeedback professional organizations. These include the Association for Applied Psychophysiology and Biofeedback (AAPB, www.aapb.org) and the International Society for Neurofeedback and Research (ISNR, www.isnr.org). The AAPB offers a list of recent research articles and abstracts, whitepapers on efficacy information, and a review of 34 disorders and treatment with research references and efficacy ratings. It also provides access to the *Applied Psychophysiology and Biofeedback Journal*. The ISNR provides a "Comprehensive Bibliography of Scientific Articles" compiled by D. Corydon Hammond. In contains over 1,000 articles under 47 categories on specific applications such as anxiety, epilepsy, and tinnitus, and general papers on such topics as theoretical treaties, adverse reactions and side effects, and professional standards. It also provides access to the *Journal of Neurotherapy*.

Another valuable resource for up-to-date research on neurofeedback is the website www.PubMed.gov. It contains over 22 million citations from the biomedical research literature including Medline, life sciences journals, and online books. It generates abstract summaries and links to full-text articles, and is operated by the National Center for Biotechnology Information (NCBI).

Endorsements

As professional training and clinical experience with neurofeedback expand and the quality of outcome and efficacy research improves, endorsements of neurofeedback as a viable and effective treatment for many emotional and behavioral problems are more forthcoming. These have come from both experts in their respective fields and well-established professional organizations such as the American Psychological Association (APA) and the American Counseling Association (ACA).

In 1997, the APA Practice Directorate and the APA Council recognized neurofeedback and QEEG as proficiencies within the scope of psychology, applied psychophysiology, and biofeedback. As a result, state licensing boards aligned their views along with the Practice Directorate. They also developed the practice code 90876 for psychophysiological psychotherapy or Biofeedback Assisted Psychotherapy as the primary code used in documenting insurance billing for biofeedback and neurofeedback (EEG biofeedback). The APA has also recognized and accepted the biofeedback and neurofeedback training and certification standards outlined by the Biofeedback Certification International Alliance (BCIA, www.BCIA.org).

In 2000, Frank H. Duffy, a professor and pediatric neurologist at Harvard Medical School and a forerunner in acknowledging neurofeedback's efficacy, said in an editorial in the journal *Clinical Electroencephalography* that the scholarly literature suggests neurofeedback should play a major therapeutic role in the treatment of many difficult problems: "In my opinion, if any medication had demonstrated such a wide spectrum of efficacy it would be universally accepted and widely used" (Duffy, 2000, p. 5). Duffy further advocated, "It is a field to be taken seriously by all" (2000, p. 7). Daniel Amen, M.D. (2001), a recognized national expert in the use of brain imaging technology and the treatment of ADHD, wrote in his book, *Healing ADD*, a biological treatment summary listing EEG biofeedback protocols for six neurologically defined subtypes of ADHD. He said, "In my experience with EEG biofeedback and ADD, many people are able to improve their reading skills and decrease their need for medications. Also, EEG biofeedback has helped to decrease impulsivity and aggressiveness. It is a powerful tool" (pp. 143–144). Russell Barkley, also a nationally recognized expert in ADHD and an ardent advocate of medication treatment and critic of neurofeedback research for ADHD, has recognized the value of the QEEG in evaluating different neurologically determined types of ADHD (Loo & Barkley, 2005). Both the APA and Chadd (Children and Adults With Attention Deficit/Hyperactivity Disorder), a client advocacy group for persons with ADHD, have recognized neurofeedback as "probably efficacious" and a valid option for the treatment of ADHD.

Hirshberg et al. (2005), in a special issue of *Child and Adolescent Psychiatric Clinics of North America*, discussed emerging brain-based interventions for children and adolescents and wrote that although there were some significant methodological weaknesses in some of the studies, "virtually all EBF (EEG biofeedback) research has demonstrated what these three most recent fMRI studies have replicated using a more complex and sophisticated imaging technology: we are able to use real-time information about brain function to alter and enhance that function" (p. 2). They went on to say, "EEG biofeedback meets the American Academy of Child and Adolescent Psychiatry criteria for clinical guideline for treatment of ADHD, seizure disorders, anxiety (OCD, GAD, PTSD phobias) depression, reading disabilities, and addiction disorders. This suggests that EEG biofeedback should always be considered as an intervention for these disorders by clinicians" (p. 12).

More recently, the American Counseling Association (ACA) has published two articles by Russell-Chapin and Chapin (2011) and Myers and Young (2012), speaking to the role of neurofeedback as a third option when counseling and medication are not sufficient, and advocating for the integration of neurofeedback into the preparation, research, and practice of professional counselors. Myers and Young (2011) concluded, "NFB offers the professional counselor a powerful tool for the diagnosis and treatment of a variety of clinical issues and is a modality consistent with the developmental, strength-based precepts that underlie the field of counseling" (p. 26).

CONCLUSIONS

Neurofeedback outcome and efficacy research are important in validating and understanding the limits of its clinical effectiveness. They are also important in helping us learn more about the underlying neurological processes involved in emotional and behavioral disorders. While the research currently demonstrates varying degrees of efficacy, this does not diminish its clinical usefulness. Valid dependent measures in controlled studies with ever-increasing sample sizes, in a variety of settings, across many types of disorders have moved the debate from, "Is it efficacious?" to "How efficacious is it?"

Research on neurofeedback continues to expand with ever-improved research design and improved brain imaging technology documenting neurofeedback's physiological impact on the brain's neurological functioning. At present, neurofeedback enjoys the endorsement of many recognized experts and professional associations for its benefit on clinical applications and optimal human performance. There are many sources to review the existing research. The future of neurofeedback research is promising, and more and more clinicians are becoming trained in its technology. Estimates have found between 10,000 and 20,000 neurofeedback practitioners in the United States and half that number in other countries (Crane, 2009). Neurofeedback appears to be well on its way of becoming the third option, and by some accounts the preferred option, when counseling and medication are not sufficient (Russell-Chapin & Chapin, 2011).

REFERENCES

Alexander, C., & McFarlane, A. C. (2010). The long-term costs of traumatic stress: Intertwined physical and psychological consequences. *World Psychiatry*, *9*(1), 3–10.

Alhambra, M. A., Fowler, T. P., & Alhambra, A. A. (1995). EEG biofeedback: A new treatment option for ADD/ADHD. *Journal of Neurotherapy, 1*(2), 39–43.

Amen, D. (2001). *Healing ADD: A breakthrough program that allows you to see and heal the six types of attention deficit disorder.* New York: Putnam.

American Psychiatric Association. (2000). *Diagnostic and statistical manual of mental disorders* (4th ed., text rev.). Washington, DC: American Psychiatric Association.

American Psychological Association. (1995). *Template for developing guidelines on interventions for mental disorders and psychological aspects of physical disorders.* Washington, DC: American Psychological Association.

American Psychological Association. (2002). Criteria for evaluation of treatment guidelines. *American Psychologist, 57*(12), 1052–1059.

Andrasik, F. (2007). What does the evidence show? Efficacy of behavioral treatments for recurrent headaches in adults. *Neurological Sciences, 28*(Suppl. 2), 70–77.

Angelakis, E., Stathopoulou, S., Frymiare, J. L., Gree, D. L., Lubar, J. F., & Kounious, J. (2007). EEG neurofeedback: A brief overview and an example of peak alpha frequency training for cognitive enhancement in the elderly. *Clinical Neuropsychology, 21*(1), 110–129.

Arns, M., de Ridder, S., Strehl, U., Breteler, M., & Coenen, T. (2009). Efficacy of neurofeedback treatment in ADHD: The effects on inattention, impulsivity and hyperactivity: A meta-analysis. *Clinical EEG and Neuroscience, 40,* 180–189.

Ayers, M. (1987). Electroencephalographic neurofeedback and closed head injury of 250 individuals. In *National Head Injury Syllabus* (pp. 380–392). Washington DC: Head Injury Foundation.

Baehr, E., Rosenfeld, J. P., & Baehr, R. (2001). Clinical use of an alpha asymmetry neurofeedback protocol in the treatment of mood disorders: Follow-up study one to five years post therapy. *Journal of Neurotherapy, 4*(4), 11–18.

Baehr, E., Rosenfeld, J. P., Baehr, R., & Earnest, C. (1999). Clinical use of an alpha asymmetry neurofeedback protocol in the treatment of mood disorders. In J. R. Evans & A. Abarbanel (Eds.), *Introduction to quantitative EEG and neurofeedback* (pp. 181–201). San Diego: Academic Press.

Beauregard, M., & Levesque, J. (2006). Functional magnetic resonance imaging investigation of the effects of EEG biofeedback training on the neural bases of selective attention and response inhibition in children with attention-deficit/hyperactivity disorder. *Applied Psychophysiology and Biofeedback, 31*(1), 2–20.

Bruder, G. E., Sodoruk, J. P., Stewart, J. W., McGrath, P. J., Quitkin, F. M., & Tenke, C. E. (2008). Electroencephalographic alpha measures predict therapeutic response to a selective serotonin reuptake inhibitor antidepressant: Pre- and post-treatment findings. *Biological Psychiatry, 63*(12), 1171–1177.

Budzynski, T. H. (1996). Brain brightening: Can neurofeedback improve cognitive process? *Biofeedback, 24*(2), 14–17.

Budzynski, T., Budzyski, H. K., & Tang, H. Y. (2007). Brain brightening: Restoring the aging mind. In J. R. Evans (Ed.), *Handbook of neurofeedback* (pp. 231–265). Binghamton, NY: Haworth Medical Press.

Coben, R., Linden, M., & Myers, T. E. (2010). Neurofeedback for autistic spectrum disorder: A review of the literature. *Applied Psychophysiology and Biofeedback, 35*, 83–105.

Coben, R., & Padolsky, I. (2007). Assessment-guided neurofeedback for autistic spectrum disorder. *Journal of Neurotherapy, 11*(1), 5–19.

Cortoos, A., De Valck, E., Arns, M., Breteler, M. H., & Cluydts, R. (2010). An exploratory study on the effects of tele-neurofeedback and tele-biofeedback on objective and subjective sleep in patients with primary insomnia disorder. *Applied Psychophysiology and Biofeedback, 35*(2), 125–134.

Crane, R. A. (2009). Infinite potential: A neurofeedback pioneer looks back and ahead. In J. R. Evans (Ed.), *Handbook of neurofeedback: Dynamics and clinical applications* (pp. 2–21). New York: Informa Healthcare.

Davidson, R. J. (1998a). Affective style and affective disorders: Perspectives from affective neuroscience. *Cognition and Emotion, 12*, 307–330.

Davidson, R. J. (1998b). Anterior electrophysiological asymmetries, emotion, and depression: Conceptual and methodological conundrums. *Psychophysiology, 35*, 607–614.

Deslandes, A. C., de Moraes, H., Pompeu, F. A. M. S., Ribeiro, P., Cagy, M., Capitao, C., . . . Laks, J. (2008). Electroencephalographic frontal asymmetry and depressive symptoms in the elderly. *Biological Psychology, 79*(3), 317–322.

Diaz, A. M., & Deusen, A. V. (2011). A new neurofeedback protocol for depression. *The Spanish Journal of Psychology, 14*(1), 347–384.

Duffy, F. H. (2000). The state of EEG biofeedback therapy (EEG operant conditioning) in 2000: An editor's opinion. *Clinical Encephalography, 31*(1), 5–7.

Duffy, F. H., Albert, M. S., McAnulty, G., & Garvey, A. J. (1984). Age-related differences in brain electrical activity of healthy subjects. *Annals of Neurology, 16*, 430–438.

Fahrion, S. (1995). Human potential and personal transformations. *Subtle Energies, 6*, 55–88.

Garrett, B. L., & Silver, M. P. (1976). The use of EMG and alpha biofeedback to relieve test anxiety in college students. In I. Wickramasekera (Ed.), *Biofeedback, behavior therapy, and hypnosis*. Chicago: Nelson-Hall.

Glueck, B. C., & Strobel, C. F. (1975). Biofeedback and meditation in the treatment of psychiatric illnesses. *Comprehensive Psychiatry, 16*(4), 303–321.

Gruzelier, J. (2009). A theory of alpha/theta neurofeedback, creative performance enhancement, long distance functional connectivity and psychological integration. *Cognitive Process, 10*(1), 101–109.

Hammer, B. U., Colbert, A. P., Brown, K. A., & Ilioli, E. C. (2011). Neurofeedback for insomnia: A pilot study of Z-score SMR and individualized protocols. *Applied Psychophysiology and Biofeedback, 36*, 251–264.

Hammond, D. C. (2005). Neurofeedback treatment of depression and anxiety. *Journal of Adult Development, 12*(2/3), 131–137.

Hanslmayr, S., Sauseng, P., Doppelmayer, M., Schabus, M., & Klimesch, W. (2005). Increasing individual upper alpha power by neurofeedback improves cognitive performance in human subjects. *Applied Psychophysiology and Biofeedback, 30*(1), 1–10.

Hardt, J. V., & Kamiya, J. (1978). Anxiety change through electroencephalographic alpha feedback seen only in high anxiety subjects. *Science, 201*, 79–81.

Herning, R. I., Better, W., Tate, K., & Cadet, J. L. (2003). EEG deficits in chronic marijuana abusers during monitored abstinence: Preliminary findings. *New York Academy of Science, 993*, 75–78.

Hirshberg, L. M., Chui, S., & Frazier, J. A. (2005). Emerging brain-based interventions for children and adolescents: Overview and clinical perspective. *Child and Adolescent Psychiatric Clinics of North America, 14*(1), 1–19.

Kaviran, S., Dursun, E., Dursun, N., Ermutlu, N., & Karamursel, S. (2010). Neurofeedback intervention in fibromyalgia syndrome: A randomized, controlled, rater-blind clinical trial. *Applied Psychophysiology and Biofeedback, 35*(4), 293–302.

Kropotov, J. D., Grin-Yatsenko, V. A., Ponnomarev, V. A., Chutko, L. S., Yakovenko, E. A., & Nikishena, I. S. (2005). ERPs correlates of EEG relative beta training in ADHD children. *International Journal of Psychophysiology, 55*(1), 23–34.

Larson, S., Harrington, K., & Hicks, S. (2006). The LENS (low energy neurofeedback system): A clinical outcomes study on one hundred patients at Stone Mountain Center, New York. *Journal of Neurotherapy, 10*(2/3), 69–78.

La Vaque, T. J., Hammond, D. C., Trudeau, D., Monastra, V., Perry, J., Lehrer, P., . . . Sherman, R. (2002). Template for developing guidelines for the evaluation of the clinical efficacy of psychophysiological interventions. *Applied Psychophysiology and Feedback, 27*(4), 273–281.

Lofthouse, N., Arnold, L. E., Hersch, S., Hurt, E., & DeBeus, R. (2012). A review of neurofeedback treatment for pediatric ADHD. *Journal of Attention Disorders, 16*(5), 351–372.

Loo, S. K., & Barkley, R. A. (2005). Clinical utility of EEG in attention deficit hyperactivity disorder. *Applied Neuropsychology, 12*(2), 64–76.

Lubar, J. F., Swatwood, M. O., Swatwood, J. N., & O'Donnell, P. H. (1995). Evaluation of the effectiveness of EEG neurofeedback training for ADHD in a clinical setting as measured by changes in TOVA scores, behavioral ratings, and WISC-R performance. *Biofeedback Self-Regulation, 20*(1), 83–99.

Mathew, R., & Wilson, W. (1991). Substance abuse and cerebral blood flow. *American Journal of Psychiatry, 148,* 292–305.

McCrone, J. (1991). *The ape that spoke: Language and the evolution of the human mind.* New York: William Morrow & Company.

Michael, A. J., Krishnaswamy, S., & Mohamed, J. (2005). An open label study of the use of EEG biofeedback using beta training to reduce anxiety for patients with cardiac events. *Neuropsychiatric Disease and Treatment, 1*(4), 357–363.

Mills, G. K., & Solyom, L. (1974). Biofeedback of EEG alpha in the treatment of obsessive ruminations: An exploration. *Journal of Behavior Therapy and Experimental Psychiatry, 5,* 37–41.

Monastra, V. J., Linden, M., Green, G., Phillips, A., Lubar, J. F., Van Deusen, P., . . . Fenger, T. N. (1999). Assessing attention deficit hyperactivity disorder via quantitative electroencephalography: An initial validation study. *Neuropsychology, 13*(3), 424–433.

Monastra, V. J., Lynn, S., Linden, M., Lubar, J. F., Gruzelier, J., & La Vaque, T. J. (2005). Electroencephalographic biofeedback in the treatment of attention-deficit/hyperactivity disorder. *Applied Psychophysiology and Biofeedback, 30*(2), 95–114.

Monastra, V. J., Monastra, D. M., & George, S. (2002). The effects of stimulant therapy, EEG biofeedback, and parenting style on the primary symptoms of attention-deficit hyperactivity disorder. *Applied Psychophysiology and Biofeedback, 27*(4), 231–249.

Moore, N. C. (2000). A review of EEG neurofeedback treatment of anxiety disorders. *Clinical Electroencephalography, 31*(1), 1–6.

Morganthaler, T., Kramer, M., Alessi, C., Friedman, L., Boehlecke, B., & Brown, T. (2006). Practice parameters for the psychological and behavioral treatment of insomnia: An update. An American Academy of Sleep Medicine report. *Sleep: Journal of Sleep and Sleep Disorders Research, 29*(11), 1415–1419.

Morin, A. K., Jarvis, C. I., & Lynch, A. M. (2007). Therapeutic options for sleep-maintenance and sleep onset insomnia. *Pharmacotherapy, 27*(1), 89–110.

Mulley, A. G. (1990). Applying effectiveness and outcomes research to clinical practice: Effectiveness. In K. A. Heithoff & K. N. Lohr (Eds.), *Effectiveness and outcomes in healthcare: The proceedings of an Invitational conference by the Institute of Medicine* (pp. 179–189). Washington, DC: National Academy Press.

Myers, J. E., & Young, J. S. (2012). Brain wave biofeedback: Benefits of integrating neurofeedback in counseling. *Journal of Counseling & Development, 90*(1), 20–28.

Nestoriuc, M., & Martin, A. (2007). Efficacy of biofeedback for migraine: A meta-analysis. *Pain, 128*(1/2), 111–127.

Obrist, W. D. (1979). Electroencephalographic changes in normal aging and dementia. In F. Hoffmeister & C. Muller (Eds.), *Bayer-Symposium, 7, (Brain Function in Old Age: Evolution of Changes and Disorders)*, 102–111.

Orlando, P. C., & Rivera, R. O. (2004). Neurofeedback for elementary students with identified learning problems. *Journal of Neurotherapy, 8*(2), 5–19.

Othmer, S. (2009). Post traumatic stress disorder—The neurofeedback remedy. *Biofeedback, 37*(1), 24–31.

Othmer, S. (2012, March 7). Remediation of PTSD using infra-low frequency neurofeedback training. *EEG Info Newsletter*, 1–5.

Passini, F. T., Watson, C. G., Dehnel, L., Herder, J., & Watkins, B. (1977). Alpha wave biofeedback training therapy in alcoholics. *Journal of Clinical Psychology, 33*(1), 292–299.

Peniston, E. G. (2007). The Peniston-Kulkosky brainwave neurofeedback therapeutic protocol: The future of psychotherapy for alcoholism, PTSD and behavioral medicine. *Applied Psychophysiology and Biofeedback, 32*(2), 73–88.

Peniston, E. G., & Kulkosky, P. J. (1989). Alpha-theta brainwave training and beta-endorphin levels in alcoholics. *Alcoholism: Clinical and Experimental Research, 13*(2), 271–279.

Peniston, E. G., & Kulkosky, P. J. (1990). Alcoholic personality and alpha-theta brainwave training. *Medical Psychotherapy, 3*, 37–55.

Peniston, E. G., & Kulkosky, P. J. (1991). Alpha-theta brainwave neurofeedback for Vietnam veterans with combat-related post-traumatic stress disorder. *Medical Psychotherapy, 4*, 47–60.

Peniston, E. G., Marrinan, D. A., Deming, W. A., & Kulkosky, P. J. (1993). EEG alpha-theta brainwave synchronicity in Vietnam theater veterans with combat-related post-traumatic stress disorder and alcohol abuse. *Advance in Medical Psychotherapy, 6*, 37–50.

Pop-Jordanova, N., & Zorcee, T. (2005). Child trauma, attachment, and biofeedback mitigation. *Prilozi/Makedonska akademija na naukite I umetnostite, Oddelenie za bioloski I medicinski nauki (Contributions/Macedonia Academy of Sciences and Arts, Section of Biological and Medical Sciences), 25*(1–2), 103–114.

Rice, K. M., Blanchard, E. B., & Purcell, M. (1993). Biofeedback treatments of generalized anxiety disorder: Preliminary results. *Biofeedback Self Regulation, 18*, 93–105.

Robbins, J. (2008). *A symphony in the brain: The evolution of the new brain wave biofeedback.* New York: Grove.

Rossiter, T. R., & La Vaque, T. J. (1995). A comparison of EEG biofeedback and psychostimulants in treating attention deficit/hyperactivity disorders. *Journal of Neurotherapy, 1*(1), 48–59.

Russell-Chapin, L. A., & Chapin, T. J. (2011). Neurofeedback: A third option when counseling and medication are not sufficient. Retrieved from http://counselingoutfitters.com/vistas/vistas11/Article_48.pdf.

Russell-Chapin, L. A., Kemmerly, T., Liu, W. C., Zagardo, M., Chapin, T., Dailey, D., & Dinh, D. (2013). The effects of neurofeedback in the default mode network: Pilot study results of medicated children with ADHD. *Journal of Neurotherapy, 17*(1), 35–42.

Saxby, E., & Peniston, E. G. (1995). Alpha-theta brainwave neurofeedback training: An effective treatment for male and female alcoholics with depressive symptoms. *Journal of Clinical Psychology, 51*(5), 685–693.

Scott, W. C., & Kaiser, D. (1998). Augmenting chemical dependency treatment with neurofeedback training. *Journal of Neurotherapy, 3*(1), 66.

Scott, W. C., Kaiser, D., Othmer, S., & Sideroff, S. I. (2005). Effects of an EEG biofeedback protocol on a mixed substance abusing population. *American Journal of Drug and Alcohol Abuse, 31*, 455–469.

Seth, R. D., Stafstrom, C. E., & Hsu, D. (2005). Nonpharmacological treatment options for epilepsy. *Seminars in Pediatric Neurology, 12*(2), 106–113.

Sherlin, L., Arns, M., Lubar, J., & Sokhadze, E. (2010). A position paper on neurofeedback for the treatment of ADHD. *Journal of Neurotherapy, 14*, 66–78.

Shouse, M. N., & Lubar, J. F. (1979). Operant conditioning of EEG rhythms and Ritalin in the treatment of hyperkinesis. *Biofeedback and Self Regulation, 4*(3), 299–312.

Singh, A. N. (2005). Multidisciplinary management of chronic pain. *International Medical Journal, 12*(2), 111–116.

Sittenfeld, P., Budzynski, T. H., & Stoyva, J. M. (1976). Differential shaping of EEG theta rhythms. *Biofeedback Self Regulation, 1*, 31–46.

Sokhadze, T. M., Cannon, R. L., & Trudeau, D. L. (2008). EEG biofeedback as a treatment for substance use disorders: Review, rating of efficacy, and recommendations for further research. *Applied Psychophysiology and Biofeedback, 33*, 1–28.

Sterman, M. B. (2000). Basic concepts and clinical findings in the treatment of seizure disorders with EEG operant conditioning. *Clinical Electroencephalography, 31*(1), 45–55.

Sterman, M. B., & Friar, L. (1972). Suppression of seizures in an epileptic following sensorimotor EEG feedback training. *Electroencephalography Clinical Neurophysiology, 33*(1), 889–895.

Stokes, D. A., & Lappin, M. S. (2010). Neurofeedback and biofeedback with 37 mingraineurs: A clinical outcome study. *Behavioral & Brain Functions, 6*, 1–10.

Suldo, S. M., Olson, A., & Evans, J. R. (2001). Quantitative EEG evidence of increased alpha peak frequency in children with precocious reading ability. *Journal of Neurotherapy, 5*, 39–50.

Surmeli, T., & Ertem, A. (2009). QEEG guided neurofeedback therapy in personality disorders: 13 case studies. *Clinical EEG and Neuroscience, 40*(1), 5–9.

Surmeli, T., Ertem, A., Eralp, E., & Kos, I. H. (2012). Schizophrenia and the efficacy of QEEG-guided neurofeedback treatment: A clinical case series. *Clinical EEG and Neuroscience, 43*(2), 133–144.

Swingle, P. (2008). *Biofeedback for the brain.* New Brunswick, NJ: Rutgers University Press.

Taub, E., Steiner, S. S., Weingarten, E., & Walton, K. G. (1994). Effectiveness of broad spectrum approaches to relapse prevention in severe alcoholism: A long-term, randomized controlled trial of transcendental meditation, EMG biofeedback and electronic neurotherapy. *Alcoholism Treatment Quarterly, 11*(1/2), 187–220.

Thibodeau, R., Jorgensen, R. S., & Kim, S. (2006). Depression, anxiety, and frontal resting EEG asymmetry: A meta-analytic review. *Journal of Abnormal Psychology, 115*(4), 715–729.

Thompson, L., Thompson, M., & Reid, A. (2010a). Functional neuroanatomy and the rationale for using EEG biofeedback for clients with Asperger's Syndrome. *Applied Psychophysiology and Biofeedback, 35,* 39–61.

Thompson, L., Thompson, M., & Reid, A. (2010b). Neurofeedback outcomes in clients with Asperger's Syndrome. *Applied Psychophysiology and Biofeedback, 35*(1), 63–91.

Thorton, K. E., & Carmody, D. P. (2005). Electroencephalogram biofeedback for reading disability and traumatic brain injury. *Child and Adolescent Psychiatric Clinics of North America, 14*(1), 137–162.

Thorton, K. E., & Carmody, D. P. (2008). Efficacy of traumatic brain injury rehabilitation intervention of QEEG-guided biofeedback, computers, strategies and medications. *Applied Psychophysiology and Biofeedback, 33*(2), 101–124.

Trudeau, D. L. (2005). Applicability of brain wave biofeedback to substance use disorder in adolescents. *Child and Adolescent Psychiatric Clinics of North America, 14,* 125–136.

Twemlow, S., & Bowen, W. (1976). EEG biofeedback induced self-actualization in alcoholics. *Journal of Biofeedback, 3,* 20–25.

Twemlow, S., Sizemore, D., & Nowen, W. (1977). Biofeedback induced energy redistribution in the alcoholic EEG. *Journal of Biofeedback, 3,* 14–19.

Vanathy, S., Sharma, P. S. V. N., & Kumar, K. B. (1998). The efficacy of alpha and theta neurofeedback training in treatment of generalized anxiety disorder. *Indian Journal of Clinical Psychology, 25*(2), 136–143.

Vernon, D., Egner, T., Cooper, N., Comptom, T., Neilands, C., Sheri, A., & Gruzelier, J. (2003). The effect of training distinct neurofeedback protocols on aspects of cognitive performance. *International Journal of Psychophysiology, 47*(1), 75–85.

Walker, J. E., Norman, C. A., & Weber, R. K. (2002). Impact of QEEG-guided coherence training for patients with a mild closed head injury. *Journal of Neurotherapy, 6*(2), 31–43.

Watson, C. G., Herder, J., & Passini, F. T. (1978). Alpha biofeedback therapy in alcoholics: An 18 month follow-up. *Journal of Clinical Psychology, 43*(2), 765–769.

White, N. (1995). Alpha-theta training for chronic trauma disorder, a new perspective. *Journal of Mind Technology and Optimal Performance, Mega Brain Report, 2*(4), 44–50.

White, N. (1999). Theories of the effectiveness of alpha-theta training for multiple disorders. In J. Evans & A. Abarbanel (Eds.), *Introduction to quantitative EEG and neurofeedback* (pp. 341–367). New York: Academic.

White, N. (2008). The transformational power of the Peniston protocol: A therapist's experience. *Journal of Neurotherapy, 12*(4), 261–265.

Yucha, C., & Montgomery, D. (2008). *Evidenced-based practice in biofeedback and neurofeedback.* Wheat Ridge, CO: Association for Applied Psychophysiology and Biofeedback.

Zoefel, B., Huster, R. J., & Herrmann, C. S. (2011). Neurofeedback training of the upper alpha frequency band in EEG improves cognitive performance. Neuroimage, 15(54), 1427–1431.

10

THE FUTURE OF NEUROTHERAPY AND OTHER PROFESSIONAL ISSUES

The brain is the last and grandest biological frontier, the most complex thing we have yet discovered in our universe. It contains hundreds of billions of cells interlinked through trillions of connections. The brain boggles the mind.

—James Watson

The neurotherapy and neurofeedback field has had many high and low amplitudes, or many peaks and valleys in its relatively short history. After surviving years of criticism, derision, and a reputation of only a "consciousness expanding" movement, NFB is emerging as a reputable and scientifically driven field. Evidence-based qualities are found in almost every discipline, and the neurotherapy and neurofeedback discipline is no different. Evidence-based neurofeedback (EBNFB) is becoming the present and future of this field.

Currently, the field seems to be growing at an accelerated pace (Swingle, 2010). Throughout this book, we have offered past and current research demonstrating NFB's efficacy. This chapter will focus on the latest research and what further research is needed. Professionalism issues will be discussed through professional organizations, ethical codes, and issues of informed consent. Standards of care will be offered, and we will emphasize several "gold standards" to guide the QEEG field. New directions, orthodoxy, and trends will be provided in the following sections.

IMPACT ON THE COUNSELING PROFESSION

At the beginning of this book, the authors stated that advances in brain research and brain understanding will change how we all conduct counseling. This time has arrived, and it has and must continue to change how we view the world and practice of counseling. In 2010, the National Institute of Mental Health (NIMH) created a vision and a mission statement and then strategized four research objectives to guide the needed research investigations over the next 5 years. Their vision statement is expansive, stating, "Envision a world in which mental illnesses are prevented and cured." The NIMH's mission statement is, "Transform the understanding and treatment of mental illnesses through basic and clinical research, paving the way for prevention, recovery and cure" (p. 1). The strategic objectives are to

• Promote discovery in brain and behavioral sciences to fuel research on the causes of mental disorders.
• Chart mental illnesses trajectories to determine when, where, and how to intervene.
• Develop new and better interventions that incorporate the diverse needs and circumstances of people with mental illnesses.
• Strengthen the public health impact of NIMH-supported research.

Meyers and Young (2012) believe neuroscience is the future of counseling and state, "Given that the research findings of NIMH and similar agencies will become the practice standards of the future, it is critical that counselors-in-training understand and can participate in the discourse relating to such research initiatives" (p. 21). It is essential that counselors and all other helping professionals familiarize themselves with critical neuroscience foundations and skills. The authors' knowledge about NT and NFB has changed how we conduct counseling, whether that is as a neurofeedback practitioner or helping professional in general. Our very first look at the client and his or her problems are from a neurologically based perspective. This adds an entirely new and different element to the conceptualization and treatment process.

PROFESSIONAL ORGANIZATIONS

There are several professional organization that serve as gatekeepers to the NT and NFB disciplines. The Association for Applied Psychophysiology and Bio-feedback (AAPB) came into existence in 1969, and in 1993, an increased demand for additional information about EEG work fostered the need for a new division on neurofeedback. The International Society of Neurofeedback and Research (ISNR) has been an essential resource for NFB and NF clinicians.

Certification is available through the Biofeedback Certification International Alliance (BCIA; http://www.bcia.org/). To become nationally certified, which is not mandatory to use NFB, BCIA requires 36 hours of didactic instruction about NFB, learning theory, and principles and a basic course on neuroanatomy, anatomy, or physiology; instrumentation, diagnosis, and treatment protocols; and ethics. Supervision or mentoring is required during the academic (10 hours) or clinical practice (25 hours) depending on the certification requested (Myers & Young, 2012). BCIA recommends that providers meet criteria for being board certified in neurofeedback by following their Blueprint of Knowledge in EEG Biofeedback. This information can be located online at http://www.bcia.org.

STANDARDS OF CARE AND ETHICAL GUIDELINES

As licensed helping professionals and members of professional organizations, we gain entry into discipline-specific policies and procedures that guide our professional behaviors and decisions. It is our duty and responsibility to protect the clients we serve and maintain an excellent standard of care. We must follow our state and federal mandates, and are obligated to uphold the ethical guidelines of our disciplines.

In the new Standards of Practice accepted by ISNR (Hammond et al., 2011), guidelines were developed for NFB practitioners to follow. Currently, there are not published ethical guidelines specifically for the discipline of NFB, but there are ethical guidelines for members of AAPB, BCIA, and ISNR, and specific licensed professions. According to Striefel (2004), the ethical guidelines for biofeedback are excellent and very applicable to NFB. The following statement occurs in the ethical principles of AAPB: "[M]embers recognize the boundaries of their competence and operate within their level of competence using only those biofeedback and psychophysiological self-regulation techniques in which they are competent by training and experience" (AAPB, 2003, p. 2).

In addition to professional competency, another critical ethical component in standards of care is that of informed consent. In the counseling profession, more counselors have grievances filed against them for lack of proper informed consent than any other reason. Kaplan (2003) stated that over 80% or more of all ethical concerns revolve around this one single issue of improper or invalid informed consent (Russell-Chapin & Chapin, 2012). In the NFB world, it is crucial that NFB practitioners are well versed in the efficacy levels and research on the effectiveness of their interventions, so clients or their insurance providers are not misled (Striefel, 2009). The AAPB guidelines mandate that written informed consent be obtained for all procedures and interventions and that clients be told of the procedures' efficacy ratings.

QEEG

As discussed in Chapter 7, quantitative EEG (QEEG) has typically been used for assessment purposes, looking for visual brainwave patterns and brain mapping and comparing those to a normative database. The first QEEG reference normative database was created for selection of NASA astronauts to fly into space during the early 1950s at UCLA (Thatcher & Lubar, 2009). Since this selection process was not for diagnostic or clinical applications, there were no inclusion and/or exclusion criteria. The first peer-reviewed publication about normative databases and the one that set the standard for future QEEG templates was authored by Matousek and Petersen (1973).

Since that time, much progress has been made to ensure that QEEG databases are valid and reliable. Thatcher and Lubar (2009) developed a Gold Standard Checklist to assist clinicians who want to use QEEG normative databases. The more standards the QEEG user can check off, the more likely a better quality assessment can be assured. Standards included in the Gold Standard Checklist are:

1. Amplifier matching
2. Peer-reviewed publications
3. Artifact rejection
4. Test–retest reliability
5. Inclusion/exclusion criteria
6. Adequate sample size per age group
7. Approximation to a Gaussian
8. Cross-validation
9. Clinical correlation
10. FDA registered.

LORETA

Low resolution brain electromagnetic tomography (LORETA), a type of QEEG, was first introduced in 1994 by Pascual-Marqui, Michel, and Lehmann), and offered a novel method of localizing the brain activity by measuring the current source density (CSD). According to Sherlin (2009),

> LORETA information can be used to help determine if the brain is operating in an electrically optimal way if there is the presence of dysregulation. The investigator, whether a clinician or researcher, will attempt to use the properties of LORETA to determine if the individual has an expected or atypical frequency maxima localization. (p. 87).

By assessing and normalizing these deep state brain-site interrelationships, mapping and treatment procedures can be accomplished on-site in a neurotherapist's office (Swingle, 2010). As with any EEG, QEEG, or LORETA analytic, there are a multitude of approaches for interpretation. This in itself is part of the validity and reliability problem. There must be a basic understanding of the fundamentals of EEG, but according to Sherlin (2009), some interpretation needs to be left to the administrator. Niedermeyer (2005), considered one of the most prominent experts on EEGs and their interpretations, believes that both science and art must be a part of an excellent EEG interpretation. This makes standardization of interpretation almost impossible (see Figure 10.1).

FUTURE RESEARCH

The direction of future research on the efficacy of neurofeedback continues to be investigated and applied to an increasing number of clinical problems and populations. As has been recommended by both critics of earlier neurofeedback research and those who have reviewed the current outcome and efficacy research, there remains a general call for more controlled studies with larger sample sizes and replication across different settings. Some of these

Electrical NeuroImaging

Linking a patient's symptoms and complaints to functional systems in the brain is important in evaluating the health and efficiency of cognitive and perceptual functions. The electrical rhythms in the EEG arise from many sources but approximately 50% of the power arises directly beneath each recording electrode. Low resolution brain electromagnetic tomography (LORETA) uses a mathematical method called an "Inverse Solution" to accurately estimate the sources of the scalp EEG (Pascual-Marqui et al., 1994; Pascual-Marqui, 1999). Below is a Brodmann map of anatomical brain regions that lie near to each 10/20 scalp electrode with associated functions as evidenced by fMRI, EEG/MEG and PET NeuroImaging methods.

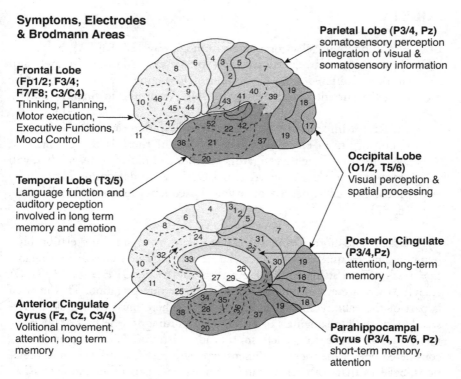

Symptoms, Electrodes & Brodmann Areas

Frontal Lobe (Fp1/2; F3/4; F7/F8; C3/C4)
Thinking, Planning, Motor execution, Executive Functions, Mood Control

Temporal Lobe (T3/5)
Language function and auditory peception involved in long term memory and emotion

Anterior Cingulate Gyrus (Fz, Cz, C3/4)
Volitional movement, attention, long term memory

Parietal Lobe (P3/4, Pz)
somatosensory perception integration of visual & somatosensory information

Occipital Lobe (O1/2, T5/6)
Visual perception & spatial processing

Posterior Cingulate (P3/4,Pz)
attention, long-term memory

Parahippocampal Gyrus (P3/4, T5/6, Pz)
short-term memory, attention

FIGURE 10.1 LORETA images and functions

Permission granted from Leslie Sherlin

studies are currently being done. However, there has been an interesting shift from research focused on investigating standard neurofeedback protocols on specific problems to more individually evaluated (QEEG based) and multi-protocol treatment of specific disorders. To date, these have found more profound effectiveness, as they better account for the individual variations not treated in group, single-protocol studies.

Another interesting change of direction in neurofeedback efficacy research is a new focus on the effects of neurofeedback on underlying neuronal networks. While it has been established that two-channel, bipolar montage neurofeedback can facilitate communication between two areas of the brain, the underlying mechanisms of this communication have been not as well understood. New fMRI brain imaging technology has allowed us to look beyond the physiological activation of specific brain locations, to also observe its underlying neuronal networks. As an example, of more recent note is increased interest in the default mode network involving activation of the medial orbital prefrontal cortex, anterior and posterior cingulate, the precuneus region, the inferior parietal lobe, and the hippocampus during the resting state (Raichle et al., 2001). The default mode network is involved in essential internal processing of external experience and has been found to become activated in children with ADHD after SMR neurofeedback during the resting state (Russell-Chapin et al., 2013). New fMRI brain imaging technology is expanding our understanding of how neurofeedback works.

Finally, an expanding area of future research is in the application of neurofeedback for normal behavior and peak performance in sports, business, medicine, and the performing arts (Strack et al., 2011; Gruzelier, 2009; Ros et al., 2009; Gruzelier et al., 2006; Ramond et al., 2005; Egner & Gruzelier, 2003). Not only can neurofeedback benefit those with debilitating emotional and behavioral problems, but it can also improve human potential and possibility, fine tuning the neurological platform necessary to excel in a variety of meaningful human endeavors.

EPIGENETICS

Our entire book has been written from the perspective that all neurotherapy and neurofeedback interventions are forms of neuromodulation, neurorehabilitation, and neuroregulaton. When these processes occur, another phenomenon, called epigenetics, may also happen. The study of epigenetics has recently been on the cover of *TIME* and *Scientific American*, and in many peer-reviewed journals. One definition of epigenetics refers to the changes in our gene sets based upon lifestyle, specific environmental factors, decision making, transgenerational evolution, and stress management (Ebrahim, 2012). Which gene sets will be turned on or off depends on many variables such as a healthy lifestyle and emotional and self-regulatory skills.

The age-old debate of "nature versus nurture" needs to be put to rest. We now understand that it is "nature and nurture" working together that determines who we are and how our DNA is impacted. It appears that an unhealthy lifestyle may be more risky than genetics, and the role of stress and chronic cortisol production cannot be overlooked (Shenk, 2010). Twin studies have demonstrated that identical twins with the same DNA at birth have uniquely different DNA after living separate lifestyles and making different decisions (Boomsma, Busjahn, & Peltonen, 2002). Doidge (2007) stated that neurons that fire together, wire together. As human beings, we choose to challenge our brains or die. Apoptosis, the definition of a dying neuron, reminds us of the necessity of working and challenging our brains. NFB and NT help clients to fire those brain cells through practice and regulation. Neurotherapy and neurofeedback techniques can teach the needed self-regulating skills essential for healthier living. NFB and NT offer neurologically based interventions to provide a method of self-regulation that gives clients a better chance for managing lifestyles and decision making. It may even impact our own epigenetics.

CONCLUSIONS

This final chapter presented essential trends in the neurotherapy and neurofeedback field. The following recommendations were suggested for the field to grow and prosper: expansion and continued research on the functions, structures, hows, and why NFB works; additional certification and future licensing adding to validity and high professional standards; and additional written ethical guidelines specifically for the NFB field expanding the new ISNR Standards of Care. However, with all that being stated, the NFB world has never been better, and evidence-based neurofeedback assists in propelling these advances even farther.

The authors end our book where we began, by discussing the new frontier of the brain and how neurotherapy and neurofeedback are an exciting part of this frontier. In the authors' combined therapy experiences of over 50 years, we have never experienced any counseling intervention as remarkable as neurofeedback. We have written this textbook because of the remarkable stories, remarkable research, and the remarkable results that our clients have expressed.

We tried to write a book that, although not totally comprehensive, presented much of the needed neurotherapy and neurofeedback information pulled together into one resource. We wrote this book knowing and realizing this was the information we searched for when we started our neurotherapy and neurofeedback journey several years ago. As we stated earlier, the way we practice our counseling trade today has been transformed for the better because of neurotherapy and neurofeedback. We have thrown ourselves into the practice of NFB. We are practicing NFB, researching NFB, teaching NFB to undergraduate and graduate students, and now writing about NFB. It is our passion, and we need and want to share the information learned with whomever is interested.

The authors' NFB supervisor asked the other day, "How much deeper do you want to go into NFB?" The thoughtful response was, "We know about six inches worth, and we need and want to learn 100 miles more!" The authors will always be students of the NFB world. There will always be new material to learn, especially as new research emerges. Jay Gunkelman, another pioneer in the NFB world, said it best: "The learning curve in neurofeedback is so steep, that we can't see the top of it" (qtd. in Robbins, 2008, p. 272). Neurofeedback is remarkable, so we are inspired and will keep learning. We hope our readers now have enough concentrated information to begin their NFB journey too. May NFB be remarkable for practitioners and consumers. May NFB be one more piece of the puzzle toward mental and physical health and neurological regulation.

REFERENCES

Association of Applied Psychophysiology and Biofeedback (AAPB) (2003). *Ethical principles for applied psychophysiology and biofeedback.* Wheat Ridge, CO: Association for Applied Psychophysiology and Biofeedback.

Boomsma, D., Busjahn, A., & Peltonen, L. (2002). Classical twin studies and beyond. *Nature, 3,* 872–882.

Doidge, N. (2007). *The brain that changes itself: Stories of personal triumph from the frontiers of brain science.* New York: Penguin Group.

Ebrahim, S. (2012). Epigenetics: The next big thing. *International Journal of Epidemiology, 41,* 1–3.

Egner, T., & Gruzelier, J. H. (2003). Ecological validity of neurofeedback: Modulation of slow wave EEG enhances musical performance. *NeuroReport, 14,* 1221–1224.

Gruzelier, J. (2009). A theory of alpha/theta neurofeedback, creative performance enhancement, long distance functional connectivity and psychological integration. *Cognitive Process, 10*(1), 101–109.

Gruzelier, J., Egner, T., & Vernon, D. (2006). Validating the efficacy of neurofeedback for optimizing performance. *Progressive Brain Research, 159,* 421–431.

Hammond, D. C., Bodenhamer-Davis, G., Gluck, G., Stokes, D., Harper, S. H, Trudeau D., . . . Kirk, L. (2011). Standards of practice for neurofeedback and neurotherapy: A position paper of the International Society for Neurofeedback Research. *Journal of Neurotherapy, 15*(1), 54–64.

Kaplan, D. (2003). Excellence in ethics. *Counseling Today, 4,* 5.

Matousek, M., & Petersen, I. (1973). Automatic evaluation of background activity by means of age-dependent EEG quotients. *EEG & Clinical Neurophysiology, 35,* 603–612.

Myers, J., & Young, S. (2012). Brain wave biofeedback: Benefits of integrating neurofeedback in counseling. *Journal of Counseling and Development, 90,* 20–28.

National Institute of Mental Health (2010). The National Institute of Mental Health strategic plan. Retrieved from http://www.nimh.nih.gov/about/strategic-planning-Reports/index.shtml

Neidermeyer, E. (2005). The normal EEG of the waking adult. In E. Neidermeyer and F. L. Da Silva (Eds.), *Electroencephalography: Basic principles, clinical applications, and related fields* (pp.167–191). Philadelphia, PA: Lippincott Williams & Wilkins.

Pascual-Marqui, R. D. (1999). Review of methods for solving the EEG inverse problem. *International Journal of Bioelectro Magnetism, 1*(1) 75–86.

Pascual-Marqui, R. D., Michel, C. M., & Lehmann, D. (1994). Low resolution electromagnetic tomography: A new method for localizing electrical activity in the brain. *International Journal of Psychophysiology, 18,* 49–65.

Raichle, M. E., MacLeod, A. M., Snyder, A. Z., Powers, W. J., Gusnard, G. A., & Shulman, G. L. (2001). The default mode of the brain. *National Science Academy, 98*(2), 676–682.

Ramond, J., Sajid, I., Parkinson, L. A., & Gruzelier, J. H. (2005). Biofeedback and dance performance: A preliminary investigation. *Applied Psychophysiology and Biofeedback, 30,* 65–73.

Robbins, J. (2008). *A symphony in the brain.* New York: Grove Press.

Ros, T., Mosely, M. J., Bloom, P. A., Benjamin, L., Parkinson, L. A., & Gruzelier, J. H. (2009). Optimizing microsurgical skills with EEG neurofeedback. *BMC Neuroscience, 10,* 1–10.

Russell-Chapin, L. A., & Chapin, T. (2012). *Clinical supervision: Theory and practice.* Belmont, CA: Brooks/Cole.

Russell-Chapin, L., Kemmerly, T., Liu, W. C., Zagardo, M. T., Chapin, T., Dailey, D., & Dinh, D. (2013). Default mode: A pilot study of medicated children with ADHD. *Journal of Neurotherapy, 17*(1), 35–42.

Shenk, D. (2010). *The genius in all of us: Why everything you've been told about genetics, talent and IQ is wrong.* New York: Anchor Books.

Sherlin, L. (2009). Diagnosing and treating brain function through the use of LORETA. In T. H. Budzynski, H. Budzynski, J. R. Evans, & A. Abarbanel (Eds.), *Introduction to quantitative EEG and neurofeedback: Advanced theory and applications* (2nd ed., pp. 83–102). New York: Elsevier Inc.

Strack, B. W., Linden, M. K., & Wilson, V. S. (2011). *Biofeedback and neurofeedback applications in sport psychology.* Wheat Ridge, CO: Association for Applied Psychophysiology and Biofeedback.

Striefel, S. (2004). *Practice guidelines and standards for providers of biofeedback and applied psychophysiological services.* Wheat Ridge, CO: Association for Applied Psychophysiology and Biofeedback.

Striefel, S. (2009). Ethics in neurofeedback practice. In T. H. Budzynski, H. Budzynski, J. R. Evans, & A. Abarbanel (Eds.), *Introduction to quantitative EEG and neurofeedback: Advanced theory and applications* (2nd ed., pp. 475–492). New York: Elsevier Inc.

Swingle, P. G. (2010). *Biofeedback for the brain: How neurotherapy effectively treats depression, ADHD, autism, and more.* Piscataway, NJ: Rutgers University Press.

Thatcher, R. W., & Lubar, J. (2009). History of the scientific standards of QEEG normative databases. In T. H. Budzynski, H. Budzynski, J. R. Evans, & A. Abarbanel (Eds.), *Introduction to quantitative EEG and neurofeedback: Advanced theory and applications* (2nd ed., pp. 29–55). New York: Elsevier Inc.

Watson, J. (1992). *Discovering the brain.* Washington, D.C.: National Academy Press.

INDEX

The annotation of an italicized "*f*" or "*t*" indicates a reference to a figure or a table on the specified page.

of 55–60, 59*f*; parietal lobe 24, 57, 116, 123; right hemisphere of brain 38, 56–7, 60, 89*f*, 141, 160; sensory motor rhythm 15, 20; temporal lobe 34, 57, 71, 112, 149; thalamus 20, 32, 55–6, 58, 101; traumatic brain injury 148–9, 168, 185–6; white matter in 24, 26, 59–60; *see also* brain waves; frontal lobe; neurons; neurotransmitters; occipital lobe; self-regulation of brain

Brain Change Therapy (Kershaw, Wade) 55, 77

brain-computer interface (BCI) 3

brain-derived neurotropic factor (BDNF) 31, 72

The Brain That Changes Itself (Doidge) 4–5

brain wave chart, 59

brainwave dysregulation: birth complications 25–7; brain injury 33–5; conclusions 44–5; diet and exercise 29–31, 111–12; disease and high fever 27–9; emotionally suppressive psychosocial environments 31–3; environmental toxins 24–5; genetic influences 21–2; medication, substance abuse, and addiction 37–9; overview 20–1; prenatal development 22–4; seizure disorders and chronic pain 40–2; stress and 35–7; surgical anesthesia and aging 42–4

brainwaves: ambient electrical activity 104–5; delta brainwaves 58, 79, 96, 100; EMG (electromyogram) interference 95, 104; gamma brainwaves 58, 96, 103, 146; during meditation 58, 78–9, 100, 141; in neurofeedback 99–100, 105–6; overview 59*f*; patterns with ADHD 58; software-driven trend analysis of 128; *see also* alpha brainwaves; beta brainwaves; sensory motor rhythm; theta brainwaves

brominated flame-retardants 24–5

Bruder, G. E. 177

Buchheim, A. 32

Budzynsky, H. K. 43, 115

Budzynsky, T. H. 17, 43, 175

Burns Anxiety Inventory 112

Burt, V. L. 37

career failures, case study 150–1

Castro, E. 24–5, 27, 29–30, 36

Caton, Richard 13

Center for Neuroacoustic Research 78

central nervous system (CNS) 62

cerebral cortex 5, 56, 59–60

cerebrum 56

Cesarean section (C-section) births 26

Chapin, T. J. 191

chicken pox virus 28

Child and Adolescent Psychiatric Clinics of North America (Hirschburg) 190

Children and Adults With Attention Deficit/Hyperactivity Disorder (Chadd) 190

chlorine contamination 25

chronic depression 111

chronic pain 40–2, 168, 183–4

chronic stress 36

classical conditioning in neurofeedback 92

client expectations in neurofeedback 120–1

client-neurotherapist relationship 135–7

client self-report 127–8

Coben, R. 186

cocaine use 24, 37, 39, 180

cognitive decline 20, 41–4, 73, 79, 103

cognitive efficiency/inefficiency 143–4, 168, 187

cognitive therapy 1–2, 68, 77, 184

Columbia University Center for Psychoanalytic Training and Research 5

computerized tomography (CT) 33

confidence lack, case study 151

Cormier, S. 77

Cornell University 16

corticotrophin-releasing hormone (CRH) 36, 63

counseling 1–2, 200–1

cranial electrical stimulation (CES) 80–1

Crawley, J. 29

current source density (CSD) 203

Cz location 155

N-acetylcysteine (NAC) 70–1, 121, 136
naproxen (Aleve) 28
National Center for Biotechnology Information (NCBI) 189
National Institute of Mental Health (NIMH) 174, 200–1
National Vital Statistics Report 25
neuroanatomy of brain 55–60, 59*f*
neurofeedback (NFB): for ADHD 3–4, 16, 17, 83, 119, 123; assessment in 109–18, 128–9; biofeedback and self-regulation 94–5; client self-report 127–8; conclusions 105–6, 130; defined 3; diet and exercise and 121–2; digital EEG neurofeedback 16; general hemispheric functions 89*f*; goals 3–4; introduction 1–3; learning and neuroplasticity 91–4; observational information 129; outcome evaluation 127–9; overview 87–8; rhythms of the brain 99–100; screening for readers 8–10; as self-regulation strategy 81–4, 82*f*; technological advancements 95–9; treatment planning 118–27
neurofeedback (NFB), efficacy research: conclusions 191; criticisms of 169–70; major applications 168, 172–88; outcome and efficacy research differences 168–9; overview 167; research-based criteria 170–2; resources and endorsements 188–91
neurofeedback (NFB), training: addiction 147; additional protocols 148; ADHD protocols 142–4; autism 148; case studies 150–4; client-neurotherapist relationship 135–7; client preparation for 137–9; conclusions 163; evaluating change during 159–61; lab design 133–5, 134*f*; learning problems 148; length of 158–9; managing distorted EEG 156–7; mood disorders 145; obsessive-compulsive and personality disorders 147; overview 103–5, 132; peak performance treatments 149; procedures for 154–63; protocol

selection 139–42; resolving problems during 161–3; sensor preparation and placement 154–6; setting thresholds for rewards and inhibits 157–8; single-channel protocols 142; tinnitus 149; traumatic brain injury 148–9; trauma treatment 147–7; two-channel protocols 140–1, 144–9
neurofeedback (NFB), treatment planning: audio-visual entrainment 124–5; client expectations 120–1; client instruction 124; completion of 126–7; evaluation of 125–6; indications, contraindications, possible side effects 118–20; meditation role in 125; overview 118; preparation for 122; self-regulation role in 122–3; training protocols 123–4
The Neurofeedback Book (Thompson, Thompson) 55
Neuroguide data base 91
neurological dysregulation risk assessment 8–10
neurons: during aging 42; excitability of 81; function of 54–5, 57–8, 59–60, 88–9, 93; in prenatal period 23
neuroplasticity: EEG and 87; learning and 91–4; neurofeedback and 106; neurogenesis and 4–6; neuronal loss 43; pioneers in 13
neurotherapy (NT): advances 17; counseling profession, impact on 200–1; defined 3; epigenetics 205–6; future research 204–5, 204*f*; introduction 1–3; LORETA information 203, 204*f*; overview 12–13, 109, 200; pioneers of 13–17, 14*f*; professional organizations 17–18, 201; QEEG evaluation 202–3; standards of care and ethical guidelines 202; *see also* assessment in neurotherapy
neurotransmitters: aging and 43; deficiencies 30–1, 60; defined 20; diet and 71; function of 58; heart brain concept 76; production of 79, 93; right hemisphere dominance 56–7
Nexus software program 82

niacin supplement 58, 71
nicotine exposure 22, 24, 71, 111
norepinephrine (noradrenaline) 31, 36, 63, 71
Norman, C. A. 93
Nurious, P. 77

obesity 29, 63, 181
obsessive-compulsive disorder (OCD) 29, 147, 176
occipital lobe: ADHD and 39, 150; brainwaves and 22, 36, 38, 101, 154; function of 57; neurofeedback and 123; QuickQ assessment of 116, 153; studies on 14–15; trauma and 33
Ohio State University 174
Olson, A. 187
omega 3 supplements 70, 121, 137
Oster, G. 78
Othmer, Siegfried 16
Othmer, Sue 16
outcome and efficacy research differences 168–9
outcome evaluation in neurotherapy 127–9

pain control 144
paranoia 57, 64, 103, 179, 182
parasympathetic nervous system (PNS) 35–6, 62–3, 76
parent–child attachment issues 32
parietal lobe 24, 57, 116, 123
Pasquine, M. 29
passive awareness state 133, 136, 138
peak performance: brainwaves and 101, 103, 141; future research and 205; neurofeedback for 83, 106, 144, 148–9
pediatric autoimmune neuropsychiatric disorders associated with streptococcus (PANDAS) 27, 29
Pembrey, M. 22
Peniston, Eugene 16, 147, 179, 181–3, 187
peripheral nervous system (PNS) 23, 24, 62, 94
peripheral skin temperature training: as client preparation 137; neurofeedback

and 73–4, 95, 138, 147; as self-regulation 122, 138; teaching of 98, 153
personality disorders 147, 187–8
Phosphotidyl Serine supplement 72
pioneers of neurotherapy 13–17, 14f
placebo effect 127, 167, 169–71, 176–8
Pollack, S. D. 32
polyvagal theory 32, 55, 64–6
Pop-Jordanova, N. 182
Porges, S. W. 32, 61–2, 64–5
postaccident frontal fibromyalgia 42
post-concussion syndrome 33–4
post-traumatic stress disorder (PTSD): brainwave dysregulation 31–2, 38–9; genetic influences 21; research on 181–3
Post Traumatic Stress Disorder Check List 112, 113–14
prematurity, defined 26
prenatal development and brainwave dysregulation 22–4
Problem Checklist 112, 114
pseudo-seizures 40
psychasthenia 180, 182
psychological and behavioral checklists 112–14
psychosocial medical history 110–12
psychosocial stressors 161
Purcell, M. 175
Pusztai, A. 30

quantitative electroencephalogram (QEEG) evaluation: for brain injury 33; confidence lack and 151; family conflict and 152; overview 105–6, 115–17, 116f, 202–3; of personality disorders 188; reliance on 128; research and 181
Quick Q assessment 90–1, 106, 116–17, 153
Quirin, M. 32
Quirk, K. 12

Ramon y Cajal, Santiago 13
Randis, T. M. 26
Ratey, J. J. 31, 72

Ray, C. G. 28
Raynaud's disease 73
Report of Post-Traumatic Stress (Child and Parent) 112, 113
Reyes syndrome 27, 28
Rice, K. M. 175
right hemisphere of brain 38, 56–7, 60, 89*f*, 141, 160
Rio Verdi University 16
Ritalin use 39, 173
Ritterfelf, U. 38
Robbins, J. 169, 170
Rossiter, T. R. 173
Russell-Chapin, L. A. 191

St. John's Wort herbal supplement 71
Saletu, B. 39
Sapolsky, Robert M. 22, 35, 37, 63–4, 68
Saxby, E. 179
schizophrenia 34, 115, 182
Schore, A. N. 31
Schwartz, J. 5
Schwartz, M. 94
Scott, W. C. 180
Seattle Pacific University 16
Sebern Fisher Bliss Protocol 143
seizure disorders 40–2, 83, 94, 123, 144
selective serotonin reuptake inhibitors (SSRIs) 39
self-regulation of brain: attachment theory 60–1; autonomic nervous system 62–4; brain neuroanatomy 55–60, 59*f*; conclusions 65–6; overview 54–5; polyvagal theory 64–5; role in neurofeedback treatment 122–3; social engagement system 61–2
self-regulation strategies: audio-visual entrainment 79–80; biofeedback 12, 73, 94–5; conclusions 84; diaphragmatic breathing 74–5; dietary supplements 70–2; exercise 72–3; heart rate variability 76–7; interpersonal connection 69–70; mental imagery and hypnosis 77–8; neurofeedback 81–4, 82*f*; overview 68; skin temperature training

73–4; therapeutic harmonics 78–9; transcranial DC stimulation 80–1
Selye, Hans 63
sensory motor rhythm (SMR): AVE equipment 79; brain dysregulation 41; chronic pain and 184; identification of 133; multifunction EEG amplifier and 96; neurofeedback for 102, 123; overview 20, 102; PTSD studies 182; seizure studies 15, 94; training effectiveness of 176
Seo, S. H. 36
Shagass, Charles 14–15
Sharma, P. S. V. N. 175–6
Sherlin, Leslie 17, 203
Shirtcliff, E. A. 32
Silver, M. P. 176
single-channel protocols: brainwaves and 149; EEG signals 140; with neurofeedback systems 97, 144, 158, 163; as training system 104, 139, 142
Single Photon Emission Computer Tomography (SPECT) 6
Sittenfeld, P. 175
16 Personality Factor 187
skin temperature training 73–4, 161, 175
social engagement system 61–2, 69
social interaction importance 56, 69, 148, 186
social introversion 180, 182
Solomon Four Square design 171
Solyom, L. 176
somatic nervous system (SNS) 62
Soutar, R. 116, 124
Spark: The Revolutionary New Science of Exercise and the Brain (Ratey) 72
Spectra glasses 79–80
Starcko, K. M. 28
Sterman, Maurice B. 15, 16, 40, 94
Stewart, R. A. 21
Stockdale, S. 93
Stolla, A. 30
Stoyva, J. M. 175
stress: brainwave dysregulation and 35–7; case study on 153; human response to 63–4; psychosocial

stressors 161; *see also* post-traumatic stress disorder
stress-depression connection 22
Stroebel, C. F. 176
Strohmayer, A. 40
substance abuse: brainwave dysregulation and 37–9; cocaine use 24, 37, 39, 180; heroin use 37, 39, 180; marijuana use 37, 39, 71, 152, 179–80; during neurofeedback 139; research on 178–81; *see also* alcohol addiction
Suldo, S. M. 187
Swingle, Paul G. 6, 21, 35, 36, 40, 43, 78, 90, 188
sympathetic nervous system (SNS) 35, 64
Symptom Checklist completion 125–6

Tang, H. 43
Tarsitani, L. 29
Taub, Edward 169
Temple University 14
temporal lobe 34, 57, 71, 112, 149
Test of Variable Attention (TOVA) 115, 128, 150, 151
thalamus 20, 32, 55–6, 58, 101
Thatcher, Robert 91
therapeutic relationships 69–70
theta alpha gamma (TAG) synchrony training 142, 145–7, 150, 153
theta brainwaves: ADHD and 58; AVE equipment 79; in drowsiness 138; multifunction EEG amplifier and 96; neurofeedback for 16, 20, 123; overview 100–1
Thomaes, K. 32
Thompson, Jeffrey 78–9
Thompson, L. 35, 36, 55, 93, 96, 100
Thompson, M. 35, 36, 55, 93, 96, 100
tinnitus 148, 149, 189
Tourette's syndrome 40
transcendental meditation (TM) 176, 180
transcranial DC stimulation (TDCS) 80–1
traumatic brain injury 148–9, 168, 185–6
trauma treatment 147–7

Trudeau, D. L. 180
turmeric spice as supplement 71, 137
twin studies 21–2, 206
two-channel protocols 97, 104–5, 139–42, 144–9

University of California, Berkeley 15
University of California, Los Angeles 15
University of Chicago 15
University of Washington 17

vacuum delivery 26–7
Vanathy, S. 175–6
vasomotor response 73
Veterans Administration (VAMC) 16
violent behavior issues 38–40, 57, 102
Virginia Polytechnic Institute and State University 16
Vitamin C 71
Vitamin D 70, 137–8
Vitamin E 72

Wade, J. W. 55, 77, 83
Walker, J. E. 93
Weber, R. K. 38, 93
Werner, E. F. 25–6
Westmoreland, B. F. 41
Whisman, M. A. 32
White, N. 188
white matter in brain 24, 26, 59–60
Why Zebras Don't Get Ulcers (Sapolsky) 63
Wilson, W. 179
within-subject replication design 171
Wurtman, R. 31
Wyrwicka, W. 15, 94

xenestrogens 24

Young, S. 201
Yucha, C. 3, 178, 183–5, 189

Zalaquett, C. 12
Zhao, Y. 42
Zoefel, B. 187
Zoloft 72–3
Zorcee, T. 182